THE CLASS OF '65

Seventeen Koinonia children waiting for the school bus, mid-1950s.

Courtesy of Conrad Browne

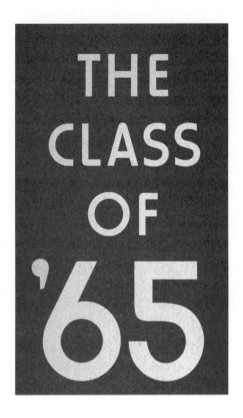

THE CLASS OF '65

A STUDENT, A DIVIDED TOWN, AND THE LONG ROAD TO FORGIVENESS

JIM AUCHMUTEY

PublicAffairs
New York

Book Design by Pauline Brown

Library of Congress Cataloging-in-Publication Data

Auchmutey, Jim.

The class of '65 : a student, a divided town, and the long road to forgiveness / Jim Auchmutey. — First edition.

    pages cm

    Includes bibliographical references and index.

    ISBN 978-1-61039-354-6 (hardcover)—ISBN 978-1-61039-355-3 (e-book) 1. Wittkamper, Greg, 1947—Childhood and youth. 2. Americus (Ga.)—Race relations—History—20th century. 3. School integration—Georgia—Americus—History—20th century. 4. High school students—Georgia—Americus—Biography. 5. Youth, White—Georgia—Americus—Biography. 6. Koinonia Farm—Biography. 7. Outcasts—Georgia—Americus—Biography. 8. Persecution—Georgia—Americus—History—20th century. 9. Class reunions—Georgia—Americus. 10. Forgiveness—Georgia—Americus. I. Title. II. Title: Class of sixty-five.

    F294.A5A83 2015

    975.8'913043092—dc23

    [B]

                                    2014041648

First Edition

10 9 8 7 6 5 4 3 2 1

*For all the people who stand up for
what they know is right.*

It is curious—curious that physical courage should be so common in the world and moral courage so rare.

— MARK TWAIN

CONTENTS

PROLOGUE   1

PART 1: Koinonia

CHAPTER 1: Farming for Jesus   9

CHAPTER 2: "We Made Our Reality"   23

CHAPTER 3: Terror in the Night   35

PART 2: Americus

CHAPTER 4: The Children's Hour   59

CHAPTER 5: Welcome to the Revolution   74

CHAPTER 6: "Not in My Town"   87

PART 3: Senior Year

CHAPTER 7: Among Panthers   101

CHAPTER 8: Still Standing   114

CHAPTER 9: A Lesson Before Leaving   121

PART 4: Continuing Education

CHAPTER 10: The Next Selma   139

CHAPTER 11: Breaking Away   152

CHAPTER 12: Growing Up   167

PART 5: Reunion

CHAPTER 13: Almost Heaven   183

CHAPTER 14: Guilt and Grace   196

CHAPTER 15: Back to Americus   207

EPILOGUE   219

Acknowledgments   *231*

Notes   *235*

Selected Bibliography   *245*

Index   *251*

Prologue

ON A COOL MORNING IN EARLY MAY, GREG WITTKAMPER GOT IN HIS Subaru Outback and started up the gravel road leading from his house in the mountains of southern West Virginia. He was going to check his post office box in the nearest town, Sinks Grove, as he did almost every day. Mixed in with the usual bills and business correspondence was a letter he had never expected to see: an invitation to his high school reunion.

High school had been the worst time of Greg's life, his nightmare years. He wasn't bullied so much as he was persecuted for his beliefs and those of his parents and of the singular religious community where they lived. Greg went to school in Americus, nine miles from Jimmy Carter's hometown of Plains, in the cotton and peanut country of southwest Georgia. At the beginning of his senior year, he made a point of riding to class with three black students who were desegregating Americus High School, an institution that had been reserved for whites since its founding in the previous century. A mob assaulted them with rocks and curses in a scene reminiscent of the disorders that greeted the first black students at Central High School in Little Rock, Arkansas, and at so many other campuses across the South.

What made this scene different was Greg's presence. He was white. He didn't have to risk his neck by accompanying the black students to school. He did it because he was raised that way. Greg had grown up in a Christian farming commune outside Americus called Koinonia (pronounced COY-no-NEE-ah, after the Greek word for fellowship). Koinonia is known today as the birthplace of one of America's best-loved nonprofit organizations, Habitat for Humanity, but the farm was anything but loved during Greg's childhood. Back then, it was notorious, resented, despised. Its residents believed in nonviolence, communal sharing, and interracial living, all of which set them against the reigning white culture of that time and place. For several years, the community was attacked and boycotted in a harbinger of the violence that awaited civil rights activists in the Deep South. Koinonia was a dangerous place to be from, especially if you also happened to be a student at a school being forced to desegregate—a student who actually *supported* that desegregation.

The last time Greg had seen any of his classmates was graduation day, in the early summer of 1965, when his name was booed and hooted during the diploma ceremony. Now they were inviting him back to their fortieth reunion. He hadn't lived in Georgia in decades. He wondered how they even knew where to find him.

Greg leafed through the rest of his mail and noticed a familiar name on a return address: David Morgan. He tore open the letter.

"I expect you will be quite surprised to hear from me," it began. "If you remember me at all, it will likely be for unpleasant reasons."

Greg remembered him all right. While David hadn't hurled insults or thrown a fist, he was part of the crowd of students that jeered as others harassed him during his three years at Americus High. They spat on him, ripped his books, tripped him on the stairs, pissed in his locker. A couple of guys even hit him in the face. Greg had heard about scapegoats in the Old Testament; he didn't know he was going to become one.

"Throughout the last 40-plus years," the letter continued, "I have occasionally thought of you and those dark days you endured at our hands. As I matured, I became more and more ashamed, and wished that I had taken a different stand back then."

Greg stared at the paper and felt his throat tighten. He was nearing sixty now, his waist thicker, his beard showing patches of gray, and he was content with his life in West Virginia, where his real estate business was going well and he had recently remarried and had a young daughter to dote on. But some hurts never go away. In everyone's memory, there's something hidden, something dark, something no one wants to think about when the lights go out and sleep won't come. For Greg, it was Americus High School. The most painful chapter of his back pages was pulling him into the past, whether he wanted to go or not.

IN THE FALL OF 1964, GREG WAS SEVENTEEN, A POWERFULLY BUILT young man who stood five foot nine and had strong, stubby hands that bore testament to hours spent working on the farm. He looked pretty much like the other guys at school. He wore his brown hair short, with a forelock that curled down from his widow's peak like a comma, and had light blue eyes that twinkled when he smiled, giving his face an elfish aspect. Not that his classmates saw his lighter side. When he was around them, he kept to himself and didn't speak any more than he had to. If the others had bothered to learn anything about him, they would have found out that he loved music and had saved up to buy an acoustic Gibson guitar, which he often used to pick out Joan Baez and Bob Dylan songs. Greg could see himself in Dylan's lyrics about victims of social injustice and "warriors whose strength is not to fight," and when he sang them, his soft, placid

Greg Wittkamper in his senior portrait.

speaking voice turned raspy and uneasy, as if there were something in the tunes that touched a burr in his soul. None of his classmates had a clue about Greg. They didn't know him, or want to. To them, he was a quiet oddball, a toxic carrier of abhorrent beliefs, a religious exotic philosophically committed to nonviolence in a world where guns and force were all too often the final arbiter.

Despite his pacifist beliefs, Greg could get angry. What he witnessed at the start of his senior year definitely made him angry.

That fall, more than ten years after the Supreme Court outlawed segregation in public education, the local school board finally admitted a
token number of blacks to Americus High. On the Friday before classes
were to begin, the principal convened a special preterm assembly so he
could prepare the student body for a passage that most of them considered unthinkable. It was the last act of a whites-only school. "We're going
to have some black students this year," he announced. "You don't have to
be their friends. I just don't want any violence."

The assembly chafed Greg. He thought the principal should have tried
to explain that the world was changing whether they liked it or not and at
least suggested that everyone be civil to the newcomers, even if they didn't
agree with them being at their school. Instead, he telegraphed to the students that he wasn't all that pleased about desegregation himself. His luke-
warm message seemed to give everyone tacit permission to be as nasty as
they pleased, as long as they didn't throw rocks or slug somebody or do
something else that might hit the news and make Americus look bad.

If no one else would welcome the black students, Greg would. He
knew all four of them far better than he knew the white kids: David Bell,
Robertiena Freeman, Dobbs Wiggins, Jewel Wise. He had socialized with
them, dated some of their kin, joined most of them in civil rights protests. The plan was for the group to ride to class in a limousine provided
by the county's most prominent black-owned business, the Barnum Funeral Home. Greg asked to go along in a show of solidarity.

On Monday, the first day of classes, only minor incidents were reported. The school board had not publicized the desegregation and was
hoping for calm compliance. The strategy seemed to be working. By
Tuesday, however, word had spread.

Greg arrived at the funeral home early that morning and climbed
into the back of the limousine with Jewel and Robertiena. Dobbs was in
front riding shotgun. David wasn't with them because his parents, fear-
ing trouble, were holding him out of school for a few days. They were
right to be concerned.

As the car approached campus, the passengers could see dozens of
people gathered outside the school along Bell Street. Through raised

windows, they saw a blur of faces distorted in pink-cheeked anger and heard their shouts:

"What are you doing here?"

"Get back to your school."

"Go home, niggers!"

Rocks and dirt clods struck the vehicle like antiaircraft flak. The incoming fire slacked off as the car turned into the campus and pulled up in front of the mobile home that had served as the administrative office since fire destroyed the main school building during the previous term. The Sumter County sheriff, Fred Chappell, a hulking man with bulging eyes and a history of animosity toward Koinonia and the civil rights movement, stood there waiting like a final barrier. He motioned for the car to keep moving, as if the people sitting inside were the ones disturbing the peace and not the mob that had surrounded them. Greg had been around the sheriff before, usually when he came out to the farm to respond to a drive-by shooting or some other act of violence, and he knew how intimidating the man could be. Chappell seemed especially menacing this morning because of an unfortunate coincidence. Greg had injured an eye in a farm accident and still suffered from occasional spells of double vision. To his horror, he looked out the window and saw two sheriffs scowling at the limousine.

The driver defied Chappell's gestures to keep moving and stopped the limo. The sheriff, his face flushed with irritation, jerked the front passenger door open and loomed above Dobbs. "Either get out now or get out of here!" he commanded.

Dobbs hesitated. Greg opened a rear door and cut between him and the sheriff, who seemed startled to see a white boy pop out of the car.

"This is it, Dobbs. We have to do it," Greg said. He pointed him toward the administrative trailer as the first bell sounded.

The black students reported to the principal's office, where special plans were being made to get them into classes late and out early so there would be less opportunity for incidents. No such plans had been made for Greg. He drifted away to his homeroom to face months of spite and resentment on his own.

———————

IT ALL CAME BACK IN VIVID DETAIL AS GREG SAT IN HIS SUBARU OPENing the mail, hundreds of miles and decades away from Georgia.

There were other letters after David's. One came from South Carolina, from Celia Harvey, whom Greg remembered as a cute, shy girl who had assiduously avoided him at school. "I'm writing this letter today to ask for your forgiveness," she wrote. Another envelope came from Alabama, from Joseph Logan, who had been cocaptain of the Americus High football team. He had enclosed a four-hundred-word sketch about an assault on Greg that he had witnessed during their senior year. "I hope your reading it does not cause unpleasant memories about AHS," he said in an accompanying note, "but I am sure it will." The most anguished letter, postmarked in Florida, was from Deanie Dudley, one of the most popular girls in the senior class, the homecoming queen. Greg smiled at the thought of Deanie; he had nursed a secret crush on her in high school, something she'd have been mortified to know about at the time. Her apology was couched in religious terms and suggested a keen sense of guilt. "I will never again say, 'How could the Holocaust have happened—how could all those Christian people in Poland and Germany have stood by and allowed it to happen?' I was present with you over a long period of time, and I never once did one thing to comfort you or reach out to you. It was cruelty."

As Greg sat on the West Virginia roadside studying the neatly penned confession, a mixture of painful memories and pent-up feelings coursed through him, and he started to weep. "You won't believe this," he told his wife when he returned home. "Something wonderful is happening."

Later, when his emotions had ebbed, he began to have second thoughts. He wondered why his classmates had waited so long to say they were sorry. He wondered what had happened in their lives to change them. Had they really changed at all, or were they simply getting older and looking for easy absolution? What would he find if he went back to Americus, the scene of so much ugliness and unhappiness? Did he really want to look into those faces after all these years and risk reopening wounds that he thought had long since scabbed over?

Could he be at peace with himself if he *didn't* go back?

PART 1

Koinonia

CHAPTER 1

Farming for Jesus

GREG WITTKAMPER WAS NEARLY SIX WHEN HE FIRST SAW KOINONIA ON a misty, unseasonably cool afternoon in the summer of 1953. He and his family had driven seven hundred miles from Louisiana to their new home in Georgia, and as they arrived at their destination, their meager possessions piled in a pickup truck and trailer, they looked like a clan of Okies fleeing the dust bowl. In a sense, they *were* refugees—refugees of conscience.

Greg's father, Will Wittkamper, was a minister who couldn't keep a job. In a decade as a clergyman with the Disciples of Christ denomination, he had been booted out of every church he had pastored, mainly because of his stubborn insistence on counseling young men to resist military service. This was not conventional advice during World War II and the surge of patriotism that followed the great victory. He was only recommending what he had done himself more than twenty years before, during the First World War, when he was imprisoned for draft evasion.

Despite his young age, Greg had already developed a sense of himself as a preacher's son. Every Sunday morning, his mother would dress him and his older brother in matching brown suits and park them in a pew with their baby brother, where they would squirm and occasionally act up as their father warned the congregation of the man-made hell that came from not heeding God's commandment to love thy neighbor. Greg was vaguely troubled by all the talk of war and hatred and hell, but he found it comforting that the man doing the talking was his daddy. When they passed the collection plate, he wondered why his family couldn't pocket the money—after all, his father was the man in the pulpit. Now they were moving to a communal farm where there would be no collection plates. Their new home would be full of surprises.

As Greg and his family turned into the dirt drive at Koinonia, children scurried out to greet them like a flock of ducklings, calling, "Here come the Wittkampers!" There seemed to be kids everywhere. Greg liked that; at least he was going to have plenty of playmates. It was the first day of July, a Wednesday afternoon, and the youngest Wittkamper son, David, was turning three. The community welcomed him with a birthday party and a freshly baked white coconut cake. Everyone seemed happy to see another family join the fold. Greg's parents were just as pleased; after years of rejection, they felt like they were finally among kindred souls.

For a boy like Greg, Koinonia looked as fun as an endless summer vacation. There were cows and pigs, tractors and trucks, wide-open pastures and wooded creek bottoms that begged to be explored. His Little Lord Fauntleroy days were behind him, as the matching brown suits went into a closet, rarely to be seen again. Now he was in a place where Huckleberry Finn would have felt at ease, a place where the grown-ups held their own worship services and didn't seem to care whether their children came to Sunday school barefoot. "It felt like we had gone to another planet," he said.

The planet had its perils. As Greg got to know the commune's children, he started hearing stories about run-ins between residents of the farm and some of the locals—things that had happened in church or in town. He was too young to comprehend where the tension came from, but he grasped its consequences as readily as a boy learns not to poke at a nest of rattlesnakes. Some people, it seemed, did not like Koinonia.

———————

WHEN THE WITTKAMPERS ARRIVED, KOINONIA WAS BARELY A DECADE old and beginning to come into its own as an experiment in Christian

The Wittkamper family shortly before
they moved to Koinonia: (from left)
Billy, Margaret, David, Greg, Will.
Courtesy of Greg Wittkamper

community. The farm occupied eleven hundred acres nine miles southwest of Americus, the seat of Sumter County, a history-haunted slice of
the Peach State best known as the site of the infamous Andersonville
prison camp, where nearly thirteen thousand Union soldiers died of ill-
ness, exposure, and starvation during the Civil War. At the heart of the
property, facing Georgia Highway 49, sat a cluster of rustic cinder-block
and frame buildings that might have passed for a World War II military
encampment. About sixty people lived there—mostly ministers and missionaries, their spouses and children—in simple cottages and cramped
apartments a short walk from the barns, cornfields, and henhouses
where they earned their sustenance. The residents worked together,
worshipped together, and ate together every day at noon when they were
summoned by a clanging dinner bell. In essence, the Wittkampers were becoming part of a large, extended family of religious dissidents and prin-
cipled misfits.

The leader of the fellowship, in fact if not title, was a Southern Baptist
minister named Clarence Jordan. He had conceived the community and
persuaded most of its members, including Will Wittkamper, to come.
It was easy to fall under his sway. Clarence was an imposing fellow who

Clarence Jordan. *Courtesy of Leonard Jordan*

stood six foot two and had a paunch that testified to his love of country cooking. He may have sounded like a typical Baptist preacher, with his down-home drawl and his endless repertoire of parables and Bible verses, usually dispensed with folksy charm and a sparkle in the eye, but this was no Main Street minister. He espoused radical ideas about some of the region's defining verities, a nonconforming worldview that took shape when he was a boy. Greg liked him instantly and felt safe and enlivened in his presence.

Clarence, as even the kids called him, came from a prominent family in Talbotton, a county seat in middle Georgia, where his father ran a bank and a general store. The Jordans (the name rhymes with *burden*, not the river in the Holy Land) had seven offspring, and Clarence, the middle child, was considered the contrary one. He read. He questioned. He argued. They called him Grump.

His conscience awakened, he explained years later, because of a disparity that troubled him. At the Baptist church the Jordans attended, his Sunday school class sang about Jesus loving the little children of the world, "red and yellow, black and white," but Clarence could see that black people weren't precious in the eyes of most white folks. Walking to and from school every day, he passed the county prison camp, where inmates were shackled and put to work on a chain gang. "I stopped and made friends with them," he recalled. "They were almost all of them black men, but they seemed more alive, more genuinely human, than the people I met in church." One August night when he was twelve, Clarence heard one of the prisoners being whipped. "His agonizing groans woke me up. It nearly tore me to pieces." Even more unsettling was the knowledge that the warden of the chain gang, the man doing the whipping, was a member of the church choir. During a revival that week, he had impressed everyone with his spirited singing of the hymn "Love Lifted Me."

As he neared the end of high school, Clarence considered becoming a lawyer so he could help secure justice for the downtrodden of the South. He changed his mind and enrolled in the agriculture school at the University of Georgia, hoping to improve conditions for the rural poor by promoting scientific farming methods. During his senior year, he decided that an ag degree wasn't enough, that if he really wanted to better the world, he should become a minister. His understanding of what his faith demanded continued to deepen. Clarence had been training as a cavalry officer in the ROTC since he had begun college. Shortly after he graduated in 1933, he reported for summer camp and experienced an epiphany while he was perched atop a horse, sword in hand, poised to attack a formation of cardboard dummies. He couldn't do it. He kept thinking about the fifth chapter of Matthew—"love your enemies"—and resigned his commission on the spot.

That fall, Clarence entered the Southern Baptist Theological Seminary in Louisville, Kentucky, and found his life's calling as well as his life partner. He met Florence Kroeger, a blonde, blue-eyed businessman's daughter, in the library where she was working and married her after completing his master's degree. He took a job directing an inner-city ministry but stayed at the seminary for a doctorate, studying the New Testament in its original Greek so he could "get it fresh from the stream," as he put it, and understand the source of his religion. One word seized his imagination: *koinonia*. It appears in the scriptures twenty times and translates into English as a communion or a fellowship (which is why a smattering of churches use *koinonia* in their names). In the second chapter of the book of Acts, the word is used to describe a community of early Christians who sold their possessions, shared their resources, and lived together in unity. That's what Clarence wanted. He fixed on the idea of forming a koinonia in the rural South where a band of believers could set an example for cooperative living, racial harmony, *and* better agricultural practices.

While he was finishing graduate school, Clarence befriended a minister from South Carolina who was thinking along the same lines. Martin England was back from Burma, where he had been serving as a Baptist missionary with his wife, Mabel, until the outbreak of World War II forced them to leave. He and Clarence talked about forming a koinonia for months and began scouting rural properties in central Alabama, where the demographics and history seemed fertile for their venture. They weren't far into the search when one of Clarence's brothers turned their attention to Sumter County, Georgia, sixty miles south of Talbotton, where he knew of a farm available for the reasonable price of $8,000. Clarence and Martin inspected the place and loved it. As they were beginning to raise funds, a contractor from Louisville who had supported Clarence's mission work handed them a $2,500 check for the down payment. No one seemed to mind that the money came from profits the benefactor had earned building facilities for the US Army.

The two ministers moved onto the property in November 1942, leaving their wives and young children behind for a time as they formally established Koinonia Farm. They had their hands full; the place was practically derelict. About a fourth of the gently rolling terrain was taken up by worn-out cotton fields that were deeply rutted, the topsoil eroded in places to hard red clay. The rest was pasture, scrubby pine woods, and swampy bottomland. Fences were down. Equipment was in disrepair. The barn was falling in. There were three tenant shacks and a farmhouse that was barely habitable. The men moved into a back room and started breaking ground for a winter garden. Once, when their mule team escaped the barn, they took turns hitching themselves to a plow. "I believe I'll make a better farmer than mule," Clarence wrote his wife. When Florence came with their two children the following spring, she could see that their new life in Georgia was going to be challenging. "I mean, it was a sorry place," she said. "There was no running water—really primitive. But it had potential."

The newcomers got busy. They repaired fences and terraced the fields. They planted peanuts and grain and set out fruit and nut trees. They managed to find building materials in the midst of wartime rationing and constructed new housing. They pooled their finances and instituted a communal system. After a couple of years, the Englands were recalled to missionary service overseas, but others heard about Koinonia and came to take their place: several college students, a conscientious objector, a minister and his family. Before long, there were a dozen people living on the farm.

One of the families who arrived during the late 1940s grew particularly close to the Wittkampers later: Conrad and Ora Browne and their children. Con was a midwesterner and had been a conscientious objector like Will, but in World War II, when he was forced to participate in risky military tests exposing him to diseases and exploring how much cold a person could endure. He went to divinity school at the University of Chicago and was a recently ordained Baptist minister when he heard Clarence speak at a conference. Utterly captivated, he persuaded his wife, a nurse, to give Koinonia a try, even though neither of them knew the first thing about farming. "I was a real tenderfoot, slight and bespectacled, with no upper-body strength," Con said. "I'd barely cut a lawn. I'm sure Clarence heaved a sigh of relief when we came."

Unlike some religious communities, Koinonia never intended to cloister itself from the outside world. Clarence envisioned it as a rural cousin of the urban ministries he knew, reaching out to improve the lives of its neighbors materially and spiritually. To that end, he introduced himself to area farmers and learned from them as he imparted modern methods from the agriculture school. He organized classes on fertilizer and soil conservation. The community started a "cow library," in which poor families could borrow a cow, return her when she was milked out, and then borrow another one. There was a vacation Bible school for children and Bible studies and hymn singings for adults.

The most successful outreach program was the farm's egg and poultry business. Clarence noticed that hens in southwest Georgia didn't produce many eggs, so he researched the matter and introduced another breed that could tolerate the heat better. Other farmers started keeping hens, and Koinonia sold their eggs in a cooperative marketing arrangement that Con took charge of. The enterprise landed Clarence on the cover of *The Southeastern Poultryman* magazine—a minister with a different kind of flock.

Funny thing about those eggs: they came in cartons with a logo that showed two hands—one white, one black—clasping in friendship. In segregated Sumter County, that raised a few eyebrows.

CLARENCE JORDAN LIKED TO CALL KOINONIA "A DEMONSTRATION PLOT for the kingdom." As long as he was demonstrating something that had to do with farming, people around Americus usually didn't object to the communal outlier in their midst. But Clarence's vision was much broader than agriculture. He wanted the fellowship to exemplify Christian brotherhood, to light a candle in a darkened room, and he knew very well that doing so might antagonize some of their neighbors. "It scared the devil out of us to think of going against southern traditions," he admitted. "White men could disappear as easily as blacks. But were we going to be obedient or disobedient?"

The tension between conviction and custom materialized early on when Koinonia hired a black man to help work the farm. Rather than make him eat by himself on the back stoop, as most people in rural Georgia would have done, he was welcomed to take his midday meal with the others. After word got around that the new people were mixing races at the dining table, a group of men stopped by to explain the way things worked in their part of the world.

"We're from the Ku Klux Klan," their leader told Clarence, "and we're here to tell you we don't allow the sun to set on anybody who eats with niggers."

Clarence thought a minute and then broke into a grin. "I'm a Baptist preacher and I just graduated from the Southern Baptist seminary. I've heard about people who had power over the sun, but I never hoped to meet one."

The men went away scratching their heads. Other matters weren't as easily defused with humor.

Koinonia noticed that the county didn't provide school buses for black children during the war, so the community used some of its gas rationing stamps to transport them to classes. That didn't sit well with local farmers who wanted young blacks to work their fields, not hold down school desks. One man was so exasperated that he wrote a letter to Clarence's father in Talbotton, informing him that his son was stirring things up. Mr. Jordan was elderly and infirm, and Clarence was so riled by the intrusion that he drove to town and confronted the letter writer. "I try to follow Jesus, and he has taught me to love my enemies, but I don't see how I can do that in this case," Clarence told him. If he ever bothered his father again, he warned, "I'll just have to ask Jesus to excuse me for about fifteen minutes while I beat the hell out of you."

The threat of fisticuffs swung both ways. Around the time Clarence was raising his hackles, a friend of his from the Baptist Student Union at the university, D. B. Nicholson, wrote Mr. Jordan about the reception his son was getting in Sumter County. While many appreciated his efforts to improve agriculture, they also felt he was "trying to go too fast in bucking the traditions of the community." Nicholson said the Jordans had already been snubbed by not being invited to a barbecue that everyone else had been invited to. He knew of one school board member who refused to speak with Clarence because he was afraid he might lose his temper and take a swing at him.

The most hurtful confrontation between Koinonia and its neighbors came, inevitably, in a house of God. Soon after they moved to Sumter County, the Jordans became members of a small church on the road to Americus, Rehoboth Baptist. Florence led a Sunday school class while Clarence sometimes preached or led songs. Others from the farm joined the choir, and a young couple got married there.

As Koinonia's views on race and pacifism became more widely known, some church members began to resent people from the commune. A group of deacons finally asked them to stop coming. They ignored the request and kept showing up. The incident that caused the final rift was almost comical. One Sunday morning in 1950, Con Browne went to church with a college student who was visiting from India and wanted to witness a Protestant worship service. Members took one look at his dark skin and thought Koinonia was trying to integrate their church. A delegation promptly visited the farm and told Clarence and the others not to return. Then a letter arrived announcing a congregational meeting to decide whether to strike them from the membership rolls. The resolution, which charged Koinonia with "advocating views and practices contrary to other members," passed by a wide margin—although not without some angst. Florence Jordan, who attended the meeting, heard weeping in the pews.

One of the deacons came to see Clarence after the vote to confess that he felt awful about what had happened. As Clarence told the story, the deacon couldn't sleep and kept imagining a choir singing "Were You There When They Crucified My Lord?" "Brother Jordan, I was there," he said. "And worse than that, I was helping do it." He asked for forgiveness.

Clarence extended his hand. "Man, I grew up in this section. I know how people feel about it. I forgave you before it ever happened."

When the deacon asked whether God would forgive him, Clarence said he didn't know, that was between him and his maker. It was the first encounter in a pattern that would become familiar in the coming years: people expressing sympathy for Koinonia in private but lacking the courage to say anything in public.

WILL WITTKAMPER WAS TWENTY YEARS OLDER THAN CLARENCE JORdan and came from a different part of the country and a different religious background. But he had traveled a similar spiritual path—albeit his was rockier—and it was that like-mindedness that eventually drew the two together and led Greg and his family to Georgia.

Will had been a pacifist since he grew up on a farm in the flat corn country of central Indiana. He was in his midtwenties when the United States entered the First World War and his draft notice came. After he refused to report for induction, the sheriff found him in a field cutting oats and arrested him. Will expected to die in prison or be executed and asked the authorities to make sure his body was returned home. The local newspaper, the *Tipton Times,* interviewed the detainee and pronounced him "mentally off on religious matters." Will did little to dispel the notion. "I have always been a queer fellow, a freak and perhaps a fool for what I have done," he told the reporter. "I am sorry but my religion stands above all to me."

Will was taken to Camp Taylor in Kentucky and put to work busting rocks into gravel with a sledgehammer. Released after the war, he returned to Indiana and enrolled at Butler University and then continued his studies at a Disciples of Christ seminary in Indianapolis. He lived with his parents for years after college, helping to run the farm, preaching and teaching school on the side. He left for a time, during the early days of the Depression, to join a religious community that was trying to get off the ground in Colorado, but a bank foreclosed on the land and the effort failed. Will didn't have much use for capitalism after that. He was well into his forties when he departed home for good, in 1938, to become pastor of a Disciples church near El Paso, Texas.

It was there that he met his wife, Margaret Gregory, a Methodist missionary assigned to a community house ministering to Mexicans on the Texas side of the border. She came from Norfolk, Virginia, where she had sold Avon products and took other jobs to help support her seamstress mother and her four brothers after her father died. Like Will, she felt a spiritual calling at an early age and held similar convictions about war and brotherhood. Once, when she was attending Ferrum College in Virginia, she asked her mother whether she could bring a young woman home for semester break. Mrs. Gregory was alarmed when the friend turned out to be a light-skinned black woman.

Margaret belonged to the Fellowship of Reconciliation, an interfaith peace organization that grew out of the Great War. When she was sent to El Paso, an acquaintance who also knew Will through the FOR suggested that he look her up. Will had never pursued the opposite sex much—by his own admission, he was a fifty-year-old virgin—but he introduced himself, and they began courting.

As a couple, they seemed like a pair of mismatched socks. Margaret was bright and bubbly, a diminutive dishwater blonde who loved children and was partial to cosmetics. Will was a wiry bantam who stood five foot seven and could be rather stern and humorless about his faith. When he heard that Margaret was volunteering at a USO club, he let her know that he didn't like the idea of her hanging out with soldiers and sailors, not so much because they were young men bursting with testosterone, but because of what their uniforms signified. He didn't like her wearing makeup either. Their biggest difference was their age. Will was twenty-two years older than Margaret. He was born in the previous century, before radio, movies, or automobiles, and vividly remembered the first time he had seen an electric light. Mrs. Gregory was displeased that her daughter was getting involved with a man old enough to be her father, a man only a year younger than she was, and in truth, it bothered Margaret as well. But she was so taken with Will's piety and intelligence—and his impressive crown of wavy black hair—that she gradually fell in love.

They married in 1943 and stayed in El Paso, both of them working and living at the Mexican community house. Their first son, Billy, came two years later. Greg, their second, named for his mother's family, arrived in 1947 when they had moved on to lead a Disciples church in Las Animas, Colorado. A third boy, David, came three years later during another pastorate in Gallup, New Mexico. While Will's fundamentalist preaching made a fine initial impression on each congregation, he was always asked to leave. Many of the men in the pews were veterans, and they weren't comfortable with a minister who considered military service morally questionable. Sometimes Margaret heard rumors that she and Will might be Communists.

Their last church was in DeQuincy, Louisiana, a small town near the Texas line. It was the first time they had lived in the South, and they liked much about it, especially the friendliness of the people and the open expression of religious faith. This time, Will and Margaret committed a new affront by inviting a mixed-race family—a family of "redbones," in the local parlance—to church. Again, acceptance curdled into opposition, and the preacher was given notice.

By 1953, the Wittkampers were weary of disapproving parishioners and fleeting pastorates. Will was sixty and wanted to settle down. Longing for an alternative way of life, he thought back to the commune that didn't work out in Colorado during the Depression. He started asking around and heard from a friend about a Christian community in southwest Georgia where property was held in common and everyone believed in nonviolence and the equality of all God's children. Will began corresponding with Clarence and went to visit Koinonia for a week. When he returned to his family in Louisiana, Greg saw him walking back from the bus station, fairly skipping as he sang out, "We're moving! We're moving!"

Margaret was less enthusiastic. She was a city girl, not a farm boy like Will. More importantly, as a southerner, she knew that their open-mindedness about race would go over no better in Georgia than it had in Louisiana. But she wanted her husband to be happy, and after he promised that he would plant her an abundance of strawberries, which she loved, she started packing. She figured they might stay for a couple of years.

IT DIDN'T TAKE LONG FOR THE WITTKAMPERS TO FEEL THE STING OF local enmity toward the commune. Soon after their arrival, the family ventured into the Disciples of Christ church in Americus for Sunday worship services. "We were greeted warmly until they found out we were from Koinonia," Margaret said. Once they were outed, the reception turned chilly. The family did not return.

Will and Margaret were used to it. For most of their married life, they had been rejected because of their beliefs about race, war, and capitalism. At least they didn't have to bear it alone now; they were among friends. Unwelcome in local congregations, Koinonia was its own church. While there was no sanctuary as such, the fellowship held daily Bible studies and weekly worship services and Sunday schools in the dining hall, under the trees, or sometimes in a barn. The gatherings were as casual as a picnic. People dressed as they pleased and listened as Will explained some passage from the New Testament, or Con read from Kahlil Gibran's *The Prophet,* or Clarence recast a parable in modern terms, turning King Herod into the governor of Georgia or the Good Samaritan into a kindhearted black man who helps a white traveler who has been mugged on the highway. Preachers and laypeople alike were free to speak; occasionally someone held forth on a nonreligious topic, like how to repair a toaster. All in all, Greg found these gatherings easier to sit through than his father's old sermons.

Despite the occasional unpleasant encounters with outsiders, the Wittkampers quickly grew to love Koinonia. Margaret enjoyed the children and the exuberant sense of togetherness—although she would have appreciated a few more creature comforts. For a time, the seating in the dining hall consisted of metal-rimmed barrels that left a circular impression on the posterior. She didn't think Christianity should be a pain in the ass. The seating was eventually upgraded, barely, with revamped apple crates.

The Spartan living conditions suited her husband just fine. Will saw Koinonia as the perfect setting to practice his austere, back-to-the-earth religion and to instill old-fashioned values in their sons. The family settled into an apartment on the second floor of the community center, quarters that Will thought were a little too cushy because they had hot and cold running water. They fell into step with communal life, which seemed to revolve around a series of endless meetings to determine everything from shopping lists to work assignments. Will tended the farm's vegetable garden and headed the trash detail, while his wife helped take care of the children whose parents were toiling in the fields and the chicken houses. Two of the Wittkamper boys would be attending elementary school in the fall. If Margaret thought the people at church had been unfriendly, they were nothing compared to what awaited Greg and Billy in the classrooms of Sumter County.

CHAPTER 2

"We Made Our Reality"

A COUPLE OF MONTHS AFTER THE WITTKAMPERS MOVED TO KOINONIA, Greg started first grade at Thalean Elementary School, three miles away on the road to Americus. It was a small country school in a huddle of frame buildings with little more than a hundred students, many of them from poor farm families. During his first weeks there, Greg noticed something about his new classmates: none of them were black.

The question of educating their sons and daughters posed a philosophical dilemma for parents at Koinonia. They considered homeschooling but decided against it because they were too busy working fields and tending chickens to run a classroom. Their only option was the public schools of Sumter County, which were as segregated as any in the South. "This causes us much uneasiness," Clarence wrote, "but thus far we have been unable, with our meager resources of money and personnel, to set up our own school system."

In his first months at Koinonia, Greg had become accustomed to seeing black people working on the farm and to sitting with them at the midday communal meal. He played with their children and wondered, once school started, where they went on weekdays. He began to notice some of them in the morning waiting for a bus—not the one he took, but another one with dark fenders indicating that it was for black children.

Their bus headed down a dirt road to another school, while his took the highway to Thalean.

Beginning first grade was a difficult adjustment for Greg. He had never attended kindergarten and knew the ABC's only as the lyrics of the familiar children's song. Spending his days in a social environment that was so divergent from the one at the commune only added to his sense of dislocation. "I felt different the first day I walked into school," he said.

When he went into Americus with his family or others from Koinonia, Greg felt a bit different there as well. The "Garden Spot of Dixie," as Americus called itself in the 1950s, was a classic cotton-belt town of eleven thousand that could have sprung from the pages of a Faulkner novel. A stone Rebel stood guard at the county courthouse, looking out at a central business district lined with handsome old brick storefronts and dominated by the Windsor Hotel, a fantastic castle-like relic of the 1890s. The principal cross streets were named for Confederate generals—Lee, Jackson, Forrest—and led south to a shady historic quarter of churches and stately columned homes built decades before with cotton money. On the other side of town, where most of the black population lived, half the streets were red clay and many of the houses were tin-roofed shacks like the ones out in the country.

For the people of Koinonia, Americus was a convenient place to buy groceries and farm supplies, pleasant enough to visit as long as they didn't look too closely at the signs demarcating the racial lines. Greg first noticed one at the Dairy Queen on US 19, where the farm's children were sometimes allowed to splurge with a soft-serve ice-cream cone. The water fountains were marked "white" and "colored," like most water fountains in public places in the South. Greg knew what that meant from an early age and understood that it represented a different way of thinking from Koinonia's. Between the signs in town and the faces at school, he was beginning to realize that he lived in a sheltered community that stood apart, an island in a rough sea.

Watermelon time at Koinonia, mid-1950s. *Courtesy of Leonard Jordan*

IT WAS A STRANGE PLACE TO GROW UP.

Being a child at Koinonia in the 1950s was like being part of an exotic tribe. And the tribe was growing; it was the baby boom era, and one of Koinonia's main crops was children. Of the sixty or so people who lived there when Greg's family came, more than a third were youngsters ranging in age from diapers to high school. The Wittkampers added another one in 1954 when their fourth son, Danny, was born.

There were a dozen families in the commune—Nelsons, Eustices, Atkinsons, and more—but the heart of the fellowship, the ones who stayed the longest and twined their lives with the Wittkampers, were the Brownes and the Jordans. Both families had four children at the time, the same as Greg's, and several were close to his age and went through school together. Con Browne and Clarence Jordan were a generation younger than Will Wittkamper; Greg came to see them as surrogate fathers, people he could confide in and come to with questions. It was Connie, as Greg called him, not his own father, who explained the birds and the bees to him.

Like most farm children, the Koinonia kids were expected to work before and after school. They milked cows, hoed peanuts, collected eggs,

Greg the farm boy. *Courtesy of Greg Wittkamper*

moved irrigation pipes. Greg started out washing dishes in the community kitchen and then helped his father in the garden, watching as he put-
tered along behind a wheelbarrow happily reciting scripture to himself.

Looking back years later, the children of Koinonia usually recalled
their upbringings fondly, describing life on the farm as a pastoral idyll,
notwithstanding the sweaty toil and the gnats and mosquitoes. What
they didn't remember as fondly was the sense that they might be in
enemy territory whenever they left the property, that they had to watch
themselves at school or in town. "It was like we had two faces: one for
the farm and one for the outside world," recalled Carol Browne, Con
and Ora's second child.

One of the strangest parts of growing up at Koinonia was the near
absence of money. Members were expected to dispose of their resources
before joining the commune, and once part of it, they rarely handled cur-
rency unless they were buying supplies or selling farm products. One of
the few times the children saw cash was when they visited a nearby country store and were each given a quarter to buy an RC Cola and a Moon
Pie. At Christmas, they received one gift worth no more than $10 and
spent hours agonizing over the choices in the Sears Wish Book catalog.

One year Greg selected a cheap radio, which he used to discover Little Richard and the rousing new world of rock 'n' roll. Buying records was out of the question; there was no budget for such frivolities.

For most of Greg's formative years, the farm did not have a television. If the kids heard about something they really wanted to watch—a boxing match, perhaps—they might visit the house of a friendly black neighbor, but such occasions were rare. Going without TV was a philosophical choice as much as a cost consideration; the parents didn't want their children binging on pabulum or falling prey to American commercialism. Billy Wittkamper had seen more TV than the others, having spent a few months with his mother's family in Virginia. After his return, he told Greg about *Howdy Doody* and all the fun shows they were missing, but the Wittkampers still didn't get a TV. Years later, when people told Greg that he resembled Wally Cleaver, he had no idea they were talking about Beaver's big brother in a situation comedy.

Groups from the farm would go into Americus occasionally to see a movie at the Martin Theater or the Sunset Drive-In. Not every film was deemed appropriate. Once, when word got around that Koinonia's youth coordinator, John Eustice, was about to take a carload of kids to town to see Elvis Presley in *Jailhouse Rock,* the dinner bell rang out, summoning the adults to an emergency meeting where they debated whether such fare would be too risqué. Elvis lost, much to Greg's disappointment. On more typical movie nights, residents would gather outside to watch dry educational films they could get for free from the library, projected onto the side of the two-story building where the Jordans and other families lived. The noisy old projector sucked bugs into its workings and zapped them into dust, which the children usually found more interesting than the films.

Despite their limited exposure to pop culture, Koinonians did not consider their lives dull. They made their own entertainment. They packed dinners and took Saturday hayrides to a spot that became known as Picnic Hill. They held sing-alongs and told stories, especially Clarence, who fascinated the children with his tales about a three-legged dog named Old Coot. They played volleyball and took dips in a swimming hole where the water was so cold it would make them gasp. They organized an Indian club, the children making their own headbands, learning tribal dances, and sleeping out in tents. Everyone got an Indian name; Greg was Arrowhead because he liked to hunt for relics along the banks of Mucka-loochee Creek. Naturally, his big brother called him Airhead.

Once, when the kids were begging to go to the county fair, their parents said no after they found out that black people were allowed to attend only on designated "colored days." The Koinonians decided to stage their own carnival, with their own animals and their own makeshift attractions. Greg starred in a sideshow as the Wild Man—half human, half beast—donning a loincloth as he growled at passersby from the inside of a chicken-wire cage. "We improvised," he said. "We made our reality."

An important part of growing up at Koinonia was the stream of people who visited. By the mid-1950s, the farm was becoming well known in alternative religious circles, largely because Clarence was spending more time on the road speaking. As many as a thousand people a year came to see the commune—a sundry collection of academics, clergy, missionaries, peace activists, spiritual questers, and vagabond ne'er-do-wells who always kept things interesting. There were Asians and Africans, Catholics and Jews, Hindus and Buddhists. "The diversity of people we met as children was mind expanding," Greg remembered.

Some of the sojourners were regulars. The kids particularly looked forward to the arrival of the Children of Light, a sect that wandered the back roads in wagons like gypsies and pitched their tents on the property to hold lively worship services that featured a pounding barroom piano. Another favorite was Leon the Hobo, a vagrant who usually came during the summer, promptly stripped off his clothes, got deloused, and stayed for months, spinning stories about traveling the country and riding the rails. A few years later, a group of earring-wearing, guitar-strumming beatniks from Atlanta frequented the farm, wooing the girls, teaching new songs to the boys, and thoroughly irritating Clarence with their reluctance to head into the fields and earn their keep. They were followed by cadres of civil rights workers and bands of hippies who thought Jesus was just all right and wanted to get back to the garden.

The visitors brought a taste of the world in all its variety to Koinonia and gave the farm's children an education unavailable to most of their classmates in the public schools. The gap in their experiences could lead to a certain smugness. Jan Jordan, Clarence and Florence's second daughter, couldn't help but feel more worldly. "I have to admit that I felt kind of superior to the other students because of all the people we met."

IN EIGHT YEARS AT THALEAN ELEMENTARY SCHOOL, NO CLASSMATE OF Greg's ever set foot on the farm, and he never went to one of their homes. Most local people were so leery of the commune that they wouldn't allow their children to go there. On one of the rare occasions one of them did, it didn't go well.

Lora Browne, the oldest of Con and Ora's children, was a year ahead of Greg at Thalean and had a reputation as one of the smartest kids in school. When she was in third grade, she asked her friend Ginger to come over and see where she lived. As they walked around the grounds, Lora pointed out a black teenager who worked on the farm and told her, girl to girl, that she thought he was handsome. "He's my boyfriend," she joked. Ginger was aghast. "You do know he's a nigger," she said.

Koinonia's liberated attitude about race was the most infamous aspect of its reputation, but there was an irony behind that stance for equality: few blacks ever became members of the fellowship. Some of them lived on the property as tenants, and many worked there over the years and appreciated Koinonia's broad-mindedness and its generosity in paying higher wages than other farms. Yet only one black family pursued full membership during the 1950s. It vexed Lora's parents, who would have loved to darken the community's complexion. "We had bathrooms and we had adequate food and clothes, and yet the Negroes didn't particularly want to come into the situation," Ora Browne lamented.

One of the main problems, Koinonia came to understand, was that a commune was alien to the religious experience of most black people in Sumter County. They weren't eager to join an organization that required members to give up their possessions when most of them didn't have that much to begin with. So they worked there, ate and worshipped there, maybe even lived there, but they didn't make the full commitment of divestment that the white families had made.

Few outsiders knew that about Koinonia. All they knew was that black people were treated as equals, and that, to them, was unconscionable.

Lora's friend didn't return to Koinonia, but when Ginger broke her leg in an accident at school, Lora visited her home, a log cabin deep in the piney woods, and stayed the weekend. Ginger and her mother couldn't have been more hospitable. Her father, a Klansman, was a different matter. When Con and Ora came to get their daughter, he peppered them with questions about the farm and its religious views, an interrogation that climaxed with the Big Horrible:

"Would you let your daughter marry a colored fellow?"

Con said he would trust his children to fall in love with whomever they chose.

"Even if he's a nigra?"

"Yes, even if he's a Negro."

"Well, it says in the Bible that niggers are inferior."

"I'd like to see that. Could you show me that passage please?"

Ginger's father stomped off to get the good book, and returned flipping through the pages. "Here," he said, pointing to a verse in Acts that uses the word *Niger*. Con explained that it was referring not to a race of humans but to Simeon Niger, a teacher in the early church who may have come from Africa and had dark skin. "It doesn't say nigger."

The awkward conversation had reached a dead end. The Brownes departed, and Lora never visited Ginger's house again.

———————

AT ONE POINT DURING GREG'S EARLY YEARS AT KOINONIA, THE ADULTS grew concerned about a seemingly innocent development: the proliferation of toy guns. It disturbed them to see their children shooting at each other even if they were just playing cowboys and Indians.

Nothing united the fellowship like its belief in pacifism. Almost every man in the commune had resisted military service in one way or another—a further source of local resentment. The subject of nonviolence seemed to come up in every other sermon or Bible study, and worship services often included a singing of "Down by the Riverside," with its spirited chorus of "ain't gonna study war no more." When Koinonians took day trips, two of their favorite destinations provided stark object lessons in the cost of armed conflict. They could drive a few miles north to the Andersonville POW camp, where close ranks of tombstones marked the final resting places of the thousands of Union prisoners who died there during the Civil War. Or they could go to the eastern edge of the county, to the state park at Lake Blackshear, where a B-29 Superfortress was displayed in a field as part of a veterans memorial. The grounded plane was the same model that had dropped atomic bombs on Japan. For the adults, it was a somber reminder of tens of thousands of lives incinerated in two hellish flashes. For the children, it was a ginormous curiosity that doubled as a playground. "We'd climb up there and sit in the cockpit and explore the whole thing," Greg remembered.

Con Browne was particularly zealous about eliminating the symbols of violence at Koinonia. "I hated guns," he said. "I talked with the children about war and the bad things guns could do. I told them that some people's religion was different from ours, that they thought strongman tactics ruled the world. We didn't believe that. We believed love was the strongest thing in the world and would win in the end."

For all the talks and sermons, the gunplay continued. The parents finally decided to put a stop to it. They wanted to teach a lesson, not merely issue an edict, so they came up with the idea of a disarmament service. The children were instructed to surrender all faux weapons—store bought or handmade—and toss them into a burn barrel as the commune stood in witness. Anyone who didn't possess an instrument of violence could clip pictures of guns out of catalogs or magazines and throw those into the flames.

The children complied, but the ritual cleansing hardly settled the issue. Knowing that toy guns were frowned upon made the kids want them more. They began fashioning their own weaponry on the sly, carving wooden rifles and making broadswords and Viking shields, hiding them from the grown-ups. "If anything, our arsenal got bigger," Greg said. "And we started making things that actually worked." One of them was a rudimentary pipe gun that used a firecracker on one end to shoot a rock out the other. "It was like a little cannon. You could knock the bark off a tree with that thing."

Con never gave up his effort to demilitarize Koinonia. Once, when his youngest son, John, came home from school with a dart gun he had received in a gift exchange, Con sneaked into his room at night and replaced it with a toy truck. After John woke and realized his dart gun was missing, he searched the house until he found it in his father's closet and reclaimed it. Con discovered the theft and ended the tug-of-war by confiscating the contraband for keeps. "I really liked that little dart gun," John said years later, a wistful note in his voice.

There were two working guns at Koinonia during Greg's childhood: Clarence's old ROTC rifle from college and an antique 12-gauge double-barreled shotgun used for hunting, killing snakes, or culling livestock. Clarence occasionally took some of the boys out to shoot rabbits, explaining that there was nothing immoral about killing something you meant to eat. As for eliminating unwanted animals, Greg's father usually played the role of the grim reaper. No stray was safe around Will Wittkamper. "A dog would come by, and Will would say, 'Stand back,'" recalled Charlie Browne, Con and Ora's oldest son, "and then he'd pull the trigger: *Boom!* And you're thinking: 'Holy shit! He shot that dog.' Will had no use for pets. If you couldn't put it in a harness or cook it or milk it, there was no damn reason to have it around as far as he was concerned."

Will was a devoted pacifist who had been arrested for his beliefs while Clarence was still in knee-highs, but that didn't mean he was opposed to the use of force. Far from it. Like other fathers at Koinonia, he practiced corporal punishment, taking the Bible literally when it said, in Proverbs 13:24: "He that spareth his rod hateth his son." Will did not spareth his firstborn, keeping him in line with a razor strop or a green switch freshly cut from a peach tree. Billy grew so resentful of his dad's whippings that he rejected many of his beliefs, including his religion, well before finishing grade school. Will began to soften his discipline under the influence of Con, who rarely punished his children. The principal beneficiary was Greg, who escaped most of his father's wrath and remained a more obedient son, more willing than his brother to follow the old man's example in matters of faith—for a time, at least.

Will's attitude about pacifism was never as simple as it sounded. He didn't even like the word; he thought *pacifist* sounded too passive, too indifferent. He preferred to think of himself as a peacemaker because the term implied effort, and he believed that it took unrelenting effort, not saintly acquiescence, to avert violence.

His sons would learn what he meant soon enough.

——————————

IN GREG'S FIRST COUPLE OF YEARS AT THALEAN, HIS POLITE DEMEANOR and eager blue eyes made him something of a teacher's pet. Most students didn't bother him or the other children from Koinonia. The school was so small that the principal and staff were usually able to monitor things, and what little harassment that occurred took the form of quick shoves or whispered name-calling. As Greg advanced in school, however, the civil rights movement began to crystallize in the South. With it came a rising level of white resentment, a general cussedness that passed from parent to child. Boys began to pick fights with kids from the interracial commune down the road.

Each time a Koinonia student was challenged, he had to decide how to respond. In the heat of such moments, biblical teachings usually did not pop into mind. Instinct took over—fight or flight.

The Browne brothers responded differently, in keeping with their different natures. The outgoing Charlie, who started first grade four years behind Greg, constantly got into scraps when others called him a Commie or suggested that his mother slept with black men. "I decided real early I wasn't going to be a pacifist, and I think some of the students liked me for that," he said. "They'd say, 'At least you'll fight with us. Those other wimps out there won't.'" His more reticent brother, John, shrank from the prospect of conflict. When he began Thalean a year after Charlie, he dreaded school so much that he would hide in a hollow tree instead of boarding the bus. Clarence persuaded him to go to class by promising to take him horseback riding.

The Wittkamper boys were another study in contrasts. While Billy tried to avoid confrontations at school, he did get into a couple of fights and found them, against all his dad's preachments, liberating and strangely cathartic. "It felt good," he said. "They left me alone after that."

Greg was torn. He wanted to emulate his big brother, to look strong and stick up for himself, but he also wanted to follow the examples of his father and of Con and Clarence, who talked about the Christian's duty to meet hatred with love. Everyone at Koinonia knew what Jesus said in the Sermon on the Mount: "Whosoever shall smite thee on thy right cheek, turn to him the other also." What seemed so clear during a Bible lesson wasn't as easy in real life, especially for a nine-year-old.

In the spring of 1956, as he neared the end of third grade, Greg faced his first test in applied nonviolence. A boy who had been badgering him since he started at Thalean followed him into the restroom and started calling him a nigger lover. There was nothing unusual about that, but this time the belligerence escalated. As Greg stood at the trough urinal, he felt a sharp jab of pain in his lower back, and then another. The little prick was kidney-punching him.

"Stop it, Bobby!" Greg warned several times. The punches kept coming.

Greg finally turned around and smacked him in the chest. The blow took Bobby by surprise, and he tumbled into the trough where his target had been trying to pee. Other boys might have burst out laughing at such a poetic turn of events. Not Greg. He felt awful. "I certainly didn't tell my parents about it. I didn't think it was a very Christian thing to do."

Greg and Bobby were called into the principal's office the next day and instructed to make up with each other. Bobby's apology seemed half-hearted, perhaps because he knew that the hostilities might not be over; his older brother had already threatened retaliation. Greg was far more upset by the altercation. He had violated a teaching of Jesus, something that came straight from the mouth of the Savior, printed in red letters in the book of Matthew, something that was the source of one of Koinonia's most precious values. As he sat beside the instigator of the incident, he couldn't help himself: he began to cry.

CHAPTER 3

Terror in the Night

IN THE SPRING OF 1953, RALPH MCGILL WROTE A COLUMN ON THE front page of the *Atlanta Constitution* under the mild-sounding headline: "One Day It Will Be Monday." His subject was anything but mild. The editor was warning his readers of ground-shaking changes that he knew would incense many of them.

The headline referred to the US Supreme Court's custom of announcing its decisions on the first day of the week. The most widely anticipated case on the docket—*Brown v. Board of Education of Topeka*—combined five challenges to racial segregation in public schools, which was required by law in seventeen southern and border states and optional in four others. The NAACP Legal Defense Fund saw the litigation as the key to ending American apartheid. When the prophesied Monday finally came, on May 17, 1954, the justices unanimously outlawed the peculiar institution that characterized education in a third of the country. Their pronouncement changed history and in one corner of Georgia unleashed passions that threatened to destroy Koinonia.

The Brown decision was met with predictable yelps of protest from southern politicians like Governor Herman Talmadge, who issued one of the first condemnations, swearing that Georgians "will not tolerate the mixing of the races" in their public institutions, regardless of what the court said. Many news commentators were more measured, at least initially. In Americus, the *Times-Recorder* held out hope that the ruling would be unenforceable: "No law or regulation can be stronger than the public sentiment behind it. If the 'public interest' is seriously taken into consideration as suggested by the high court, then it will be many years before the schools in most communities of the South are desegregated."

It was an accurate prediction. Greg was finishing first grade when the *Brown* ruling came down. He would be a twelfth grader before he saw any black students in the hallways. Because of the court's vague enforcement directive—a year after the decision, it instructed school systems to desegregate "with all deliberate speed"—leaders in the Deep South were able to take their sweet time when it came to enacting the decreed changes. The twilight of segregation in the public schools would be long and arduous.

In the months after *Brown,* the attitude of many white southerners hardened and a backlash took hold. In the nation's capital, three-quarters of the senators and congressmen representing the states that had belonged to the Confederacy signed the Southern Manifesto declaring the decision unconstitutional. In Mississippi, the first White Citizens Council was formed—a sort of Rotary Club dedicated to resisting integration by any means, especially economic pressure such as firing employees or throwing tenant farmers off their land. The councils spread under various names to dozens of communities across the region; an Americus version was chartered in February 1956.

As they looked around Sumter County almost two years after *Brown,* the group's organizers could see only one entity outside the black community that publicly supported racial equality: that eccentric band of Christians out on Highway 49. People around Americus had long been suspicious of Koinonia, but it was easy to stomach the place as long as those people kept to themselves and didn't try to export their dissident views to the local populace. In the fourteen years since its founding, the farm had faced gossip and grumbling and a degree of shunning but only occasional outright hostility.

That was about to change.

———————

IT WAS A DELICATE REQUEST. IN MARCH 1956, A MINISTER FRIEND OF Clarence Jordan's asked him to help two students enroll in the Georgia State College of Business, a school near the capitol dome in Atlanta. The college, which later became Georgia State University, was all white; the students were black. They needed the signatures of two university system alumni and thought the leader of Koinonia, a graduate of the flagship school in Athens, was a logical candidate for one of them.

Clarence wasn't looking to pick a fight with the state's higher education hierarchy, but he figured these students had as much right to attend the college as anyone. He met them during a trip to Atlanta and took them to see the president of the institution. Word must have leaked out because reporters were waiting for them when they left. Someone was trying to desegregate the university system, and that was news.

As it turned out, Clarence was ineligible to sign the applications because he wasn't a graduate of that particular college. But the fact that he had *intended* to sign was enough. He woke the next morning to find himself on the front page of the Americus newspaper. Governor Marvin Griffin, a south Georgian who had pledged to keep the state's public schools segregated "come hell or high water," took notice and phoned the sheriff in Sumter County to ask who "this Jordan fellow" was. "Clarence came back from Atlanta and said this was what the spirit led him to do," Con Browne remembered. "We didn't know he was going to do it, but we wouldn't have objected. I didn't think it was going to cause us problems."

Was he ever wrong. A line had been crossed. Within days, local misgivings about Koinonia turned into belligerence, and the farm became a magnet for all the anger and resentment that had been building since the *Brown* decision.

It started with threatening phone calls in the night, usually to the Jordans. Then the vandals went to work. Fences were cut, sugar was dumped into gas tanks, almost three hundred fruit trees were chopped down. The farm's roadside market made an irresistible target. It was located five miles from the community on US 19, the old Magnolia Highway to Florida, and was marked by several signs identifying it as the "Koinonia Farm Market." The signs were shot up repeatedly and hauled off so they couldn't be repaired.

In June, the county government piled on. The farm was getting ready for Camp Koinonia, its annual summer camp for thirty children, white and black, when it learned that the commission had won an injunction blocking the eight-week program from opening. The grounds: health code violations. When that didn't stick, the grounds were changed to decency because the kids might witness pigs giving birth. By the time the matter came up for a court hearing, Koinonia had accepted an invitation to move the camp to another site in the mountains of Tennessee. Greg attended and had a swell time—he didn't miss the pregnant sows at all.

Back in Georgia, vandalism toward the farm was taking a dangerous turn. One Monday night, a car pulled into the driveway of the roadside market and deposited several sticks of fizzing dynamite. The explosion severely damaged the front of the structure and wrecked a freezer and a meat display case. More than a hundred country hams were lost, although a few were saved. The Klan-charred hams tasted especially good, everyone joked.

Koinonia decided it was time to speak out. The fellowship placed a full-page ad in the *Times-Recorder* in an attempt to introduce itself, starting with the correct way to pronounce that funny-looking Greek name. Koinonia was essentially a church, the ad explained, that worshipped daily and counted among its residents a number of ministers and missionaries. "It is true that a few of our beliefs differ from those held by some people in this section. But the right to differ is a precious American heritage. The Fathers of this nation, coming from countries where religious differences were not tolerated, sought to preserve and perpetuate their newfound liberty by writing into the Constitution: 'Congress shall make no law respecting the establishment of religion, or prohibiting the free exercise thereof.' . . . We pledge ourselves to respect the rights of those who differ with us. We believe the citizens of this county will give us the same consideration."

That was wishful thinking.

The newspaper itself deplored the bombing, hinting at a more acceptable course of action: "Surely there are more honorable ways of waging a battle than through violence and possible bloodshed." Koinonia was about to get waylaid by one of those honorable methods.

———————

AS BAD AS THE BOMBING HAD BEEN, A MORE FUNDAMENTAL THREAT TO the community arrived in the mail over the summer. Four insurance companies were canceling six polices covering the farm's buildings and equipment. In the coming months, Koinonia was cut off by its gasoline distributor, its butane supplier, its building materials company, its fertilizer and seed sellers, its mechanic and auto parts dealer, and, worst of all, the Americus bank that had financed the farm's operations since 1942. One of the few men who offered any explanation was Willis Shiver, head of the lumber company whose materials had been used in most of the community's structures. He wasn't dealing with them anymore, he said, because of "pressure from levelheaded businessmen."

Translation: The White Citizens Council was boycotting Koinonia.

One by one, stores stopped selling to people from the farm. They had to drive to nearby Albany or Columbus for groceries. They had to make mail-order purchases because the Sears Roebuck in Americus refused to deal with them. Margaret Wittkamper tried to buy back-to-school shoes for her sons at Belk, and when she was ready to check out, she noticed a police officer enter the store and motion for the clerk. He returned and said it was against the law for him to sell anything to her.

"There's no law like that," she protested.

"Yes, but the people in Americus are upset about you all at the farm, and I just can't let you have those shoes."

Koinonia couldn't sell much of anything locally, either. The demand for its produce, hams, and eggs shriveled, and its only customers were a few black-owned markets in Albany. "Chain stores as well as independent grocers refused to stock our eggs, even though they had white shells and were laid by all-white flocks in white buildings," Clarence wrote, trying to make light of the situation. "Perhaps it was because the yolks were colored!"

The most bizarre embodiment of the boycott was a sad little man everyone knew as Slappey. He wasn't quite right. He pursed his lips and cracked his knuckles and pulled at his scraggly, thin hair in a state of perpetual fidgetiness. His task, as he saw it, was to trail Koinonians to make sure no one did business with them. "Don't buy any of them nigger eggs," he'd call out in a shrill voice when Con Browne tried to make deliveries. Con figured someone was paying his cab fare because he didn't drive and seemed to pop up in every store. Slappey claimed the citizens council was bankrolling him to keep an eye on the Communists.

He had seemed friendly enough before the violence started, when he used to visit the farm and play with the children on the trampoline or amuse them by throwing his voice and making it sound like Jiminy Cricket was trapped inside an apple crate. But after the white community turned against the farm, so did Slappey. He became a racist caricature. His vigilance could be downright creepy.

Once, outside the courthouse, he sneaked up behind Clarence and kicked him in the rear end. Another time, in the middle of Americus, he noticed someone from the farm with her niece, who was visiting. He looked her up and down admiringly and said, "You'll make some nigger a fine wife." Then there was the time he followed Lora Browne and her mother into Walgreens, where they were drinking Cokes at the soda fountain. He waited until they were finished and smashed their glasses, cutting his hand and bleeding all over himself as he explained that he didn't want anyone to have to press their lips against the same tumblers.

There were actually a handful of businessmen in the area who were willing to disregard the boycott, albeit carefully. One of them resided nearby in Plains.

Jimmy and Rosalynn Carter belonged to one of half a dozen families in Sumter County who were known to be tolerant about race. Though both were natives and had grown up with segregation, they had spent their early married years living on bases around the country as he climbed the ranks in the navy. The military, recently desegregated by order of President Truman, provided a marked contrast to the social order of southwest Georgia.

When his father died in 1953, the Carters moved back home to run the family peanut warehouse. Not long afterward, they went to hear a visiting preacher at Plains Baptist Church, who noticed his old friend Clarence Jordan entering the sanctuary and introduced him. "About a third of the people got up and walked out," Carter recalled. "That was the first time I knew anything about Koinonia." The town folks filled them in. "They said it was Communist," Rosalynn Carter said.

When the White Citizens Council later approached Carter about joining, he said no. His refusal to go along with the crowd cost him some business, although it was nothing on the scale of the blacklisting against Koinonia. Carter quietly offered to shell the farm's peanuts—Con Browne remembered taking some to his warehouse—but there were never many transactions because Koinonia was unable to get fertilizer and fuel and was forced to move away from row crops. Years later, when Carter ran for president, reporters would examine his limited contact with the besieged community only seven miles from Plains and look for clues about his moral character. That campaign led to the White House, of course, where Carter's chief of staff had a familiar name: Hamilton Jordan, Clarence's nephew.

———

IT GOT WORSE.

A few days after Thanksgiving, the reopened market was blasted with buckshot, ruining coolers bought to replace ones that had been ruined in previous attacks. On the night after Christmas, the gasoline pump at the farm was drilled with four rounds of steel-jacketed bullets. On New Year's Day, the sign at the entrance was riddled with rifle fire. The property damage reached a noisy climax on the night of January 14, 1957, when another charge detonated at the market, blowing it into pieces that were found hundreds of feet away. Koinonia elected not to rebuild this time, leaving the blackened remains as a testament for motorists on US 19.

One of Greg's future classmates, David Morgan, saw the smoldering wreckage as his family drove by on the way to visit relatives. The fourth grader had never heard of Koinonia and didn't understand what it was, except that people didn't like it. It scared him to think that something like that could happen near his seemingly peaceful hometown. In the coming years, he would remember his glimpse of what fear and hate could lead to.

Wreckage of the Koinonia farm market after the second bombing, 1957. *Courtesy of Conrad Browne*

With each incident, the law was called to investigate, and in unincorporated Sumter County, that meant Sheriff Fred D. Chappell. He was new to the job and wore civilian clothes, pants hiked high, two inches of nylon socks showing, instead of a uniform and the Mountie hat favored by many southern sheriffs. He was heavyset and jowly and had a foul temper that could turn his face purple and lead him to spew a stream of racial slurs. When he came to Koinonia after the latest shooting or bombing, he did not seem very motivated to get to the bottom of things, perhaps because he suspected that the victims were perpetrating the attacks.

"I don't find any clues, and I don't get any cooperation from those folks," Chappell told the Associated Press. He went on to say that people around Americus "have had it up to here" with Koinonia and related a report he had received about a white girl and two black boys from the farm walking down the street eating from the same bag of popcorn (a report later debunked—they weren't from the farm and the white girl was a fair-skinned black girl). "They're operating more openly now than ever before, and somebody is going to get hurt."

On the first Friday in February, someone did almost get hurt—almost killed, in fact.

Early that evening, Greg and some of the children were playing volleyball on a lighted court beside a peach orchard when they saw two cars creeping down the bend in the highway leading to the farm. The vehicles were so close that it looked like the first one was towing the second one. The children stopped their game to watch. It seemed odd; maybe one of them was having mechanical trouble. Then they heard several pops in rapid succession and the sound of something pelting the branches like a blowing sleet storm. Greg caught a glimpse of the guns as they discharged from the car windows, bursts of fire flicking from their muzzles like tongues from snakes.

"Hit the dirt!" someone screamed, and the kids dove and scattered.

Inside the house near the road where the Brownes lived, Lora had just come in from volleyball and was putting her little brothers to bed. She bent over to remove John's shoes when a crack sounded and a bullet pierced the wall inches above her head. A college student who was staying at the farm and had been sitting with the young ones yelled, "Get down! The house is going to explode." Lora corralled her brothers, and the three of them crawled into the bathroom shower, where she thought they might be safer.

After the volleyball court shooting, Greg said years later, "We thought they were going to take us out and hang us on crosses."

Once the mysterious cars had vanished into the night, Sheriff Chappell was summoned. As best he could piece together, at least two gunmen had attacked the farm. The first volley came from a shotgun, the second from a .22-caliber rifle. When he heard that Con and Ora Browne had not been there at the time of the shootings—they were in Americus—the sheriff formulated a theory of the crime to fit his biases: the Brownes had done it. They had shot at their own daughter and damn near hit her in an attempt to elicit outside sympathy and contributions. Clarence was livid; he wasn't sure why they even bothered to call the sheriff anymore when all he did was test their commitment to nonviolence.

A few weeks after the assault, Lora's fifth-grade teacher pulled her aside and asked, "Did you almost get shot?" Her sister in the North had sent her a copy of a church bulletin that included an item about an embattled community near Americus, Georgia. It was the first time anyone at Thalean Elementary School had mentioned the troubles to Lora. Her teacher was shocked. So was Lora, but for a different reason. She couldn't understand how an intelligent person could live in Sumter County and not have some idea of what was happening. Most people didn't seem to know, or want to know.

There were more close calls—shots fired at residents, shots fired into cars, more shots fired into houses, once from a machine gun. The most brazen attack came one night when a sniper targeted a window where Clarence usually sat reading. He had gone to bed, but the slug almost hit their oldest daughter, Eleanor, who was home from college.

With no expectation of police protection, Koinonia organized a night watch. Residents strung lights along the highway and posted sentries armed only with flashlights in cars parked along the shoulder. To fortify the houses nearest the road, they piled wood against exterior walls and rearranged furniture inside where it could stop the bullets. The children joined in during their playtime and dug pint-sized foxholes where they could look out for the approach of enemy pickups until their parents made them come in before sundown.

One of the night watchmen was a professional soldier, Con's brother-in-law—Uncle Carl to the kids—an army paratrooper stationed at Fort Benning in nearby Columbus. During a visit to the farm, he reported for duty in full uniform, his chest beribboned with decorations he had been awarded during the Korean War. He brought his rifle, but Con and Ora asked him to put it away, so he reluctantly sat through the night unarmed at his guard post by the highway. "So your dad's not going to stand up for you?" he told Lora. "I'll stand up for you. If they think they're going to kill my niece, they've got another thing coming."

IT WAS TIME TO APPEAL TO A HIGHER AUTHORITY: THE HIGHEST-RANKING soldier himself, the commander-in-chief. "Dear President Eisenhower," the letter began. "A community of nearly sixty men, women and children is facing annihilation unless quick, decisive action is taken by someone in authority. I am therefore appealing to you as a last resort." Clarence laid out the crimes against Koinonia and pleaded for federal intervention, but the architect of D-Day did not respond. Eisenhower's attorney general, Herbert Brownell, answered the letter, saying that while the attacks were regrettable, they were a matter for state and local law enforcement.

That was not comforting. The state revenue department had been combing through Koinonia's account books for weeks. The governor had ordered the Georgia Bureau of Investigation to examine the commune for evidence of subversive activities. Sumter County had impaneled a grand jury to look into the farm and the incidents there—a grand jury whose members included some of the same men who were boycotting the farm.

"A number of us have been summoned and we have spent many hours before them being quizzed in Gestapo fashion," Clarence wrote. "They seem to be convinced that we are the authors of all the violence for the purpose of working up sympathy, publicity, and money. They confiscated all of our financial records and also our mailing list, and photostated every card. The whole procedure has been one of the most discouraging things I have ever witnessed in my life."

The grand jury found what it wanted. Its April presentment took more than five thousand words to fault almost every aspect of Koinonia. Among the conclusions: the farm had indeed orchestrated the violence and reaped $27,500 in donations as a result. Its newsletter was a "propaganda sheet," and its mailing list of fifteen hundred included known Communists. It had brainwashed local blacks into participating in its communal system, which amounted to peonage. The community was not faith-based by any reasonable definition. "We find its claim to Christianity is sheer window dressing and has no precedent in the religious annals of the United States."

At least there were no indictments.

The grand jury got one thing right: Koinonia's plight was attracting publicity. The persecution of the farm produced the worst headlines to come out of Sumter County since the revelation of scandalous conditions at the Andersonville POW camp during the Civil War. Publications from *Time* to *Redbook* to the *New York Times* sent correspondents to Americus and documented the local animosity toward the farm. "The

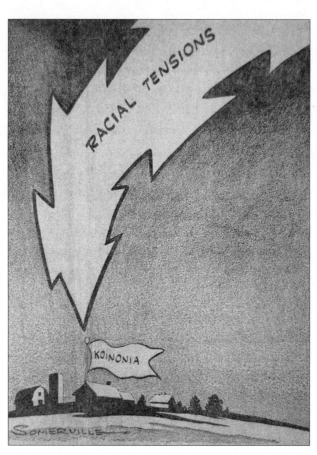

An editorial cartoon in the *Atlanta Journal* depicted
Koinonia as a victim of the tempestuous times.

misconceptions about the community are as many and as tinted as the
rumors that circulate the town," a stringer for *Newsweek* reported to
the Atlanta bureau. He went on to relate the story of a man who went
to the farm to pick up some potatoes, wandered behind a barn, and
claimed to have seen three women washing clothes: one white, two
black—all naked. "Other rumors have it that Koinonia is a group of
free-lovers, communists, home-sexuals [sic], nudists, spies, and mon-
grelizers of the races. The subject causes uneasiness or awe."

Religious journals like *The Christian Century* eagerly followed the
Koinonia story and depicted it as an American morality play. The great

theologian Reinhold Niebuhr, writing in *The Messenger,* the publication of the Evangelical and Reformed Church, called the grand jury report a "monstrous injustice in the name of justice" and mused about the way the Supreme Court's school decision had made good people better and bad people worse. On a more secular note, Eleanor Roosevelt, the patron saint of liberalism at the time, wrote about the farm in her syndicated column: "All of us who believe that there are no second-class citizens in the United States, and that we must learn to live together peacefully regardless of race, color or creed, have an obligation to give what help we can to those in the Koinonia Community."

Help did come. Churches sent care packages and supplies. (Greg wore donated trousers for years.) People wrote supportive letters and enclosed contributions. One woman drove all the way from New Hampshire to deliver a single sack of fertilizer. Dorothy Day, the Catholic activist and journalist, arrived on a bus from New York and volunteered to stand watch. One night, when a shot struck the vehicle in which she was sitting, Ora Browne ran to her aid and, noticing that she was shivering, offered her a coat. Day waved it off. "That ain't cold, baby. That's scared."

Koinonia turned to its contacts in the black community to address two of its most pressing needs: banking and insurance. A black-owned bank in Atlanta was pleased to have its business. In an effort to find insurance, Clarence sought the advice of someone who had faced a similar round of reprisal cancellations in Alabama, the leader of the Montgomery bus boycott, the Reverend Martin Luther King Jr. (Clarence had spoken from his pulpit at Dexter Avenue Baptist Church when another man was pastor and would speak there again at King's invitation in 1958.) In his reply, King let him know that the Georgians were not alone. "You and the Koinonia Community have been in my prayers continually for the last several months. The injustices and indignities that you are now confronting certainly leave you in trying moments. I hope, however, that you will gain consolation from the fact that in your struggle for freedom and a true Christian community you have cosmic companionship."

Koinonia eventually found coverage through a novel program called the Christian Brotherhood Insurance Plan. Two thousand people across the country signed pledges to insure the farm for up to $100,000, splitting any claims equally among them. Insurance, it seemed, was a fundamentally communal proposition.

At the time the violence started, fifteen black people were living at Koinonia—about a quarter of the farm's population. In the winter of 1957, members of the Ku Klux Klan, who were presumed to be behind the shootings and bombings, began a campaign of intimidation intended to drive the black residents away. They burned crosses and torched outbuildings at Koinonia and on nearby farms that were occupied by black families with ties to the community. The sight of flaming crosses was unnerving for people who had been raised on stories of lynchings and vigilante whippings. Rufus and Sue Angry, a black couple from Sumter County who lived at Koinonia with their children and wanted to become members, were particularly concerned that they might be singled out for punishment.

Most of the farm's black residents moved away as the population dropped by a third within a matter of weeks. Koinonia arranged to send the Angrys to New Jersey, where a communal farm called Hidden Springs was available. Some of the Georgians wanted to establish a sister community there, or at least a refuge. Others wanted to move the whole operation there and be done with Dixie.

Another group in Sumter County had the same goal.

One Sunday afternoon, Margaret Wittkamper was outside pushing a baby carriage with her youngest son, Danny, when she looked up to see a procession approaching the farm. "There was a long string of cars coming real slow, and they had their headlights on, so I thought it was a funeral," she said. It was a motorcade of seventy vehicles, and it was carrying members of the Knights of the Ku Klux Klan. They had been holding a rally at the fairgrounds in Americus and were coming with a proposition.

Margaret noticed Slappey, Koinonia's old nemesis, get out of a car, and she asked him what was going on. "Whose funeral is this?"

"It might as well be yours," he answered.

Another Klansman appeared and intoned, "Show me to your leader." It sounded like bad dialogue from a science fiction movie, and Margaret couldn't help but giggle. But the men were dead serious. They wanted to know whether Koinonia would consider an offer for its property. They wanted them to sell out and leave south Georgia.

———————

A RAY OF HOPE APPEARED IN THE SPRING OF 1957 WHEN HERBERT BIRD-sey, a farm supplies merchant in Macon, offered to provide Koinonia whatever feed and seed it needed from his stores in Americus and Albany. He had read about the boycott and didn't understand why anyone would turn down sales like that. The farm took advantage of his overture and bought seven hundred pounds of chicken feed. There would be no more purchases.

The first indication of trouble came on Friday, May 17, when Birdsey received a phone call from a man in Americus who loudly demanded to know who had given instructions "to sell to Communists down here." Birdsey said he had. Offended by the man's abusive tone, he hung up.

That weekend, around 1 A.M. on Sunday morning, several sticks of dynamite were tossed at the store in Americus from a car speeding down Forsyth Street. The explosion heavily damaged the front of the building and blew out fourteen windows in the Citizens Bank, the chamber of commerce, and the county courthouse, where the glass face of the venerable clock was chipped out between the numerals two and three. When Birdsey arrived later that morning to inspect the damage, his manager resigned on the spot, saying he had never wanted to do business with Koinonia in the first place. The establishment never reopened.

Among the stream of curious people who came by to see the crime scene was Greg's future high school classmate Joseph Logan, then finishing fourth grade at Furlow Grammar School. Joseph had never met anyone from Koinonia and was only hazily aware of its existence. Still, the episode made an impression on him. His father's insurance agency had been on that block. His mother worked in an office across the street. Joseph examined the three-inch gash in the sidewalk where the dynamite had gone off and wondered who might have been hurt if it had happened on a weekday.

Attacks on an unpopular farming community out in the country were one thing; a bombing on one of the city's main streets was quite another. Civic leaders decided that things had gone far enough. "Regardless of how we feel toward Koinonia," the *Times-Recorder* editorialized, "this violence, from whatever source it comes, must be stopped." The city, county, and chamber of commerce backed up the newspaper's words by offering a reward of $1,100 for information leading to the perpetrators.

On the Sunday after the blast, a delegation of ten businessmen and community leaders drove to Koinonia after church to talk with residents about how they could resolve the conflict. The delegation included the mayor, the chairman of the county commission, the editor of the *Times-Recorder*, and the president of the largest bank. They met with eight full members of the community—including the Jordans, Brownes, and Wittkampers—in the Jordans' living room.

Charles Crisp, the head of the Bank of Commerce, spoke for the visitors. He was the eldest of them and the bluest blood in town, the grandson and namesake of a man who had served as speaker of the US House of Representatives during the 1890s. He tried to couch his message as a moral appeal.

"Now your experiment has provoked the sensibilities of the vast majority of our people. Some of our people feel that you are out here to create trouble and chaos or to make money, which, if that's true, why, there would be no use for us to come out here. We come out here on the basis that you are serving what you believe to be Christian principles and are dedicated Christians. You say you are and we accept that. Now our philosophy is that the first duty of a Christian would be to—well, peace on earth, goodwill to men—to make brotherly love in the community. Unfortunately, your experiment has not done that; it has set brother against brother. It has created bitterness. It has created hatred. It has created every emotion that is contrary to my concept of Christianity."

He got to the point. "It is our belief that unless this experiment is moved to other fields that tempers will get to such a point that somebody is going to get hurt. We deplore it; we don't want it. We want to appeal to your good judgment to pray over it and think over it and see if you don't think you'll be serving the best interests of your Lord to move and leave us in peace."

The people who ran Sumter County were giving Koinonia an ultimatum: get out or there would be blood, and it would be on their hands. It was essentially the same offer the Klan had made earlier that year.

Clarence thanked the gentlemen for coming and considering the problem. "Suppose we did leave," he said. "Would it be an admission to the rest of the nation and to the rest of the world that Sumter County could not or would not preserve law and order within its bounds? Would it be an admission on our part that we felt people were not free in Sumter County to worship God as they saw fit, so long as they did not harm anyone?"

"We would take that responsibility," Crisp said.

"Another thing," commission chairman George Mathews interjected. "There's no way in the world for us to furnish you with police protection out here, and we don't have any control over folks slipping around at night and throwing a stick of dynamite, not only on your place but up there on the streets of Americus." Later in the discussion, Mathews opined that the sheriff was doing a good job of investigating the crime, and then he added an offhanded remark that was closer to the truth of the situation. "Somebody asked me the other day who that was threw that dynamite up on the sidewalk, and I told him if I knew I wasn't going to tell anybody, because I don't want any of it in my automobile, 'specially with me in it."

It was a telling admission. The county's chief executive was saying that he was too scared of the bombers to try very hard to find out who they were. Of course, this was the same man who earlier that year had told an Atlanta freelancer writing for *The Nation* what he thought about Koinonia. "We aren't going to have that gang down here stirring up our Americus niggers. . . . We got no room for people like that here, and we don't aim to have them around much longer." No wonder he wasn't chosen to speak for the delegation.

The two sides talked awhile longer and then broke up with little agreement or understanding. A few weeks later, Koinonia invited the men back and suggested that a third party—perhaps someone from Georgia who understood southern attitudes—could mediate. The proposal went nowhere. If nothing else came of the summit meetings, at least the violence tailed off. While no one was prosecuted for the bombings or the attacks on the farm, word apparently went out to the Klan and its ilk that further terrorism would not be tolerated, even if the authorities more or less agreed with the terrorists.

As for the suggestion that Koinonia relocate to a more hospitable setting, Clarence was asked about that after a speech he gave that year. He answered with some of the most passionate words he ever spoke:

> I want to tell you why we don't sell out and move away. Fifteen years ago, we went there and bought that old eroded piece of land. It was sick. There were gashes in it, and it was sore and bleeding. I don't know whether you've ever walked over a piece of ground that could almost cry out to you, "Heal me, heal me." I don't know whether you feel the closeness to the soil that I do. When you fill in those old gullies and terrace the fields, you begin to feel the springiness of the sod beneath your feet, and you see that old land come to life. When you walk through a little ole pine forest that you set out as little seedlings and now see them reaching for the sky and hear the wind through them. When you walk a little further over a bit of ground where your child is buried. [The Jordans lost a newborn son in 1955.] And you go over to a hill where your children and many visitors have held picnics. When you walk across a creek that you've bathed in during the heat of summer.

His voice suddenly rose in indignation. "And men say to you, 'Why don't you sell it? Move away.' You might as well say, 'Why don't you sell your mother?'"

He continued in a softer tone. "Somehow God has made us out of this old soil, and we go back to it and we never lose its claim on us. It isn't a simple matter to leave it."

———————

NOT ALL THE THREATS CAME FROM BOMBERS AND NIGHTRIDERS. THAT summer, more than a year after the violence started, Greg's family faced a calamity that millions of parents in the fifties feared almost as much as the risk of nuclear war.

The water in the swimming hole seemed especially cold when some of the kids went for a dip late one afternoon. Climbing out, Greg noticed that his youngest brother, Danny, was shivering uncontrollably and that his skin was bluish. They wrapped him in blankets and put him to bed. He awoke the next morning unable to move his legs. His parents took him to the hospital and heard the dreaded diagnosis: infantile paralysis—polio.

Greg and the other Koinonia children who attended Thalean had been inoculated with an early version of the Salk vaccine at school, but Danny, not yet three, was considered too young to receive it. He spent most of his youth on crutches or braces, his mother shuttling him to an endless series of exams and operations at charity treatment centers. When Danny started school a few years later, his condition afforded him a measure of protection from harassment. Once, when a boy popped him in the face and he fell to the bathroom floor, a couple of other kids came to his defense. "What are you doing?" one of them said sharply. "Leave him alone. Can't you see he's crippled?"

After Danny came down with polio, the Wittkampers faced another health crisis when Will almost died of pneumonia. Greg watched through the window of their cottage as the adults in the community gathered around his father's bed to pray for his soul—his condition was that critical. But Will was a tough old bird. Once he recovered, he became a health-food nut, making smoothies, which he called "green shakes," with half-spoiled food and plants that most people wouldn't put in their mouths. "They were the worst things you ever tasted," Greg said.

Will was an early environmentalist who didn't believe in using chemicals, which put him at odds with Clarence, who considered pesticides a practical tool of modern farming. Will also thought that Christian stewardship called for reusing everything, including spent nails, which he collected in buckets of water to let them rust and then spread across the garden to amend the soil. It peeved Clarence, who pointed out that even partially disintegrated nails could puncture tractor tires. "Your father has some strange ideas," he told Greg. "Do you know why this soil is red? Iron. It doesn't need any more iron."

While Clarence appreciated Will's efforts in the garden, he didn't think it was necessarily the best use of time or resources. What Koinonia really needed during the boycott, he thought, was a new source of income.

———————

WITH NO PLACE TO SELL ITS EGGS OR ROW CROPS, KOINONIA LOOKED around for another business to sustain the community—one that would be less susceptible to local hostility. The members settled on pecans, which thrived in south Georgia and could be turned into a number of products sold nationwide by mail order. They planted pecan trees to supplement their existing orchards, and until the young trees bore fruit, bought nuts from the federal government and from farmers in Alabama who didn't know or care who they were dealing with. They purchased grading and sorting equipment from an Italian family in Albany who were getting out of the pecan trade. Clarence studied up on commercial baking and candy making, and one of the poultry houses was converted into a kitchen producing confections and dense fruitcakes soaked in wine. The solicitations went out under a pointed slogan: "Help us ship the nuts out of Georgia."

In the meantime, Koinonia set up an assembly line of slaughter to liquidate its former business. For days on end, Will Wittkamper yanked the heads off thousands of laying hens, while Greg plunged the bloody carcasses into scalding water and sent them on to the kitchen to be plucked, processed, and frozen. They had more fricassee on their hands than anyone knew what to do with. In the coming months, the farm served so much poultry that some residents grew queasy at the smell of stewing birds. "We ate chicken till we grew feathers," Con Browne said.

Con was in Americus that November taking mail-order packages to the railroad express office when he became the victim of another spasm of hatred. A man approached his car demanding to know what he was doing, and then jerked off his glasses and hit him in the face with brass knuckles. Con fell back into the passenger seat bleeding, and the man pounced on him, striking him repeatedly. The railroad express manager took him to a doctor and drove him back to the farm, where he went to bed with his wounds. Greg stopped by the house to look in on him and flinched at the sight of his raw, lacerated face.

A short while later, Sheriff Chappell knocked on the door. He wasn't there to investigate the assault; he was there to arrest Con. A city policeman had noticed that he was driving a car with an illegal license tag, and the sheriff intended to book him for it. He took Con from his bed, bandaged and groggy, and hauled him to jail, where he locked him up with a convicted murderer. The Browne children saw their bruised father carted off. It was all their mother could do to keep them from kicking the sheriff in his shins. "I actually went to find an ax," Charlie Browne remembered. "I was going to chop his head off."

The assault of Con Browne and his subsequent arrest dramatized like nothing before the trauma and frustration of living at Koinonia during the terror years. Schooled as they were in Christian nonviolence, the children understood why they were not supposed to fight back. But that didn't quell their emotions. They were angry. They wanted to hurt the people who were hurting them. Some of them could not accept that their parents wouldn't make it stop or at least move them all away. "I thought my father wasn't man enough to defend us," Charlie said. "For a long time, I was kind of ashamed of him." Greg directed blame outside the farm; the attack on Con and his subsequent arrest taught him, at the tender age of ten, to be leery of law enforcement officers.

The adults discussed whether it would be better to evacuate the children. The question caused them considerable pain. "I've wondered many, many times how much good we were doing by letting those people ride by here and shoot at us," Clarence said years later during one of his final interviews.

Con had a particularly hard time squaring the responsibilities of fatherhood with the requirements of his faith. He resolved that, while he wouldn't commit violence in defense of his children, he would stand between them and anyone meaning to harm them. Taking a bullet for his kids may have been a valid position intellectually and morally, but it didn't reassure his family and it didn't still the doubts churning inside Con's subconscious. He started seeing a therapist in Columbus. He was having a terrible dream: one of his children had been killed, and all he could do about it was to lay the body on the courthouse steps in Americus.

The farm's dilemma reminded Greg of the Old Testament story of Abraham. When God asked him to sacrifice his son Isaac as a show of faith, he bound him to an altar and started to slit his throat before an angel intervened and stopped him. It seemed to Greg that the people at Koinonia were putting a lot of trust in angels.

PART 2

Americus

CHAPTER 4

The Children's Hour

KOINONIA'S TROUBLES DIDN'T END WHEN THE BOMBINGS AND DRIVE-BY shootings stopped. The conflict between the farm and the outside community simply moved to another setting, one that put Greg and the other children on the front lines.

In the fall of 1960, three Koinonia teenagers were ready to start high school, one from each of the fellowship's core families: Lora Browne, Jan Jordan, and Billy Wittkamper. Sumter County had dual school systems—one in Americus, the other outside the city—in addition to separate facilities for whites and blacks. The Koinonia students normally would have attended the white county high school in Plains, but as the offspring of ministers, they were expected to go on to college, and the city high school in Americus had better preparatory classes. The farm also had to consider its history with the schools. The Jordans' oldest daughter, Eleanor, had gone to Americus without incident, but their oldest son, Jim, had the misfortune of starting at Plains shortly after the desegregation cyclone touched down. He was hounded so mercilessly that he left the school after one day. Their parents agreed that Lora, Jan, and Billy ought to go to Americus High, where they hoped they would be treated better.

There was just one problem: the school board refused to enroll them. The city had a transfer arrangement with the county and rarely rejected an applicant; of the thirty who applied in 1960, twenty-seven were accepted. No one thought it was a coincidence that all three rejects came from Koinonia. The boycott was continuing, only this time it wasn't about insurance or chicken feed; it was about children.

After appealing the board's decision unsuccessfully, Koinonia debated what to do next. The parents were reluctant to go to court because that seemed to them an unchristian act of aggression—but wasn't discrimination unchristian? Seeing no other choice, they called the American Civil Liberties Union and filed a lawsuit. Their lawyer invited journalists to the farm to write about the children, to show the public that they didn't have horns and cloven hooves, so Lora, Jan, and Billy gave interviews and dutifully posed for photos holding a library book none of them had read, as if they were studying for exams. "Well, you *look* normal," the reporter said. Another reporter quoted a school board official as saying that they didn't want the Koinonia students because they might "infect" the other kids with their ideas. While the suit was pending, Florence Jordan homeschooled the three while their younger siblings continued to attend their classes. "I thought they were lucky dogs not to have to go to school," said Greg, who was starting his eighth and final year at Thalean Elementary. He knew that the outcome of the case would soon affect him.

The suit was heard a month into the school term. Judge William Bootle, an Eisenhower appointee who would figure in some of the most important civil rights decisions in Georgia, presided over the hearing in federal court in Macon. Six witnesses appeared for Koinonia—the students and their fathers—and six appeared for the school board. Their testimony provided a rare public airing of Sumter County's tangled attitudes toward the farm.

A young lawyer named Warren Fortson offered particularly illuminating testimony. Fortson came from a politically connected family near Augusta—his brother Ben was Georgia's secretary of state—and had been in Americus only a few months. The question of whether to admit the Koinonia students came up at his second board meeting. All he knew about the farm was that people detested it and that a county grand jury had condemned it. He read about the investigation and wondered how fair it had been, but since he was new in town, he thought it wise to defer to the other members when they argued that the presence of the Koinonia children would disrupt classes.

"I was as much worried about a lot of the parents of the children creating a disturbance as I was the children," Fortson testified. "I was acutely aware of the man in the street's opinion, and I have also heard some of those expressions voiced against the people at Koinonia, and I knew it was just right for a rather explosive situation to occur if we allowed those children in the school system."

An explosive situation? Judge Bootle pressed Fortson about who he thought would light the fuse.

"I felt that people in Americus or the children in the Americus system would cause the trouble."

"Well, Mr. Fortson, has law and order broken down in Americus to the point that they cannot control their own citizens and the children in the schools?"

"Well, let's put it this way," Fortson replied. "Before I ever came to Americus, there was a considerable . . . outbreak of civil violence. It happened before and it could happen again."

That was the nut of it: there had been bombings and shootings in Sumter County, and not that long ago. The school board was afraid that violence might break out again if the Koinonia children were allowed to enter the city high school, so it took the easiest course and excluded them altogether.

Judge Bootle wasn't buying it. Four weeks after the hearing, he ruled that the students had been rejected solely because of their parents' religious and social beliefs. "This will not do," he declared, ordering the three admitted to classes immediately. The decision was a foretaste of the civil rights struggles to come in southwest Georgia, and it met with widespread anger. The next time Bootle visited Americus to preside over US district court, in January 1961, protestors gathered outside and hanged him in effigy. By then, they had something else to be furious with him about; he had ordered the desegregation of the University of Georgia.

In the wake of the Koinonia lawsuit, at least one school board member reexamined his stand and made an effort to research the matter. Fortson had been impressed with Clarence Jordan's eloquence in court. A few weeks after the ruling, he visited the farm and learned more about the community over a fried catfish lunch with the Jordans. He came away liking them and feeling more sympathetic for their perilous position in the county. As for that grand jury finding that Koinonia was teeming with Communists, Fortson privately dismissed it as "crap—standard McCarthy stuff."

———————

AMERICUS HIGH SCHOOL OCCUPIED A 1938 REDBRICK STRUCTURE WITH a cupola on top that made it look like it belonged on a colonial plantation in Virginia—Mount Vernon's middle-class cousin. It was located a couple of blocks off the city's main drag in a shady neighborhood of older homes that abruptly gave way at the end of the school property to an unpaved street where black people lived in smaller frame houses. Around five hundred students—all white—attended grades nine through twelve. After missing nine weeks of school, Lora, Jan, and Billy joined their number in early November. The court offered an escort of federal marshals, but the families declined because they disliked the idea of armed guards coercing acceptance at the point of a gun barrel. As Clarence told his daughter, "Now, Jan honey, we won the case in court, but there isn't a court in the land that can make these folks like you."

On the night before she was to start classes, Lora received a phone call from an elementary school friend warning that she could no longer be seen speaking with her in public. They might be able to speak on the bus or over the phone at night. "But if I talk to you in class," she said, "no one will talk to me." Her friend had been at Americus High since September and knew what sort of reception awaited the Koinonia students. Jan got a similar call from the brother of her best friend at Thalean and thought to herself, "Uh-oh, this is not going to be fun and games."

It wasn't. The three of them were met with hostility from the beginning. Classmates refused to sit with them at lunch, and a few tossed food at them. Someone poured acid in Lora's locker and ruined her gym clothes. Jan's textbooks were stolen or vandalized repeatedly, and she ran through a dozen sets of replacements. They were called Commies and

Greg (left, with his brother Billy) tries out a banjo for friends, including Jan Jordan (center) and Lora Browne (right), 1962. *Courtesy of Lora Browne*

race mixers so often that they tuned it out like so much white noise—although Lora was amused by the inventive vitriol of one boy who labeled her "a goddamn nigger-loving Communist Watusi Jew." That kind of covered it. In a backhanded way, the school board had been right: their presence was disruptive. The hostile atmosphere certainly disrupted Lora's studies, as she went from being one of the top students in grade school to making Fs before she recovered her academic footing. It seemed like the only people at Americus High who treated the Koinonia children kindly were the black ladies working in the cafeteria; when they saw her in line, Jan noticed, they'd nudge each other and give her heaping portions.

Billy may have had the toughest time of it. The southern code of chivalry dictated that no one lay a hand on the girls, but there were no such compunctions when it came to boys like the eldest Wittkamper son. Along with the taunting and vandalism the others experienced, he got pushed on the stairs and popped in the back and received threatening letters. Reflecting on it later, he would laugh and say that it could have been worse. Billy had stuttered since childhood and played it up whenever he was menaced by others. "I think they thought I was a moron and left me alone sometimes." He warned Greg that high school was going to be nothing like what they had known at Thalean.

Jan would tell her father what she and the others were going through, but the only advice he usually imparted was to turn the other cheek. It occurred to her that the children were being persecuted for their parents' beliefs. She grew resentful and began to question her own faith. One day, relating an especially bad incident, Jan watched as her father's eyes filled with tears, and she understood that he was as frustrated and powerless as she was. After that, she stopped telling Clarence about everything that was happening.

As rough as it was, Jan and Lora remained at Americus High after their first year. Billy did not. Near the end of the school term, his parents asked him whether he would rather continue his education somewhere else. Billy despised the high school and hated the heat, humidity, and insects of southwest Georgia, so he leapt at the chance to escape. The Wittkampers sent him to the Chicago area, to Reba Place, a Mennonite community with long-standing ties to Koinonia. It turned out to be one of the best things that could have happened to Billy, but it wasn't so good for Greg, who wouldn't have his older brother to lean on when he entered the crucible.

––––––––

GREG WAS INITIATED INTO AMERICUS HIGH SCHOOL WITH A FAVORITE weapon of teenage pranksters everywhere: a rubber band–propelled paper clip.

As he started ninth grade in the fall of 1961, he had to deal with the provocations of a junior named Tommy Bass, who liked to sneak up behind him in the hallways and fire paper clips into the small of his back with a rubber band. They stung like shotgun pellets. Tommy was good; his attacks were so quick and stealthy that Greg could never catch him in the act. He had little doubt who was shooting him, though, so he went to the principal's office to try to stop the nonsense. K. W. McKinnon—Mr. Mac to students—may have looked like a bespectacled milquetoast, but he was known as an old-school disciplinarian. Jan and Billy had warned that the principal's penchant for order did not extend to looking out for Koinonia children. Greg understood what they meant when he reported that he was being nettled with office supplies.

"Did you see who did it?" McKinnon asked.

Greg had to admit that he had not actually seen the culprit.

"Then there's nothing I can do. I need proof."

Angered by the principal's seeming lack of concern, Greg reached for the first rebuttal that popped into his mind. "Well, if you won't do anything, maybe we should bring in some federal marshals."

"Go ahead," McKinnon replied coolly.

It had not been an auspicious introduction to authority at Americus High. When Greg went home and told some of the adults about the exchange, Clarence suggested that he shouldn't make threats he couldn't back up. It had been almost a year since Koinonia had declined the court's offer of marshals to escort the students. The cavalry would not be galloping to the rescue.

There was another Koinonia teenager entering the high school that fall, and she carried herself quite differently than Greg. Carol Browne, Lora's younger sister, was starting eighth grade as part of a new class that had been added to the school. A high-strung thirteen-year-old who was so skinny that students inevitably nicknamed her Olive Oyl, she didn't take guff from anyone. When kids started pestering her and calling her a nigger lover, she responded combatively, "Why not? I trust them more than you." She begged her parents to let her fight the bullies at school, but they told her no, under no circumstances.

Greg took a different tack. After his encounter with the principal, he concluded that his best survival strategy would be to lie low and keep quiet. When slurs and insults came his way, as they did almost every day, he tried to ignore them and didn't talk back. He was determined to be invisible.

Nothing about Greg's appearance or demeanor should have drawn undue attention. At fourteen, he looked like many teenagers in the years before Dylan and the Beatles, when boys modeled themselves after Elvis or Ricky Nelson if they didn't have a crew cut or a flattop. Greg wore his hair long and greasy, swept back into a ducktail: he could've been the lost Everly Brother. He didn't raise his hand in class. He seldom spoke unless he was spoken to. He didn't volunteer for any clubs or go out for any teams.

Greg quickly realized that his brother had been right: high school was going to be more trying than grade school. The harassment clearly intensified, but most students never jeered at him or shoved him on the stairs or stung him with paper clips; the juvenile vigilantes were always a minority. Most of his classmates simply shunned him. Age had something to do with it. As children move into their teens, they become more susceptible to peer pressure. Like Lora and Jan the year before, Greg noticed that students who had once been approachable at Thalean would no longer talk with him openly. They might say something on the bus ride home, but at school they seemed afraid to be seen near him. When he sat down for lunch, people moved away from his table as if he had come in reeking from cleaning the hog pens. From 8 A.M. to 3 P.M., five days a week, he was at once utterly conspicuous and completely isolated.

Greg's new classmates didn't know much about Koinonia. Many of them couldn't even pronounce the name properly; they called it Corn-nee-ah, like it was a weed that popped up in the cornfields, or Co'nia, skipping over a syllable like they were ordering Co'Cola in a south Georgia drawl. They didn't know about Koinonia's religious beliefs, why it supported racial equality, or how its communal system worked and why it didn't necessarily make the members Communists. All the students knew was that their parents said Koinonia was bad, that Greg was the only member of their class who came from the place, and that it had literally taken a federal case to get him and his like into the school. The boy was radioactive. It was best to stay away from him.

———————

AMONG THE FRESHMEN WHO OBSERVED GREG THAT FALL WERE SEVERAL who would write him letters of apology many years later. He knew none of them because he came from a county elementary school and they had attended one that was part of the city system in Americus. They made little impression on him at the time, but they all knew who he was; he might as well have worn a scarlet *K* on his chest.

Celia Harvey, a demure banker's daughter and devout member of First Methodist Church, was curious about Koinonia in the way a good girl might be curious about a leather-clad motorcycle gang. She had heard awful things about the farm. "People called it a cult. There was a lot of discussion about why their kids were coming to our school. I felt sorry for them. I kept thinking: 'How can their parents allow them to be here? My parents wouldn't put me in a position like that.' I didn't think it was right, as young and vulnerable as they were."

Celia made a point of staying away from Greg. So did her best friend, Deanie Dudley, a pretty car salesman's daughter who had a friendly word for almost everyone she met. She didn't want to be rude to Greg—not directly—so when she saw him coming down the hall, she turned away or pretended to be hunting for something in her locker. "I would look at him and wonder who he was and why he believed things everyone else disagreed with. I couldn't understand why those people were here in the first place. Why would they come to the Deep South and start a commune? It didn't seem like a wise thing to do."

David Morgan, a vocational instructor's son who was something of a smart aleck, had no personal animosity for Greg. But he did want to be liked, so he snickered when the other boys called him names and said nothing when he witnessed the tripping and shoving. As a red-blooded male, he was mystified by Greg's nonviolent response. "I always wondered why he didn't fight back. You could see from his physique that he could have taken care of himself."

Of all the classmates who later apologized to Greg, perhaps none was as dubious of what he represented as Joseph Logan, the wavy-haired son of an insurance salesman. Joseph had heard the rumors about Koinonia—about the Communism and race mixing—and wanted to keep his distance from anyone who came from the farm. "We were told that when they came in from the fields, they threw their clothes into one pile, and the next day, they may get their clothes back and they may not. You may get a black person's clothes from the day before." His young mind shuddered.

Joseph Logan.

Joseph was a good kid: diligent, well-behaved, churchgoing, an A student, and certainly not a troublemaker. But he was also a football player, and the company he kept explained a lot about his frame of mind. Americus High was the focus of white pride and identity in Sumter County, and its football team was at the tip of that tribal allegiance. The Panthers were a winning program, making the playoffs in 1961, taking the state championship the following year, and churning out star players like Dan Reeves, who went on to play professionally with the Dallas Cowboys and to coach two teams to the Super Bowl. Joseph dreamed of joining the AHS tradition and, despite his average size, made the varsity as a hard-blocking offensive lineman during his sophomore year. The other players looked at his curly hair and nicknamed him Buckwheat, after the kinky-headed boy in the *Our Gang* comedies. Joseph didn't care; he laughed along with the guys. He took the credo of teamwork and athletic groupthink to heart. His coach became the ranking authority figure in his adolescent world, his teammates the most influential peers. They weren't the kind of people who questioned the way things were. "We despised Koinonia and all it stood for," he said. "You have to put up with a wart until it goes away; that's how we felt about Greg."

In other circumstances, Joseph and Greg might have been team-mates. Greg would have made a fine gridiron prospect. He was strong for his age, his upper body pumped up from hours of lifting hay bales on the farm, and he could run like a colt. When they picked sides for football in physical education class, he was usually one of the first guys chosen, his objectionable background temporarily overlooked. Greg could do more chin-ups in a minute than anyone else and could climb the rope to the gymnasium ceiling with ease—an exercise that panics many a young teenager. One coach, watching him run, asked him to try out for the track team. Greg said he was too busy with farm chores and told him no.

There was more to it than that. PE was mandatory; competing on the track or football teams was elective. Greg had no interest in going out of his way to glorify Americus High School on the fields of athletic endeavor. He certainly didn't want to attend football games, the biggest events on the school calendar, where he would have made an easy target for his enemies. He secretly pulled against the team and would have been pleased if it had gone 0–10. If his classmates were going to have nothing to do with him, he was going to have nothing to do with their most exalted pastime.

As the school year wore on, Greg got through his classes by withdrawing from his surroundings and creating a sort of mental bubble around himself, tuning out other people and daydreaming about arrowhead hunting and other things he enjoyed doing on the farm. He was an indifferent student who didn't like to spend time inside reading when he could be outside tinkering with a tractor or walking through the woods. He drifted through his courses and paid only intermittent attention to the lectures. His grades slipped, and he flunked Latin and algebra, where a particularly mean-spirited teacher seemed to delight in asking him questions he couldn't answer. His silence and lack of engagement only added to the sense that he was an alien presence, someone who could be ignored or picked on without consequence.

Even the yearbook editors dumped on him. In the 1962 annual, *The Panther,* his freshman portrait was misidentified as "Grey Whitthamper," as if he were a pile of dirty laundry.

GREG MIGHT NOT HAVE ENDURED FOUR STRAIGHT YEARS AT AMERICUS High. Fortunately, he didn't have to. While he was in ninth grade, his family decided to move about as far north as they could move and still remain in the Lower 48 of the United States—not because of what was happening to their son at school, but because of the farm's struggle to survive. As a side benefit, Greg received a temporary stay from harassment that helped replenish his sanity.

The years of violence and boycott had diminished Koinonia, chasing off residents to the point that virtually no one lived on the farm except the Brownes, Jordans, and Wittkampers. The adults held lengthy discussions about whether to shut down the community or join another group. There was a possibility in North Dakota. Koinonia had a long relationship with a family there, the Maendels, who had supported the Georgians during the years of persecution and had taken in Jim Jordan after he fled Plains High School. The Maendels were Hutterites, members of a sect that originated in Austria and bore similarities to the Amish and the Mennonites in that they wore plain clothing and believed in pacifism and simple, communal living. Their farm had hosted a Hutterite colony, but they were reevaluating their affiliation and considering their options. In the spring of 1962, Will and Margaret Wittkamper volunteered to relocate their family and explore a merger between Koinonia and the North Dakotans.

Greg stayed behind for a couple of months to finish his freshman year. It was the loneliest time of his life. Unwelcome in class, separated from his brothers and parents, he felt like he had been abandoned and began to brood and have fleeting thoughts of suicide. His mood lifted when he boarded a northbound Greyhound in June and saw a comely, blue-eyed brunette traveling by herself. They sat together and talked for hours, Greg telling her all about Koinonia and the way its young people were being treated in school. She seemed to understand. As she got off the bus in Indianapolis, he impulsively kissed her good-bye, and she kissed him back. He couldn't remember feeling more lighthearted.

Greg arrived in North Dakota to find a communal setup not un-like Koinonia. Joe and Mary Maendel had fourteen children and were a virtual colony unto themselves, living on a farm called Forest River that spread across six thousand acres on the boundless plains near the Canadian border. Greg and his brother David worked long hours collecting and grading eggs from a ceaseless production line of twenty thousand hens. That fall, they attended public school without incident, and Greg's marks improved dramatically. He made up algebra with the help of a sympathetic teacher and earned Bs on his report card. He started reading more and found that it could be enjoyable. Outside the classroom, he joined the track team—the only extracurricular activity he ever participated in—and ran the hundred-yard dash. The other students knew he lived in a religious community and thought some of their customs were peculiar, but they didn't regard Greg and David as freaks. For the first time, high school seemed kind of normal.

The Wittkampers felt welcome at Forest River despite the cultural differences. The Maendels worshipped in the Hutterite fashion, speaking in a German dialect and separating the men from the women in church. They wore black clothing like the Amish and disapproved of certain accessories like belts, which they considered an unnecessary expression of human vanity. That wasn't an issue since the Wittkampers brought very little with them from Georgia and allowed their hosts to dress them. But other issues were looming.

The Maendels were thinking about making Forest River a full-fledged Hutterite colony again. That meant inviting other members of the faith to live there and adhering more strictly to its rules. Among them were two that the Wittkampers could not abide. The Hutterites prohibited music outside church. Will had a problem with that: he loved to sing and play the cello, and could take a bow to a wood saw and produce eerie-sounding tunes that seemed to issue from another century. His sons didn't like the music restrictions either. One day, when a group of Hutterite elders were visiting to evaluate the community, Greg saw them outside his open window, put Dvořák's Fifth Symphony on his record player, and cranked up the volume. He might as well have lit a cherry bomb.

The other rule had to do with whiskers. According to tradition, husbands were supposed to wear a beard while single men kept a clean-shaven face. Will thought that was silly. Though he was entitled to a beard and had cultivated one for some time, he promptly shaved it off to show what he thought of all the strictures. Margaret was getting tired of the family's new home as well, especially the winter weather, which depressed her. She learned a new word—*snirt*—to describe the mixture of snow and dirt that lingered through early spring.

The Wittkampers decided that they weren't cut out for North Dakota winters and Hutterite ways. At the end of the school year, they departed for Koinonia in a gray 1949 Plymouth sedan that the Maendels, generous as always, had given them for the trip. Greg drove most of the sixteen hundred miles back to Georgia. It was the first time he had ever taken a car out on the highway, and he was excited to be behind the wheel using his learner's permit, but his adventure was tinged with sadness and apprehension. He would liked to have stayed at Forest River, belt-less or not; to him, almost anything would have been better than going back to Americus High School.

———————

WHEN GREG'S FAMILY RETURNED IN JUNE 1963, KOINONIA WAS STILL IN transition. With fewer people living there, the fellowship decided that it would no longer be a true commune where members pooled their resources and earned no income for their labors. It adopted a quasi-capitalistic model, with each resident assuming work responsibilities and receiving a stipend. Will Wittkamper would get $100 a month for tending the garden. Greg would earn $25 a week for taking care of a hundred cows, a consuming task that involved everything from baling hay and setting out feed to castrating bulls and birthing calves. Clarence Jordan would remain the de facto leader of the farm, but he would spend more time on the road speaking and more of his time at home writing. He had been working on a new project, an outgrowth of some of his talks at Koinonia, translating the New Testament from Greek into the vernacular language of the South in an effort, as he explained, "to help cotton-picking Christians understand what their pea-picking preachers had been saying." The first volume of what Clarence called the "cotton patch" version of the Gospels would soon be published.

There was one other change at Koinonia that grieved everyone. As the adults saw it, the farm could no longer support three families. They came to the painful realization that one of them would have to go. It couldn't be the Jordans. Clarence was indispensable; not only was he the community's cofounder and spokesman, but he knew more about agriculture than anyone else. The Wittkampers weren't going anywhere. Will was entering his seventies, losing his hearing, and could no longer be expected to find a job to support his wife and sons. "You all do what you want," Margaret declared, "but we're going to stay here until we die."

That left the Brownes. Con was in his midforties and had better employment prospects than Will. He arranged a job as associate director of the Highlander School, the training center in Tennessee where Rosa Parks had learned about nonviolent resistance before the Montgomery bus boycott and where Koinonia had moved its interracial summer camp when the Sumter County authorities shut it down. As the Wittkampers were coming home, the Brownes were reluctantly packing up after thirteen years and leaving for Knoxville, where Lora and Carol would have to finish school. There would be two fewer Koinonia kids at Americus High, one more reason for Greg to be wary of going back.

His classmates had not forgotten him. That spring, when they signed each other's copies of the 1963 Panther yearbook, one of Joseph Logan's pals ended his inscription with a jab at the boy none of them had seen in months:

"P.S. Hasn't it been great with no *Greg*?"

CHAPTER 5

Welcome to the Revolution

AT SOME POINT IN HIS ADOLESCENCE, EVERY PREACHER'S SON SEEMS drawn to a friend who knows his way around the shadow world of temptation and gratification. When Greg returned to Georgia in the early summer of 1963, he found such a friend helping out in the pecan plant at the farm.

Collins McGee did not move to Koinonia to become a member of the commune; he came to work. The goateed young black man did everything from handling livestock to putting up hay to repairing tractors. He was a couple of years older than Greg and far more experienced in the sweet mysteries of life that a sixteen-year-old boy is naturally curious about—namely, the pursuit of women and alcohol. After he came back from North Dakota, Greg no longer stayed with his family in the house they had occupied before but instead took up residence in a room across from Collins, under the old Jordan quarters. They quickly became running buddies, in part because Greg had something Collins needed. He didn't own a car, and Greg, now old enough to drive legally in Georgia, had access to that clunky old Plymouth he had steered back from the Hutterite farm.

Collins was from Americus and seemed to know everyone in the black community. When Greg drove him into town for errands, Collins would take him to the places he frequented and show him a side of

Collins McGee and Greg on the farm, mid-1960s. *Courtesy of Leonard Jordan*

Sumter County few whites ever saw up close. They shot pool together, listened to the blues in juke joints, and hung out along Cotton Avenue, where the black cafés and businesses were congregated in between all the streets named for Confederate generals. Sometimes they drove out in the woods to buy moonshine, which Collins preferred to most store-bought spirits. Greg had tried beer and brandy, but he had never tasted liquor. He kind of liked it.

People in the dives eyed the young paleface suspiciously at first, but Collins vouched for him. "He's OK," he'd say. "He's from the Farm." That's what they called it—the Farm, like it was the only one around. Being from there was recommendation enough; it meant Greg wasn't like most of the other white kids. "It meant that I was on *their* side. They treated me like I was some kind of minor celebrity. I was the honky they tolerated."

As Greg got to know Collins, he could see that there was more to him than a thirst for the nightlife. He was smart and funny. He was intense and worked as hard as two men. Best of all, he was caring and took a sincere interest in his younger friend. Greg told him about his troubles at Americus High in a way that he had never confided to some of his family members. He came to regard Collins as an older brother, especially now that Billy was spending most of the year in Illinois completing high school.

The first thing most people noticed about Collins was his physique. He was short and solid and as thickly muscled as a young Joe Frazier. He exuded fearlessness. "We thought he could kill a bear with his bare hands, and he'd try it, too," said one of his best friends in Americus, Sammy Mahone. "There was nothing he wouldn't do."

That derring-do served Collins well in the cause that mattered more to him than anything: civil rights. During the year Greg was away, young black people in Sumter County had started to come together in a protest movement, with Collins McGee and Sammy Mahone among its leaders. Little more than a month after Greg returned, marchers hit the pavement in Americus, and all hell broke loose. For weeks, Collins would head into town to attend mass meetings at the black churches accompanied by his new bud and driver, and afterward they'd shoot pool and maybe take a nip. Greg had never known Americus could be so interesting.

GREG HAD ACTUALLY EXPERIENCED THE RIGHTEOUS FERVOR OF A CIVIL rights rally before. His introduction came in Albany, thirty-five miles south of Koinonia, where the movement mobilized in southwest Georgia a few weeks after he started high school, in the fall of 1961.

With a population of fifty-six thousand, All-BENNY (as the natives pronounced it) was the only city of much size in the agricultural quarter of the state below Macon and Columbus. More importantly, it was the site of Albany State College, a black school where students were keenly aware of the lunch counter sit-ins that had spread from black colleges in Nashville, Atlanta, and Greensboro, North Carolina. In September 1961, the organization that grew out of those protests, the Student Nonviolent Coordinating Committee (SNCC), dispatched two field representatives to Albany, where the NAACP and local civil rights groups had been stirring. They formed a coalition, the Albany Movement, and launched the largest campaign against racial discrimination in a southern city to date.

The revolution began at a bus station. The Interstate Commerce Commission had issued a ruling against segregation in bus and train terminals, and activists across the South were itching to test it. On November 22, the day before Thanksgiving, five students were arrested for refusing to leave the area of the Trailways station reserved for whites. Two of the students declined to post bond and stayed in jail through the holiday, eliciting widespread sympathy because they were away from home and missing their families' turkey dinners. Hundreds of people turned out for the movement's first mass meeting and to protest outside city hall on the day of the trials.

Another round of demonstrations began in December after a group was arrested for trying to desegregate the train station. The city responded with mass incarceration on a scale never before used against the civil rights movement. More than five hundred protestors were locked up, far too many for Albany to detain, so the overflow was sent to a makeshift gulag of jails in surrounding counties. Running low on people and resources, the leaders of the Albany Movement summoned the biggest name they could to publicize their struggle; they asked Martin Luther King Jr. to come from Atlanta to speak at back-to-back church assemblies.

King intended to rally the troops, not join the street protests. In the emotion of the moment, however, he agreed to lead a march and was promptly arrested along with Ralph David Abernathy, his closest associate at the Southern Christian Leadership Conference (SCLC). The two were driven to Americus under the guard of an officer carrying a Thompson submachine gun and delivered into the custody of Sheriff Chappell, who threw them into a cell together in his new county jail. King spent two nights there and was galled by the rudeness of the sheriff and his deputies, who kept calling him "boy" and worse. Chappell refused to let reporters speak with his distinguished guest, telling two of them, "Ain't you glorified that damn nigger enough?" A few days later, bailed out and back in Atlanta, King drolly characterized the high sheriff to a journalist: "I had the displeasure of meeting the meanest man in the world."

Over the next few months, Albany descended into a war of attrition. The city refused to negotiate, and the movement tried to apply pressure with boycotts and continued protests. There were more arrests—including King, again—and an endless series of mass meetings that were celebrated for their revival spirit and passionate singing. Still, by the summer of 1962, little had changed in the racial status quo.

Up the road at Koinonia, people did what they could to support the cause. The farm welcomed civil rights workers for rest and relaxation, hosting picnics and hayrides and sometimes looking after the children of jailed activists. Charles Sherrod, SNCC's leader in Albany, was a frequent visitor, as was C. B. King, the lawyer who represented most of the arrested protestors. Although Koinonians themselves did not join the demonstrations as a rule, they often went to the meetings to show that at least some white people in the area were sympathetic. "Many of these people had stood by us and helped us through the years of severe persecution," wrote Dorothy Swisshelm, a social worker from Cincinnati who had come to Koinonia to live and regularly attended the rallies with others from the farm. "It was now our turn to stand by them."

When Swisshelm and a group of other white women from Koinonia went to their first mass meeting, people eyed them nervously, as if they might be police spies. Greg had a similar feeling when he encountered C. B. King in an alley beside an Albany church and noticed the lawyer's eyes flash with alarm. "I think he thought I was a redneck there to assassinate him." But once the crowd knew they were from Koinonia, the visitors were warmly accepted and sometimes treated as honored guests. "They sat us up front and introduced us," Lora Browne recalled.

The meetings, usually held at two Baptist churches across the street from each other, were a revelation for most of the Koinonians. Greg had never heard such loud and joyful music. "Everyone sang at the top of their lungs. Our singing was very calm at the farm—I mean, we used Methodist hymnals." Lora had never been in a black southern church before and was almost embarrassed by the outpouring of emotion. "People were shouting amen and fainting and hanging out the windows. I thought they were going to jump out of the balcony. It couldn't have been more of a culture shock if we had been in Tanzania."

At one assembly Greg attended, Clarence Jordan was invited to speak. He told a typically folksy story about two hunters out to bag a bear. One of them chases the beast into a cabin and tells the other one, "Here he is. You skin him and I'll go out and get you another one." Clarence assured the faithful that Koinonia wasn't going to be like the first hunter; it was going to stick around and help them skin the bear of racism.

In truth, Clarence and others at the farm had reservations about the movement. They believed the best way to encourage equality was to set a Christian example in the manner they lived, not to attack segregation in the courts or on the picket lines—a *live-in,* Clarence called it, not a sit-in. While he supported the movement's goals wholeheartedly, he disapproved of confrontational tactics such as boycotts. Koinonia knew what it was like to be boycotted. He did not regard it as an act of nonviolence, regardless of which side was behind it.

As the protests in Albany dragged on, Clarence requested a meeting with Martin Luther King so they could discuss their different understandings of nonviolence. Vincent Harding, a Mennonite minister from Chicago who had come to Georgia to work for civil rights, knew both of them well and set up the conference, which he witnessed. "Martin had great respect for Clarence and Koinonia and all they had been through. As I remember, Clarence came to the house where Martin was staying in Albany and went into the bedroom, where Martin was resting, and they talked for an hour or an hour and a half. It was a serious conversation. Clarence laid out his deep concerns about the problems that he saw with a boycott. Martin didn't want to disagree too vigorously, but it's fair to say he did not share those hesitations."

The two concentrated on their areas of agreement. Koinonia would continue to help the movement in accordance with its convictions and make the property available to civil rights workers. That commitment was about to intensify.

IN THE SPRING OF 1963, A HARVARD STUDENT NAMED JOHN PERDEW was reading about the protests in Birmingham, Alabama, where police had attacked demonstrators with water cannons and snarling German shepherds. News coverage of the savage repression accomplished what

months of marches and arrests in Albany had failed to do: it swayed public opinion in favor of stronger civil rights laws. The events inspired Perdew to write SNCC and volunteer to spend his summer working with
the group in the South. He was instructed to report to a place in deep
rural Georgia that he had never heard of—Koinonia Farm—where an
orientation session would begin on Sunday, June 16. He and two Harvard
classmates hit the road in his '56 Ford.

The movement was boiling over that week. On Tuesday, Governor
George Wallace made his infamous "stand in the schoolhouse door" in
a vain attempt to keep black students out of the University of Alabama.
That evening, President Kennedy, who had been disturbed by the brutality in Birmingham, announced on national television that he was sending
a civil rights bill to Congress that would outlaw discrimination in public
venues. Shortly after midnight, Medgar Evers, the field secretary for the
NAACP in Mississippi, was shot and killed in the driveway of his home
in Jackson. It all happened within twenty-four hours, as if the boundless
pain and promise of American race relations had been compressed into
one three-act drama.

Enter Americus. In early 1963, SNCC sent a team of organizers from
Albany to mount a voter registration drive in Sumter County. It was fertile ground; although more than half the county's population was black,
none of its elected officials were. The organizers lived at Koinonia for
several weeks and then found a place to stay in town. "We knew Clarence
had issues with some of the things we were doing, and we didn't want to
get into a conflict with him," explained one of the SNCC field secretaries,
Don Harris, a Rutgers University graduate from New York City.

After they left the farm, the organizers often returned to socialize
and share information. They became friendly with the young people,
who were quite taken with Harris and the others because they seemed
so cool and confident. That spring, when Lora Browne decided to attend
the junior-senior prom to show that Koinonians could be regular teenagers, too, she asked a white SNCC worker to take her. Soon afterward,
he got arrested and jailed, as activists are wont to do. He was sprung just
in time to escort her to the dance, where he loudly asked administrators

why Lora's family had to go to federal court to get her into high school. They were not elected king and queen of the prom.

The Wittkampers were settling back into life at the farm when Perdew and twenty other summer volunteers arrived for the SNCC orientation. Greg and Collins drifted in and out of the sessions as their work allowed and got to know the newcomers, most of whom were college students from the North. The SNCC veterans gave them a primer on nonviolent protest: how to behave, how to get arrested, how to go limp and become dead weight when the police haul you to jail, how to protect yourself by curling into a fetal position and covering your head, what it feels like to be struck by a billy club.

Little of this was surprising or new to Greg. He had been weaned on Christian nonviolence and been targeted for his beliefs for as long as he could remember—hell, he'd been shot at. At the same time, he had never been arrested, so he paid attention.

For Perdew, a white college professor's son from Denver, the orientation was considerably more worrisome. "If you are arrested," he remembered one speaker saying, "don't expect to be bailed out; there's no telling how long you might be in jail. We do not have the resources to post bail, and you will be a more effective witness for the battle against racial injustice by staying in jail."

That sounded ominous.

After the talks and training, the session ended, as civil rights gatherings usually did, with music. Everyone sang freedom songs, many of them customized for the local fights to come. One of them invoked Martin Luther King's favorite lawman: *"Ain't gonna let Sheriff Chappell turn me 'round, turn me 'round, turn me 'round."*

Three weeks later, those lyrics sprang to life.

———————

THE SUMTER COUNTY MOVEMENT WAS DRIVEN BY TEENAGERS, MOST OF them students or recent graduates of the black high school in Americus. Galvanized by the collegians in Albany and the children who filled the

Ad for a segregated drive-in from the Americus High School yearbook.

jails in Birmingham, they were impatient to attack white supremacy in their hometown. "SNCC tried to discourage us," remembered Sammy Mahone, one of the group's leaders. "They didn't think we were ready to protest public accommodations. But the students insisted we do it."

Their first target was the Martin Theater, the biggest symbol of segregation in Americus, where black moviegoers had to walk down a long, dark alley to buy tickets at a separate window and then climb the back stairs to the balcony. The theater had figured in racial incidents before; in a rare instance of a white person running afoul of Jim Crow laws, a Koinonia resident was once charged for sitting upstairs with some black friends. Greg had done the same thing several times, settling into the colored section with Collins. On the night of July 11, eleven teenagers approached the main box office to buy tickets for *The Young Racers*, a forgettable flick about sexy young people on the grand prix circuit in Europe. Not that the teenagers cared about what was on the marquee overlooking Forsyth Street. When they were turned away and refused to leave, they were arrested for blocking the sidewalk and given sixty days' probation. A week later, a larger group—including some of the ones on probation—returned to the theater and were again intercepted by the police.

This time, the punishment was harsher. The protesters were locked up, and some of the organizers were put on work details. Sammy Mahone had to clean out the city's sewage treatment tanks under shotgun guard.

"It was 90 degrees, and I was down there shoveling shit with a pitchfork. Some of it would fall back on you and run down your back."

As the arrests stacked up, the authorities did what Albany had done and farmed out prisoners to surrounding counties. Three dozen girls from the ages of ten to sixteen were taken to Lee County, south of Americus, and held for days in a derelict facility known as the Leesburg Stockade. They were confined to a single room of twelve by forty feet and slept on a bare concrete floor. They were fed cold, half-cooked hamburgers and drank water from a dripping shower head. The one toilet was clogged, and they had to squat over the drain to relieve themselves. One of their overseers, a white man, tossed a snake in with the youngsters just for laughs.

Parents couldn't find out where their daughters were being kept at first, and when they did, were allowed only minimal contact with them. The plight of the girls wasn't revealed to the wider world until a photographer working for SNCC, Danny Lyon, sneaked onto the stockade property and took pictures while his driver was distracting the guard. The images were published in black newspapers nationwide. The *Chicago Defender* ran some of them under the headline: "Americus Hellhole for Many."

The young people at Koinonia were sorely tempted to join the demonstrations. While Greg and Collins and Jan Jordan were regulars at the mass meetings, only Collins took to the streets, once getting a bloody nose when a cop billy-clubbed him. Greg was new to the movement and uncertain of where a blue-eyed white kid fit in with the black freedom struggle. Besides, he had a job at the farm, a job he was actually getting paid for now—he didn't particularly want to take an involuntary leave inside a jail.

When Jan asked her father for permission to join the protests, Clarence said he'd rather she didn't. He thought it was dangerous and counterproductive to provoke the segregationists. If she went to a soda fountain with a black girlfriend because they wanted a Coke, that was fine; but if she went there for the sole purpose of testing the law, he would not approve. "If you get arrested under those circumstances," he told her, "I won't bail you out."

For the time being, Jan and the others at Koinonia did not participate directly in protests. They found other ways to help.

That summer, several of them worked with SNCC volunteers to put out a newsletter about the movement, *Voice of Americus*. They printed it at the farm on the same mimeograph equipment used to produce Koinonia's newsletter. The publication continued for two years and carried articles from black and white students, including Greg, who contributed an illustration showing an intricate spider web that symbolized the deceitfulness of white supremacy. Or something like that.

Whether it participated in protests or not, Koinonia had already contributed immeasurably to the movement in southwest Georgia, if only by example. "When people saw that little group wasn't going to let the Klan run them off," said Mabel Barnum, whose family ran the largest black funeral home in the county, "they knew from that time on that you don't have to be scared of the Klan."

On a hot Thursday night in early August, more than two hundred people surged out of a rally at Friendship Baptist Church and onto the streets of Americus singing "We Shall Overcome." The police ordered them to disperse, and when they didn't, fired shots overhead, scattering some of the crowd. They waded into the remaining demonstrators with clubs and blackjacks, targeting the three SNCC organizers they believed were fomenting the unrest: Don Harris, John Perdew, and Ralph Allen. The civil rights workers used their training in nonviolent resistance and lay inert like sacks of cornmeal. Sheriff Chappell stood over Harris and tried to make him get up by poking him with an electric cattle prod—a "hot shot," they called it. The three were roughed up—Allen required stitches—and arrested. Angry onlookers threw bricks, breaking windows and injuring several officers.

On the following night, there was another rally, another march, more clubs and bricks, more injuries and arrests. It was the second small riot in as many days. In the aftermath, Greg went to Americus with Zev Aelony, a sometime Koinonia resident who was working for another civil rights organization, CORE (the Congress of Racial Equality), and helped him interview witnesses and take affidavits documenting allegations of police brutality. Aelony was a true-blue do-gooder from Minnesota who had read about Koinonia while he was staying in a kibbutz in Israel. He was inspired to discover that a band of Christians could be so serious about sharing their resources and standing up for their convictions, so he moved to Georgia and lived with them off and on for several years, despite the fact that he wasn't, strictly speaking, one of them. He was Jewish. Clarence welcomed him anyway, saying that his belief in nonviolence made him part of the fold.

Aelony's investigation of the earlier arrests was abruptly halted on August 17 when he was nabbed during another march and thrown into jail with the SNCC leaders. To keep them behind bars indefinitely, the county's solicitor general devised a novel legal gambit: he charged them with inciting insurrection under a Reconstruction-era statute that had last been used to prosecute a black Communist labor organizer, Angelo Herndon, during a notorious show trial in the 1930s. If convicted, they faced a possible death sentence.

The four languished in jail for more than two months. Allen and Perdew shared a cell and were able to keep up each other's spirits, although they came to hate the sound of the sheriff's pet Chihuahuas scampering over the hard floor with their toenails clicking. Harris maintained a cocky demeanor, irritating Chappell to no end by calling him "Doc," as if this were a Bugs Bunny cartoon and he were Sheriff Elmer Fudd. Aelony caught the worst of it; he was thrown in with several white prisoners and cuffed around more than once.

The Americus Four, as the activists were known, became a cause célèbre. Campus rallies were held, politicians issued statements, newspapers editorialized about justice in Georgia. At the March on Washington on August 28, SNCC chairman John Lewis, speaking ahead of King's "I Have a Dream" oration, called for the immediate release of the four from the steps of the Lincoln Memorial.

A few weeks later, midway through their imprisonment, Claude Sitton of the *New York Times* wrote an article about the case, terming it "a situation without parallel in the South." He tallied the clashes of July and

August—two riots, seven injured police, twenty-eight injured demonstrators, more than 250 arrests, thirty-eight still in jail—and concluded that the Sumter County Movement had been all but crushed by the ruthless application of the law. "There is no apparent hope for a compromise."

Well into the article, Sitton related the tale of the religious farming commune that had been persecuted by night riders and main street merchants during the 1950s. He had covered that violence for the newspaper and found, upon his return, that some people in Americus still blamed Koinonia for the racial troubles that were now threatening to overcome their way of life.

CHAPTER 6

"Not in My Town"

A FEW WEEKS INTO GREG'S JUNIOR YEAR, ONE OF HIS CLASSES HELD A show-and-tell session. The theme was current events; students were supposed to bring a newspaper clipping and discuss the story. Plenty of possibilities appeared in the headlines during the late summer and early autumn of 1963: the March on Washington and Martin Luther King's "I Have a Dream" speech, America's growing entanglement in Vietnam, the killing of four Sunday school girls in a hate bombing at a church in Birmingham. Greg chose a local story. He talked about the Americus Four, the civil rights workers who were still in the Sumter County jail facing capital charges of insurrection.

Standing before the class as if he were delivering a book report, Greg read the article aloud, trying not to roll his eyes at the part about the young men being "outside agitators" who might have Communist connections. In his discussion afterward, he freely shared his opinion. "This writer obviously doesn't know what he's talking about because these guys are my friends, and they aren't Communists."

When Greg finished, most of the class stared. Only then did it dawn on him that he had confirmed their darkest suspicions: that he hung out with pinkos and lived in a community that harbored the kind of people who got arrested for treason.

For Greg, reentering high school in Georgia felt like stepping back into a cold shower. He had grown accustomed to being treated like a normal young person during his sophomore interlude in North Dakota. Now that he was starting his second stretch at Americus High, the hectoring resumed as if he had never left. The same wise asses called him names, the same tough guys fired spitballs and paper clips, the same girls completely ignored him. Nothing had changed. The prospect of retracing the worst time of his life left him more depressed than ever.

At one point that fall, Greg grew so resigned and apathetic that he stopped bathing. He walked around for days in a peculiar and increasingly funky statement of dissent, figuring that if his classmates were going to shun him anyway, he'd give them good reason to keep their distance. "I guess I wanted people to smell my pain. I really hit a low."

Greg's mother spoke with him about the message he was sending. "Until now," she said, "the kids didn't have a good reason to dislike you. Now you're giving them one. You're letting them win." Principal McKinnon called him in and suggested that he would stand a better chance of making friends if he didn't stink like a goat. Even Collins McGee weighed in; he thought Greg's hair was too long and slicked back and made him look like a common peckerwood—not the best guise for a white boy who was trying to make connections on the black side of town. Collins prescribed a shorter cut with a clean, straight neckline that he called a "tape job." Greg ditched the Brylcreem and started combing his locks forward in short bangs. Oddly enough, his new do made him look like some of the athletes who enjoyed messing with him.

None of it helped. Showered and shorn, Greg simply made a better-smelling target.

His friends at the farm and in the movement worried about him. Zev Aelony wrote from the county jail, where he was languishing on the insurrection charge that Greg had spoken about in his show-and-tell: "How [are] Greg and Jan? Concerned about their reception in school."

Jan Jordan, now a senior, was one of two other students from Koinonia at the high school that fall. The other one was David Wittkamper, who was entering eighth grade and was a year younger than his brother had been when he first had to run the gauntlet. He was ill-equipped to take it.

David was a sensitive child, shy and insecure, and when the boys found out that the slight thirteen-year-old was from Koinonia, some of them took delight in knocking him around. They tore the books out of his hands, pushed him down, and tripped him during a footrace, ripping his clothes. Once he suffered a black eye and a bloody nose. Most of the roughhousing happened after school or between classes, where teachers did little to stop it. On the bus ride home, Greg would see his brother crying and try to comfort him, telling him that he knew what he was going through. David would have nightmares about his family being attacked and then wake up, get ready for school, and catch the bus for another round of abuse. "It was like going to torture every day," he said. Not surprisingly, he was failing most of his courses. Sometimes he daydreamed about suicide.

One of the worst moments for David happened on the Friday before Thanksgiving—November 22, 1963—the day President Kennedy was assassinated. The terrible news was even more traumatic for the eighth grader because, at first, he misunderstood what had happened.

David was in history class that afternoon when one of the boys who had been beating up on him rushed into the room calling out, "They got him! They shot him down!"

David froze for a few seconds, imagining that the someone who had been shot down was his brother. It wasn't an unreasonable fear; Greg was despised, and the Koinonia children had been targets of gunfire. When David realized that the victim was the president of the United States, his horror turned to shock and then to revulsion when a few hotheads clapped and cheered as the class learned that Kennedy had died of his wounds. "Calm down!" the teacher objected. "That isn't right." A similar outburst occurred in Greg's algebra II class. Not everyone celebrated—certainly not the girls, nor most of the boys—but there were enough instantaneous whoops to underscore how detested the president had become in certain quarters of the South. He may have been the leader of the free world, but John F. Kennedy supported civil rights, and for some children and their parents, that was all that mattered.

In Americus, as across America, students were sent home early that afternoon. The Wittkampers listened to radio coverage of the national tragedy well into the evening, Greg's mother quietly weeping.

The student newspaper reports the fire, 1964. *Courtesy of David Morgan*

TWO MONTHS AFTER THE KENNEDY ASSASSINATION, THERE WAS AN-
other shock—a local one. No one perished this time, but for many in
Sumter County, the loss was profoundly sad nonetheless. Americus High
School burned down.

It happened on the last Sunday in January. Around 10 o'clock that
night, passersby noticed smoke coming from the august colonial-style
building and called the fire department. As the first men arrived to investigate, an explosion erupted and a wall collapsed. The structure burst into
flames, fueled by heart-of-pine floors that had been burnished for years
with oil-based cleaning solvents. Although there were lingering suspicions of arson, the most likely cause was that someone had neglected to
turn off a gas burner in the chemistry lab.

The light from the fire could be seen for miles and attracted a crowd
of people who watched helplessly, tearfully, as a beloved part of their town
was destroyed. Greg's classmate David Morgan walked from his home
two blocks away and never forgot how hot the winter night felt. Greg
rode to Americus with a carload of people from Koinonia. By the time

they got there, the flames were waning and the main building had been reduced to a heap of rubble and the sooty remnants of the entry façade. The library, the language lab, the typing room, the home economics department, sixteen classrooms, the administration offices—all were lost.

While other students mourned, Greg could muster little sentiment for a place that had been the setting of so much unhappiness. He admired the school building itself and did not enjoy seeing it laid to ruins. But he had seen fires before—fires that had not been accidents. During the terror years at Koinonia, he had witnessed the eerie glow of tenant houses torched in the night at the hands of parties unknown. As he stood watching this latest conflagration, a practical thought popped into his head: maybe he wouldn't have to go back to school there.

But he did, and sooner than he expected. In fact, the fire made things worse for Greg.

It took only three days for Americus High to reopen. Trailers were moved onto campus, and classes were held in subdivided spaces in the youth center, the newer annex, and other detached buildings that had not been damaged. In the stopgap configuration, students had to walk outside between periods, around corners, past shrubbery. Some of the kids took advantage of the enhanced cover and began to harass Greg more openly, out of sight of their teachers. Going from class to class became more hazardous. He came to miss the days when they were usually under one roof.

Beyond the fire, the early months of 1964 were eventful for Greg. Koinonia was bustling with visitors who were using the farm as a staging ground for the southern leg of a transcontinental peace walk to protest US government policy toward Cuba. At the same time, Greg was beginning to enjoy some of the fruits of capitalism. After the old Plymouth he had been driving conked out, he saved money from his livestock duties and bought a used car in Atlanta, a cherry-red 1959 MG two-seater. His classmates, clueless about the workings of Koinonia, wondered how a socialist like Greg could afford to buy such a sporty automobile.

His most cherished acquisition—the first thing he bought with his earnings—was a J-50 acoustic Gibson guitar, which he got for $175 at a pawnshop in Albany. He played songs by Joan Baez, Bob Dylan, and other folk singers, whose protest lyrics he much preferred to the early music of the Beatles, which was all the rage among his peers but too teenybopper for Greg. As usual, he was out of step with his classmates.

As Greg's second year at Americus High came to a close, there was one final trauma: he almost got killed. During the last weekend of spring term, he was working at the farm, helping to repair a wagon used to pull hay behind a tractor, when the heavy steel carriage fell on top of him and struck his back and his head. Blood gushed from his mouth and ears and seeped out of the corners of his eyes. One side of his face was skinned clean, and the nerve that controlled movement in his left eye was injured, giving him double vision for months. He had to wear a patch until the nerve mended, which made him look a little like a beatnik.

Greg was taken to the emergency room in Americus and spent the night swallowing and vomiting his own blood. He had suffered a concussion and had to stay in the hospital for a week. He missed his final classes, but even in the hospital, he couldn't escape one more indignity from his schoolmates. One day, laid up in his bed, he saw several of them in the hallway pointing at him through the open door. They must have thought he looked funny in his bandages because they were laughing at him.

———————

OF THE THREE KOINONIA STUDENTS ADMITTED BY FEDERAL COURT order, only one made it all the way through Americus High. While Billy Wittkamper escaped to Illinois and Lora Browne's family moved to Tennessee, Jan Jordan endured the slings and arrows for the entire four years.

Jan tried not to let her emotions show—Greg thought she was more stoic than any of them—but the constant badgering got to her as well. One incident in her speech class stood out. On a day when she was supposed to deliver an oral presentation, she returned from lunch to find her textbooks strewn across the classroom. "I don't think I can give my speech today," she told the teacher, bolting down the hall in tears. A few minutes later, she came back from the restroom to witness a dramatic display of belated justice. The boy who had trashed Jan's books was standing in front of the class looking distressed, and the teacher, Mrs. Fennessy, was conducting an angry inquisition.

"What have you learned today?" she demanded.

"Not to knock someone's books on the floor," came the meek reply.

"What else have you learned?"

"To say I'm sorry."

"What else?"

"I've learned not to be so prejudiced."

Mrs. Fennessy wasn't finished.

"Do you feel like crying?" she asked the boy. Then she turned to the class. "Do the rest of you feel like crying? Well, I feel like crying."

Jan was thunderstruck. For the remainder of the year, no one bothered her in speech class. She wished there had been more no-nonsense teachers like Mrs. Fennessy and more students like the two girls who had broken ranks and started eating lunch at her table in the cafeteria. Jan never doubted that there were decent people at Americus High School. As for the ones who behaved less decently—the name callers and food throwers—she had begun to take a philosophical view. She didn't really blame them; if she had been born to different parents, she might have acted the same way.

But all that was nearly behind her now.

As her high school days dwindled, Jan clung to a D average that barely qualified her to graduate with the Class of 1964. She had never earned high grades, given the stress and distractions, and she was relieved to be donning a gown and collecting a diploma at all. Fittingly, the final scene did not go smoothly.

Among the friends Jan invited to the commencement exercises at the football stadium was Collins McGee, who was still working and living at Koinonia. When he learned that Collins wasn't planning to attend, Clarence Jordan asked him a pointed question. "Are you not going because you don't want to, or are you not going because you're a Negro?"

That clarified matters; Collins decided to go.

At the commencement, Jan was standing in line with the other students when her father walked up and told her that Collins had been stopped at the gate and denied entry to the section where the other

families and friends—all of them white—were seated. The school authorities offered to let him sit in the grandstand, where a few places remained
near the top, but they didn't want to upset people and cause a scene by
allowing a black person into the reserved area. In their fear of causing
trouble, they provoked a different kind of scene.

Jan found the superintendent, Clay Mundy, and told him that she
wanted no part of the ceremony if her friend couldn't be treated like everyone else. The processional music was about to start.

"What do you want to do?" her father asked.

Jan exited the queue of students and climbed into the grandstand.
She watched the exercises from the top row, conspicuous in her white
gown and mortarboard, seated with her father, mother, younger brother,
and Collins. During the roll call of graduates, the person at the microphone skipped over her name, as if she didn't exist.

After the service, Clarence confronted the superintendent and
blessed him out. In parting, he made a prophecy that sounded like a
threat. "Next year," he said, "this school *will* be integrated."

He followed up on it. The Jordans placed an ad in the *Times-Recorder*
giving Jan's account of what happened at the commencement, headlined:
"Why I Did Not Graduate with My Class at Americus High." Several
times over the summer, Clarence phoned or wrote the school board to
check what they were doing about their segregation policy. His letter of
July 29 laid out what he expected of the board members:

> Almost two months have elapsed since my previous letter to you, and as
> there has been no response, I take it that you do not intend to reply. . . .
> I can assure you that your "head-in-the-sand" position will become in-
> creasingly difficult—and miserable—in the days ahead. The experience
> of other communities surely teaches us that our problems do not go
> away if we but hide our faces from them long enough. Nor will they
> evaporate into the mists of accusations, rumors, and evasions. They
> must be faced—courageously, intelligently, and openly. It is my deep
> wish that you may thus respond, so that our community—both white
> and Negro—may be spared the suffering which so often follows in the
> wake of unwise, stubborn leadership.

Clarence was unaware that a plan to admit a token number of black students to Americus High was already in the works, at least in one person's mind. If he had known who that person was, he would have found it ironic indeed.

———————

WARREN FORTSON, THE SCHOOL BOARD MEMBER WHO HAD GONE ALONG with rejecting the Koinonia students a few years before, had come a long way in his thinking. When he moved to Americus and joined a law partnership in 1959, he was too busy with his job and his family to spare much thought for relations between the races. Later, during the Albany Movement, he regarded the long-running battle as someone else's problem, even though it was unfolding less than an hour's drive down US 19. "People in Americus reacted to Albany like people in America did to World War II in the beginning," he later explained. "People said: That's happening over there. I hope it doesn't happen here."

Then it did.

The turning point for Fortson came when the mass arrests started in Americus. On the way to his law office, he passed a vacant building that had once housed the local newspaper. One day in August 1963, he saw that the city had turned it into an emergency jail overnight. Forston thought it looked like a holding pen for frightened livestock. "That thing was chock-full of kids. Eighth graders, ninth graders, tenth graders—kids. When I saw all those children locked up, I thought: not in my town."

Fortson resolved to work as quietly as he could to ease Americus through the inevitable racial transition. Later that year, he phoned John Perdew, one of the Americus Four, who had been freed with the others by a federal judge after more than two months in jail on treason charges, and invited him over to his house for a beer. Perdew was wary. One of his SNCC buddies advised him not to go because it might be a trap. He went anyway and stayed late into the night talking with Fortson, who impressed him with his sincerity. "He said he was so sick and tired of Jim Crow and he wanted to bring it down," Perdew remembered. Fortson asked him to stay in touch and let him know what was happening in the movement—and to be sure to call from pay phones so they wouldn't be discovered. He also initiated back-channel communications with two black people he knew from his legal practice: Lena Turner, a young activist who had been arrested in protests, and Robert L. Freeman, an educator and minister who also headed the local chapter of the NAACP. His daughter, Robertiena, was a star student at the black middle school.

As a member of the school board, Fortson's biggest concern was peacefully desegregating the city schools, especially the flagship, Americus High. It wasn't going to be easy.

Local opinion on the issue was apparent in 1960 when the Georgia legislature created a commission to hold hearings around the state about whether to close public schools or submit to federal law and begin to integrate them. The first hearing was held in Americus. Of the fifty-seven people who testified, all but nine favored segregation at any cost. In essence, they said that they would rather eliminate the school system and rely on private academies than allow white and black children to mingle in the classroom. "I believe our people can educate their own," said banker Charles Crisp, one of the civic leaders who once had tried to get Koinonia to sell out and move.

Pushed to the brink, state officials came to a different conclusion. Governor Ernest Vandiver backed away from his pledges to perpetuate segregation and asked lawmakers to repeal a constitutional amendment denying state education funds to any systems that integrated. That left the decision to local school boards. In the fall of 1961, Atlanta allowed nine black teenagers into its formerly white high schools, earning praise from President Kennedy, and a few other city systems across the state soon did likewise. But in most of Georgia—and definitely in Americus—schools remained as segregated as ever in 1964, ten years after the Supreme Court had spoken.

That summer, a few weeks after Jan Jordan's tumultuous graduation, Fortson was chatting with some school board members after a meeting had broken up when one of them acknowledged the elephant in the room. "You know," he said, "we're going to have to address this race question." Seeing his opening, Fortson went home and drafted a proposal to admit a handful of black students into Americus High. He knew the board would be apprehensive and closely divided. To bolster his case, he contacted Perdew and asked him what might happen in the black community if the schools weren't desegregated. Perdew understood that he was being invited to play the bad cop, so he complied by predicting that there could be civil disorders. "I think some people might riot and cause damage in the downtown area."

That was just what Fortson wanted to hear.

He took his integration plan—and his hot intel about the risk of doing nothing—to the next board meeting. The members hashed it out until well after midnight. One of them resigned on the spot as it became apparent that he was going to lose. In the end, the board agreed with Fortson, and the next day Clarence Jordan received an understated call informing him, "Clarence, we no longer have a policy of segregation." People on both sides of the issue were astounded, given the town's history of resistance. One civil rights activist in Atlanta called it, simply, "the surprise."

Forston expected a backlash. "We knew there were going to be people who raised hell about it, but it was something we had to do. We had been sitting there watching Albany commit suicide. We didn't want that to happen to us."

———

THE BOARD HAD APPROVED A FREEDOM OF CHOICE PLAN THAT CALLED for volunteers to transfer into the high school. With only a few days left before the start of classes, black leaders scrambled to find students who would be willing to wade into what promised to be choppy waters. Four teenagers were selected, three sophomores and a junior. All of them were veterans of the 1963 protests and had been arrested, so they had a clear idea of what white people could do when they were challenged. David Bell and Jewel Wise, both quiet, well-behaved sophomores, had been charged in the demonstrations at the Martin Theater. Dobbs Wiggins, a junior with a feistier personality, had been jailed for picketing. The Reverend Freeman's daughter Robertiena, a sophomore, had spent thirty days locked up in the Leesburg Stockade.

Robertiena was the most obvious choice. The energetic fourteen-year-old had been groomed to walk through this doorway her entire life.

Robertiena Freeman.

She first realized the expectations her parents had for their children when she was a little girl and wanted to join some of her friends in the neighborhood as they headed into the fields to pick cotton. "I want to go," she told her father. "They're my friends, and I want to go to the cotton fields with them." She might as well have asked to join a minstrel show.

Freeman was a proud Morehouse man who had graduated from the prestigious college in Atlanta and also held a doctorate in theology. Besides his pastorate at Bethesda Baptist Church, where some of the mass meetings had been held, he was an administrator and teacher at the middle school for blacks. His wife taught in a neighboring county. He informed their daughter that she was not going into the cotton fields, and when she protested and demanded to know why not, he explained that it was because of who they were and what their family represented. "We stand for change," he said. "I don't want to get upset over something they've done to you in the cotton fields."

Robertiena got a better understanding of what he meant after the protests started in 1963 and the family's home on Forrest Street was targeted because of Freeman's involvement in the movement. A brick crashed through their picture window, shots were fired from the street, and someone painted "KKK" on the driveway. For a time, armed men had to stand guard at the house.

Despite the recent history of violence, Robertiena was her usual chipper self when her father raised the possibility of attending Americus High. "Daddy, I want to go integrate that school," she told him in her high, eager voice, sounding as if she had been asked whether she wanted to go out for cheerleading. "I'd like to go over there and make some white friends."

As it turned out, she would have only one white friend—and he was as unwelcome at the school as she was.

PART 3

Senior Year

CHAPTER 7

Among Panthers

On Monday, August 31, 1964, Americus High School was desegregated without incident. At least that's what the *Americus Times-Recorder* and the Associated Press and the *New York Times* reported. They didn't have the whole picture. One of the black students, Dobbs Wiggins, was struck in the back with two Coca-Cola bottles as he walked between classes. He informed the principal and his homeroom teacher, and both said there was nothing they could do unless he could identify the thrower. That afternoon, as Dobbs left school and crossed the street, more projectiles were hurled in his direction and a car full of white boys almost ran him down. Dobbs did not think his first day had gone without incident.

But it *was* relatively calm compared to what the school board had feared. In not making a big public announcement about the desegregation of Americus High, board members had hoped that the presence of four black teenagers in a white student body of five hundred might attract less attention, as if people wouldn't notice that they had barely darkened a gallon of milk with a few drops of chocolate syrup. Except for the bottles chucked at Dobbs, the wishful ploy more or less worked for about twenty-four hours. And then dawn broke on the second day of school, and Americus woke up to what was happening. Greg's classmate David Morgan aptly characterized the reaction of many white people: "That town was spring-loaded in the pissed-off position."

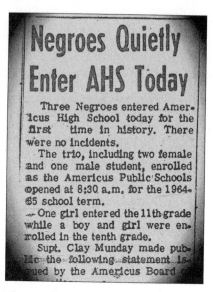

Negroes Quietly Enter AHS Today

Three Negroes entered Americus High School today for the first time in history. There were no incidents.

The trio, including two female and one male student, enrolled as the Americus Public Schools opened at 8:30 a.m. for the 1964-65 school term.

One girl entered the 11th grade while a boy and girl were enrolled in the tenth grade.

Supt. Clay Munday made public the following statement issued by the Americus Board

The *Americus Times-Recorder* ran an eight-paragraph item about the desegregation of the high school in 1964.

Early Tuesday morning, Greg climbed into his red MG and drove to Barnum's Funeral Home on the north side of Americus, where three of the black students had agreed to rendezvous for the ride to campus. They all knew him from civil rights meetings and from palling around with Collins McGee, so it wasn't unexpected when he phoned the night before and offered to show his support by accompanying them to school. "We were glad he was there," one of the students, Jewel Wise, remembered. "He was in the same predicament we were in. They were out to get him, too, so we felt a camaraderie." The funeral home had agreed to provide a car and driver to help the students get to and from school safely and to avoid the kind of attacks Dobbs had suffered. As they boarded the black limousine, no one mentioned the irony that they were traveling in a vehicle typically used to ferry mourners to a graveyard.

A mob was waiting outside the school. Through the car windows, the passengers saw the scene unspool like a newsreel, perhaps some old footage from Little Rock: bricks, rocks, shouting, cursing, florid faces, middle fingers. It could have been a hundred people, it could have been three hundred—no one inside the sedan was thinking about counting as their pulses quickened and their breathing shallowed. "It looked like everyone in Americus had come to campus to have a riot," said Robertiena Freeman, who was sitting in the backseat. The car pulled up in front of the glowering sheriff, his head a crimson balloon, and the occupants got out as another rock came flying toward them, narrowly missing Jewel. The black students hurried into the administrative office, where no one seemed pleased to see them.

The disorder outside Americus High did not surprise Greg. As a survivor of the terror campaign against Koinonia, he had anticipated trouble. The ruckus actually exhilarated him. It stoked his sense of righteousness. "I knew I was part of something important and long overdue. I felt like I was carrying a banner." In classes that day, none of his teachers and very few students discussed the momentous social revolution unfolding at their school. The only mentions came from some of the boys, who lashed out at Greg. "You think you've won the battle, but we're going to win the war," one of them said, putting it in terms a Johnny Reb would have appreciated.

Greg's feeling of triumph deflated that evening when he spoke by phone with Jewel. There had been a change in plans. To head off further unrest, school officials had decided that the black students would go to classes five minutes late and leave five minutes early. When Greg asked to go on the same schedule, he was refused. He had assumed that he would be able to hang out with the four, have lunch with them, lock arms and form a united front. That wasn't going to happen. He was a senior and they were a year and two years behind him, so they weren't likely to be taking the same courses. He didn't see much of them around campus for the rest of the year, and neither did the other white students, except in classes, where teacher supervision kept down the opportunities for misconduct.

That left Greg as the most convenient fall guy. It didn't entirely make sense; he wasn't a member of the school board and he hadn't voted to admit blacks. But he had made a public display of his support for integration—and he was from Koinonia—and those were more than enough to make him the most despised person in school. "People thought he was worse than the black students," said fellow senior Celia Harvey. "You'd hear them say he was a traitor to his race."

———————————

THE COMING OF BLACK STUDENTS TO THE HIGH SCHOOL WAS ONLY PART of the reason for the surly mood in Americus. Many white people across the South and beyond were spitting mad at the federal government that autumn for what they saw as an unwarranted meddling with local customs. The bill that President Kennedy had introduced outlawing segregation in most public places had become a holy cause to his successor, Lyndon Johnson, who bulled it through Congress over the diehard opposition of filibustering senators from Dixie. Two days before the Fourth of July, the president signed the Civil Rights Act of 1964, driving a stake through the heart of legal discrimination. Many Americans rejoiced, but to most of Greg's classmates and their families, it seemed like a civilization was shattering before their eyes.

When the law took effect, Greg was still recovering from the grisly farm accident that had landed him in the hospital and given him double vision. He came to town occasionally that summer to attend civil rights rallies with Collins, but he wasn't as involved as he had been the previous year. There wasn't as much going on in Americus anyway, not in public view. There were headlines elsewhere—riots in Harlem; Lester Maddox chasing black people from his Atlanta restaurant with an ax handle; the disappearance of three civil rights workers during the Freedom Summer voting education campaign in Mississippi—but Sumter County seemed to be taking a breather from the mass demonstrations that had packed the jails and stockades in 1963.

The most notable local incident occurred on the night after the civil rights bill was signed when six SNCC activists decided on the spur of the moment to test the law at the Hasty House, a blue-collar café on US 19. It wasn't such a good idea. The group took their seats amid glares and grumbling and gave the waitress their orders. She brought the food after a long delay, slamming the dishes and glasses on the table. As they left and returned to their car, a cluster of young white men who had been watching from a service station across the street approached and attacked them with tire irons. The activists managed to drive away, but in the confusion they left behind one of their party, the only white member: John Perdew, the accused "insurrectionist" who had attended the nonviolence training session at Koinonia the summer before. The tire iron posse descended on him and beat him bloody. A policeman witnessed the violence and did nothing to stop it.

There were a few other outbursts in Americus during the days after the law took effect. A white mob formed at the Martin Theater to keep blacks from sitting downstairs. Fifteen white teenagers went on a spree through a black housing project, tossing bricks and cherry bombs—and the police actually arrested some of them.

Greg avoided the disturbances. Going to a white restaurant to witness the death throes of Jim Crow was the last thing he wanted to do during the summer between his junior and senior years. When he left Sumter County eighteen months later, almost all the "white only" signs had come down, in accordance with the law, but everyone knew there were some places that black people—and their white friends—still should not go. But things were changing, however grudgingly. In one bow to the new reality, the King and Queen Drive-In, a burger joint that had run ads in the high school yearbook with the disclaimer "Serve Whites Only," dropped the line in the 1965 edition of *The Panther*. In Americus, that was undeniable progress.

After he signed the civil rights act, President Johnson confided to his aide Bill Moyers, "I think we just delivered the South to the Republican Party for a long time to come." The backlash showed up in the presidential election that fall. While Johnson scored a landslide victory nationally, the Democratic ticket was trounced in places like Sumter County, where a dramatic reversal of party fortunes occurred. Kennedy had taken 70 percent of the vote in 1960 against his Republican rival, Richard Nixon. Four years later, Johnson won only 31 percent against Barry Goldwater, a vehement critic of the civil rights legislation. They took a straw vote in Greg's government class, and Joseph Logan, trying to be cute, wrote in the name of an even more strident opponent of the law: George Wallace.

It could be hazardous to support LBJ in Americus during the mean season of 1964. Lillian Carter, the future president's mother, helped manage the Johnson campaign in the county. Children yelled at her, and her car was vandalized. Her daughter-in-law, Rosalynn Carter, came home one afternoon to find one of her sons in his room crying. His classmates in Plains were giving him a hard time because of his family's political loyalties. The tears were because someone had pulled a chair out from under him during choral practice and he had hit the floor.

Greg wasn't the only white person in Sumter County being punished for his beliefs. It just felt that way sometimes.

———————

THE FIRST WEEKS OF HIS SENIOR YEAR WERE WORSE THAN ANYTHING Greg had experienced at Americus High. The abuse moved beyond name-calling and guerrilla spitball attacks. In keeping with the angrier atmosphere, the boys who tormented him became more brazen and physical. They elbowed him as he walked down the hall, tried to knock the books out of his arms, occasionally launched a loogie in his direction. The instigators were always boys, typically hoodlum types or jocks who saw it as their duty to enforce the school's traditions, all the while playing to an audience of onlookers who stayed on the sidelines laughing and taunting. Joseph Logan was a member in good standing of the peanut gallery. While he never touched Greg or threw anything at him, he cackled one day as one of his football teammates tried to boot him down a stairwell with his foot. To Joseph, the ramped-up hostility was obvious and easily explained. "Everyone blamed him for integrating the school."

Greg expected rough treatment from the boys; he was more affected by the cold shoulder he got from the girls. Not a single one would talk to him, the only exceptions coming during forced exchanges required by the course work. Once, in Spanish, students were assigned to bring a picture and start a conversation based on it with a classmate. Greg brought a picture of a calf and turned to Deanie Dudley, the homecoming queen, and asked whether she thought the baby cow was cute: "¿No es lindo este becerro?" He knew perfectly well that Deanie didn't want to speak with him; he was being impish and wanted to put her on the spot. "No," she tersely replied, almost crawling under her desk from embarrassment.

After Greg gave a presentation in another class, one of Deanie's friends confided to her, "I think he has beautiful blue eyes." Deanie agreed, but she didn't dare admit it out loud. "I couldn't even say yes because someone might overhear me and read something into it," she later recalled. "I was petrified of even making eye contact with Greg. He was a nice-looking guy, and we definitely could not go there."

Greg understood why the girls were trying so hard to act as if he weren't in the same room. To show him any kindness would have been social suicide. But did they have to move against the wall or turn their backs when he walked by? When he made his way down the halls, the milling students parted as if an invisible wedge preceded him. It made him feel not just disliked but unwashed, like a leper. It corroded his self-esteem. It hurt. Years later, when he thought about high school, the part that was most likely to make him well up with tears was being so thoroughly excluded.

Along with Spanish, Greg took four courses that fall—English, speech, typing, and government—plus a study hall period. Because of the fire during his junior year, his classes were scattered in different buildings, and he had to walk through a sort of no-man's-land to go from one to the other. A couple of weeks into the term, a dozen guys ambushed him outside at the bottom of a flight of stairs, where they forced him behind a stand of bushes and started shoving him back and forth like a hot potato. It was all he could do to stay on his feet.

"OK, Wittkamper," the biggest one said, "this is it. We're going to kill you. This is all your fault." Greg didn't recognize him, but he could see that he was holding a blackjack. Mercifully, he didn't use it. Instead, he hauled off and whacked him in the jaw with the back of his hand.

Greg was stunned and throbbed with pain. Trying to get a closer look at his assailant, he noticed another face in the pack, a familiar one, a boy who had been a playmate of his at Thalean Elementary School years before. He singled him out with a stare.

"Paul, I'm ashamed of you for being here."

"I'm ashamed of you because you won't fight," Paul snapped back.

The group quickly dispersed. Greg entered his next class rubbing his jaw and asked the teacher whether she had heard the disturbance outside. They had spoken several times, and he had found her friendly. Whether she was telling the truth or simply didn't want to get involved, she said she had heard nothing. Greg later reported the incident to Principal McKinnon, and as usual he said he was powerless to do anything without names and witnesses. The attack shook Greg. He had endured two years of harassment at the high school, but he had never been physically assaulted so flagrantly. "My God," he thought, "is this what my senior year is going to be like?" His jaw was sore for a month.

Back at the farm, Collins heard about what had happened and offered to give Greg lessons in the manly art of self-defense. One of the reasons Collins was so chiseled was that he had been a Golden Gloves amateur boxer. He knew how to cover his head, feint and jab, bob and weave. While he understood that Greg was philosophically committed to nonviolence, he thought he could benefit from some instruction in case he found himself in a situation where he had no alternative. Greg agreed, and the two of them started sparring in the pecan-processing plant. The way things were going, he might need a Plan B.

To one woman, Greg and the black students at Americus High were heroes, and she wanted to do something to recognize them.

Frances Pauley—Aunt Frances, as Jewel Wise called her—was a matronly white churchwoman who directed the Georgia Council on Human Relations, a civil rights advocacy group in Atlanta. She had logged hundreds of miles visiting small towns and rural areas across the state, trying to lay the groundwork for the racial transition that was coming one way or another. She knew Sumter County well and had butted heads with its leaders during the disorders there. "I still think Americus was one of the worst towns I ever worked in," she wrote in her memoir. "Segregation came first; money came second. Most places put money first, and you could talk to them. But in Americus the bankers didn't move, and

Greg with other young people at Jekyll Island receiving an award during the fall of his senior year, 1964. Two of the first black students at Americus High are immediately to his right: Dobbs Wiggins and Jewel Wise. *Courtesy of Greg Wittkamper*

consequently Americus didn't move. I was powerless. I did well to get out with my own neck, looking back on it."

Pauley often stopped by Koinonia and visited with Clarence Jordan, so she knew what the students from the farm were going through. When the high school desegregated, she was there to observe and continued to monitor the situation through the fall. On the last weekend in October, she invited Greg and the pioneering black students to the Jekyll Island resort, where the human relations council was holding its annual meeting. They were going to get an award.

Greg drove the group to the Georgia coast, where they strolled the beach and relaxed away from the tension of attending a school where they were not welcome. They were each given certificates of appreciation at a banquet and praised for their courage and composure. David Bell, speaking for the others, acknowledged how difficult it had been. In the first two months, he had heard countless racial slurs and had swallowed his anger when someone placed a sign outside his typing class that said, "Come by and feed the monkey." He had been suspended for fighting when a football player walked up to him in the hall and punched him in the face, and he had not swung back. All four of the newcomers had been 'buked and scorned, in the words of the old spiritual, and it didn't look like it was going to stop anytime soon. But the cause was larger than their personal comfort, and David vowed that they would persevere and remain at the school until graduation.

That was not going to happen. A few days after the trip to Jekyll, one of the pioneers decided he had had enough.

When the proposition of integrating the high school had come up in August, Dobbs Wiggins hesitated to volunteer because he wondered whether he could put up with the provocation he was sure to face. He had kept his cool during his arrest for picketing during the civil rights protests, but he was part of a group then. He would be on his own at Americus High. Dobbs had spent time in reform school for truancy and knew how to handle himself in a scrap; he was strong and confident. As the Coke bottles started flying, however, he felt himself coming to a boil and wasn't sure he could trust himself not to fight back. "I didn't want to get into a confrontation with some white students and embarrass the civil rights movement," he said. Nor did he want to flunk out. He told his father that he couldn't concentrate on his studies while he was worrying about survival. "I felt like I needed to do well and set a good example for the black community if I was going to stay there, and I wasn't sure I could do that."

So he left school and moved to Atlanta, where he continued his education in a less intimidating setting.

To most of his former classmates, Dobbs's departure was good news, their first victory in the struggle to keep the high school white. It was one down, three to go—four, if you counted Greg. And they did.

THE LONELIEST TIME OF THE DAY FOR GREG WAS THE LUNCH HOUR. IN the classroom, students were usually treated equitably and teachers kept them relatively quiet and well behaved. In the lunchroom, students had more freedom. They sat with whomever they pleased and acted more like the high-spirited teenagers they were. They always looked like they were having a good time, socializing, gossiping, joking, laughing. Greg had no part of it.

One autumn day in the cafeteria, he was leaving the serving line with his lunch when some boys motioned for him to come over to their table. "Hey," one of them said, "why don't you sit with us?"

This gesture of sudden hospitality should have seemed suspicious, a spider's come-on to a fly. But Greg was hungry for any sort of interaction. During his junior year, he sometimes had sat with Jan Jordan at lunch, but now that he was the only Koinonia kid in the school, he was invariably alone. He tried to make his isolation as inconvenient and awkward for the other students as he could. Instead of taking a seat off to the side of the cafeteria, where he could easily be ignored, he positioned himself in the middle of a row of half a dozen tables, his back to the windows, in the manner of a poker player trying to keep people from sneaking up behind him. As the lunch room filled, students would be forced to sit closer and closer to him, a dance of discomfort that Greg rather enjoyed.

Now this boy was asking him to sit with him and his buddies. Greg looked around the room and calculated the risk. He thought that there were too many students, too many teachers, for them to try anything. Maybe they really did want to talk. Sure, why not. He walked toward their table and pulled out a chair.

As he was putting down his tray, he noticed something flying toward him. It was sloppy joe day in the cafeteria, and someone had launched one of the messy sandwiches toward his head, bun and all. Greg jerked backward as if he were evading a punch. The airborne food narrowly missed him and struck another boy, who was so angry that he retaliated, not against the launcher, but against Greg, mashing a sloppy joe into his face. The reddish filling glopped down his chin and onto his white shirt.

Greg was furious. His first impulse was to flip the table and rampage like a bull. He fought back the urge to scream or cry, sighed heavily, and sat down. The lunchroom had cleared out like a saloon in a gunfight. A minute later, the sheriff himself—Principal McKinnon—appeared, looking distraught, and asked what had happened.

"I think it's pretty obvious," Greg told him.

"This is terrible," the principal said, showing concern for once. "If you want to, you can go home."

"No, thank you," Greg said. "I'll stay."

He went to the restroom, washed his face, and blotted his shirt. His chest bore a soggy stain the size and color of a medium pizza. Greg decided to leave it. He wanted everyone to see what had happened; he wanted to wave his bloody shirt. That afternoon, in his English and government classes, boys pointed, laughing and nudging, but no one said a word to him.

Greg had ridden the bus that day. When he got off at the farm after school, Clarence Jordan spotted his soiled clothes, tilted his head quizzically, and strode briskly toward him. He apparently thought the reddish smear was blood. As he came closer and saw that it wasn't, he opened his arms and gave the seventeen-year-old a hug.

A few days later, Clarence approached Greg in the community dining hall and told him that he had been discussing his predicament with one of his few friends in Americus, Lloyd Moll, the president of Georgia Southwestern College. "He had a situation like this in his high school," Clarence began. "A kid was getting picked on, and it went on and on, and he finally broke and fought back, and they left him alone after that. Now I'm not telling you what to do; I'm just tossing it out there. But I've watched you work, and I've seen you throwing bales of hay out here in the fields, and I know you're as strong as an ox. So maybe the next time one of them picks on you—not some puny guy, but someone your own size or bigger—maybe you should just haul off and beat the tar out of him. Just something to think about."

Greg was astonished. Clarence Jordan, a prominent apostle of nonviolence, a man so committed to his convictions that he didn't even want Koinonia children to play with toy guns, was giving him permission to whoop ass. Greg was tempted to use that permission like a shield, to go back to school and coldcock the first jerk who laid a finger on him. As he thought it over in the next few days, though, he came to realize that it wouldn't be that simple.

"If I'm going to fight them," he told Clarence, "I have to win. They're not going to roll over just because I'm stronger. They have to save face. So if I fight back, I have to be willing to hurt them badly. Sometimes I *do* want to hurt them, but I don't want to hurt them badly. They're just aping what their parents believe. I guess I'm doing the same thing. If our cribs had been switched at birth, they'd be me and I'd be them."

As Greg saw it, he had no choice but to take the abuse. The worst was still to come.

CHAPTER 8

Still Standing

ONE AFTERNOON DURING THE FALL OF HIS SENIOR YEAR, GREG WAS slouched at his desk waiting for Mrs. Bailey's government class to begin. It was midautumn, and the windows were still open to the lingering warmth of the season in south Georgia. Greg was daydreaming as usual, his eyes half closed, his legs splayed into the aisle, when another student walked by and brushed against one of his feet. It was Thomas Jordan—no relation to Clarence—a football player whose black-rimmed glasses made him look like an accountant in training. Reacting to the minimal contact, Thomas spun around, cursed, and pointed his finger accusingly at Greg.

"You tripped me!"

Greg sat up straight and listened as Thomas thoroughly tongue-lashed him. The outpouring of venom was unexpected; T.J., as most of the guys called him, had joined in some of the hounding, but he was far from the worst. Greg looked around for Mrs. Bailey, hoping the teacher could defuse the situation, but she hadn't arrived. "Oh, come on," he muttered below his breath, "quit being such a baby."

Thomas couldn't make out what Greg had said, but another class-mate thought he heard the remark and told him that Greg had used a fighting word. "You called me a *bastard*?" Thomas said. "I'm going to kick your ass, Wittkamper."

Greg didn't take the threat seriously. In his experience, people who wanted to beat up somebody didn't announce their intentions in front of a room full of witnesses; they just waited until school was out and then lowered the hammer. It was the final period of the day, and fisticuffs did not break out after the bell sounded. Greg went home to Koinonia convinced that T.J. didn't mean what he had said, that he had only been talking big because he thought that was expected of him.

But the threat did not vanish.

Few things incite the minds of adolescent males like the prospect of a good old-fashioned fracas. Throughout the next day, word spread through the hallways that there was going to be a fight after school—better yet, a fight involving the most reviled member of the student body. Greg heard the rumors and thought he'd better tell a responsible adult that something bad might be about to happen. He had study hall after lunch in Mrs. Crabb's class. He'd tell her. She'd listen.

GLADYS CRABB WASN'T FROM THE DEEP SOUTH. SHE CAME FROM MARY-land, where racial lines weren't as sharply drawn, and started teaching at Americus High in 1959, just before the civil rights movement awakened in southwest Georgia. She had Greg in her twelfth-grade English class and could see that he was shouldering a burden no other student had to bear. She realized that most of her colleagues and neighbors were leery of Koinonia because they considered it a den of Communism, but she didn't think this quiet, conscientious boy was a Marxist. She sympathized with him and made a point of asking him only questions in front of the class that she knew he could answer. When other students mistreated him, she showed her displeasure subtly, with a frown or a gentle comment, but never with a lecture or a reprimand. She didn't want the kids to turn against her, she just wanted them to broaden their minds and act more mature. Greg would come to her study hall early and talk with her before anyone else arrived. She was the only teacher he felt comfortable confiding in.

Gladys Crabb.

On this afternoon, Greg told her about his encounter with Thomas and the hotly anticipated fight. "What do you want me to do?" Mrs. Crabb asked. "Do you want me to come out there with you? Do you want me to tell the principal?"

Greg didn't want a lady English teacher coming to his rescue, so he asked her not to do anything. "I've got to face this sooner or later," he said. "I just wanted someone to know." Mrs. Crabb never forgot the tone of sad resignation in his voice.

In government class, where the alleged tripping had occurred the day before, Thomas repeated his threat to kick Greg's ass. Greg was growing more concerned, but he still wondered whether T.J. really wanted to mix it up. Why hadn't he named a time and place to meet? Everyone knew the protocol for an after-school fight: you had to make an appointment, like gunslingers challenging each other to a duel.

Near the end of the school day, when Principal McKinnon's voice came over the intercom to make announcements, he ordered Greg to report to his office. Some of the students sniggered and said he was in trouble for using a profanity in class. Greg assumed the principal had heard about the possibility of a fight, probably from Mrs. Crabb, and wanted to stop it before anybody got hurt. Maybe, he thought naively, Thomas would be there and they could talk through their differences.

When the final bell buzzed, Greg went to the principal's office and asked to see Mr. Mac. The secretary said he was in a meeting and would be there soon. Greg didn't much like the principal and figured he wasn't really in a meeting, he was just hoping Greg would stay in his office long enough for Thomas to grow tired of waiting and leave campus. Greg wanted no part of that evasion. He didn't want people to think that he was hiding out in the principal's office, that he was a Communist *and* a coward.

"If Mr. McKinnon wants to talk to me, he can find me tomorrow morning," Greg told the secretary as he moved for the door. "I've got to go home and feed the cows."

GREG HAD BEEN DRIVING TO SCHOOL IN THE RED MG THAT HE HAD bought cheap in Atlanta. He parked in the black neighborhood a couple of blocks from the school, his car hidden from potential vandals in the yard behind an elderly woman's house. He left the principal's office and walked briskly through the sand-and-gravel parking lot beside the baseball grandstand, the oldest surviving structure on the campus. In the distance, he saw Thomas and three or four others standing there waiting. "Uh-oh," Greg thought, "this is for real." He quickened his stride and imagined that he could outrun them if he had to, like a halfback breaking into the clear. If he could just make it to the black neighborhood, he'd be in the end zone—no one would follow him there.

But Thomas had teammates. As Greg drew closer, more boys moved out from behind the grandstand: two dozen, three dozen, maybe more. It looked like half the school. Greg's mind raced. "My God, am I going to get lynched? Are they going to stone me?"

Thomas stepped into his path. He was still wearing his black-rimmed glasses, which made Greg question again whether his heart was in this. Maybe he was being pushed into it. Maybe he was as scared as Greg was.

"I'm giving you five seconds to put down your books," he announced. Greg was toting a bulky stack of textbooks; he had to carry them around because his locker had been pissed on and generally trashed, and he could no longer use it.

As he stood in front of Thomas weighing the ultimatum, an under-classman sneaked up from behind and kicked the books out of his grasp, scattering them across the parking lot. Greg was angry now. He squared off against the underclassmen and heard people shouting, "Fair fight! Fair fight!" His recent conversation with Clarence about nonviolence flashed into his mind. Clarence had suggested that sometimes, under ex-traordinary circumstances, perhaps a Christian, especially a young and strong one, was justified in fighting back. Maybe this was one of those times. Maybe Greg should duke it out. His hands were empty, available to deploy as weapons.

"Hit him!" someone shouted.

"Knock the hell out of him," someone else called.

Greg felt the circle of boys closing around him. He was badly out-numbered and knew it wouldn't be a fair fight. As he turned away from the underclassman and back toward Thomas, the mob finally got what it had been screaming for. Thomas balled his right fist and swung, striking Greg directly on the left cheek. He staggered and felt his knees buckle, but he didn't fall. Through the stars in his eyes and the ringing in his ears, a biblical vision came to him. He imagined Thomas as a young Roman soldier and himself as Jesus. It was a passion play, and he knew his part.

Greg stepped closer to the boy who had just hit him and jutted out his chin as if awaiting another blow.

"I love you, Thomas," he said.

The two stared at each other. Thomas said nothing. He looked con-fused. His arms seemed to fall limp.

Just then, a coach and a plainclothes policeman pushed through the crowd to break up the confrontation. They had been watching from a car across the street.

"Do you need an explanation?" Greg asked one of the men.

"No. Get your books and get out of here."

Greg scooped them up and started to walk away, and another biblical scene came to him as the crowd parted before him—Moses and the Red Sea. He headed across the street toward the black neighborhood where he had parked. Despite the presence of the adults, a few students tossed gravel and dirt clods after him, and many more shouted and called him names. Greg did not acknowledge them. He slowed down and walked deliberately, as if to show that the debris and the catcalls couldn't touch him. When he reached a safe distance, he turned around and wiped his shoes on the curb as if he were scraping cow plop off the soles. Almost everyone there came from a churchgoing family, but it's doubtful that many of them understood the significance of the gesture. It came from the Bible, the ninth chapter of Luke, when Jesus tells his disciples what to do if they attempt to preach the gospel in a town that rejects them: "And wherever they do not receive you, when you leave that town, shake off the dust from your feet as a testimony against them." The verse was well known at Koinonia. It made everyone think of Americus.

Among the classmates who witnessed the one-sided fight that afternoon were Joseph Logan and David Morgan. At the time, they drew opposite lessons from it.

Although David jeered and hooted with everyone else beside the baseball stands, he was having misgivings. The threat of violence had always made him uneasy. He didn't talk about it much, but he had been bullied himself as a sixth grader—typical playground stuff that had nothing to do with politics or unpopular beliefs. While he didn't make the connection then between what he had experienced and what Greg was going through, it no doubt influenced his sympathies. "I knew it was wrong to goad him into a fight when we knew he wasn't going to fight," David reflected later. "My raising was better than that. I felt kind of ashamed to even be there." But in the fall of 1964, he kept those reservations to himself. He didn't dare object to Greg's mistreatment, not if he wanted to be liked.

Joseph, on the other hand, was only disappointed that Greg didn't get hit more than once. Joseph had worked his way up to cocaptain of the football team, and he instinctively stood with his teammate T.J. It was that tribal loyalty again. "We didn't like Greg, and Thomas was going to beat him up, and we all wanted to see someone beat the crap out of him," Joseph said later. As Greg walked away from the mob and scraped his feet, Joseph cursed at him, still blind to the moral dimensions of what he had seen.

AFTER THE SHOWDOWN, GREG DROVE HOME AND WENT ABOUT HIS usual farm work. He hitched a load of hay to a tractor and hauled it into the fields to feed the cows, his cheek sore from the punch. After dinner with his family, he pulled his mother aside and told her that he had been attacked while what seemed like half the boys in school cheered; she looked pained but had little to say except that this sort of thing had been happening to believers since the birth of Christianity. He later confided in his friend Collins, who agreed that his boxing lessons probably wouldn't have done Greg much good in the presence of so many angry young men spoiling for blood. Despite the trauma of the day, Greg slept well that night. He was relieved. The worst had happened, and he had survived.

For the first time that fall, Greg looked forward to school the next morning. He wanted to show everyone that he hadn't been hurt, that the intimidation hadn't worked, that he and everything he represented weren't going away. Principal McKinnon, who had been eager to talk the day before, did not send for him. In fact, no one in the administration asked Greg about the act of violence that had been perpetrated on school property. The only adult who said anything to him was Mrs. Crabb, who had heard about the incident and asked Greg whether he was all right. Throughout the day, none of the students uttered a word to him— especially not Thomas, who looked uncomfortable in his presence during government class. It was like nothing had ever happened.

But something fundamental had changed in the conflict between Greg and his classmates. He was the center of attention more than ever. He could sense the other students' eyes following him and could tell that they were whispering about the boy who wouldn't fight back. He watched them in silence, back in his bubble, feeling for the first time that he might be doing some good after all.

CHAPTER 9

A Lesson Before Leaving

THE EMOTIONAL LIFT THAT CAME FROM STANDING UP TO THE CROWD did not last. After Thomas struck him in the jaw in front of dozens of boys, Greg felt noble and vindicated for a few days, but as Thanksgiving came and went, he sensed that nothing had really changed. The badgering and shunning continued as before. To Greg, the confrontation behind the baseball grandstand had seemed like the turning point in a great moral struggle. To his classmates, he now realized, it must have been nothing more than an unrequited fight. If it had affected any of them more deeply, it was not yet apparent.

As the Christmas break approached, Greg was losing his resolve. His grades were flagging, and he didn't think he was learning much of anything. He wondered why he was staying in school at all. One of the main reasons he had stuck it out so far, he had to admit, was pure sibling rivalry. Greg wanted to show that he was tougher than his older brother, who had lorded over him and sometimes scuffled with him when they were young. Billy had left Americus High after one year, and Greg was midway through his third, so he had already won that contest. Proving himself a worthy second son no longer seemed a compelling motivation.

That December, Greg told his mother that he didn't plan to go back to school after the holidays. He wanted to quit. "Mom, they don't care what I think, and I don't care what they think. I've been smacked in the face and I've worn my food—I've taken their best shot—but it hasn't changed anything. It isn't doing me any good. It just seems like a big waste of time."

Greg could talk to his mother like that, bare his vulnerabilities, confess his fears and worries. Margaret might not have much practical advice to impart, but she could cloak him in maternal love and bolster his strength to face another day. It was different with his dad. Will seemed to come from an earlier time, a late-pioneer era when people placed a greater value on being stoic and self-reliant. When his son came to him about the latest tribulations at school, Will tended to fall back on biblical truisms, as if to say: "We're Christians. People are going to throw stones. It isn't right, but you'd better get used to it." Greg didn't confide much in his father anymore.

Margaret wanted her son to earn his high school diploma and didn't think he should quit school just yet. She urged him to give it one more chance. "Go back that first day after the holidays, and if you still want to quit after that, we'll support you. Just give it a day. At least do that."

Greg reluctantly marched back into the trenches.

———————

IF ANY STUDENT RIVALED GREG FOR UNPOPULARITY, IT WAS ANDY WORthy, a gangly, flat-topped senior whose acned face and Coke-bottle glasses typecast him as the class nerd. Poor Andy tried to fit in. He was usually there when people picked on Greg, laughing and grinning as if joining in the mockery would win him admittance to the fraternity of regular guys. It didn't. They made fun of Andy, too. It was so easy with those homely looks.

Not long before the holidays, Andy approached Greg in a sympathetic manner and started to say something to him, one misfit to another. At least that's how Greg read it. He cut him off before he could say a word. He couldn't forget the times Andy had scoffed at him. Greg would size up his scrawny frame and reckon that he could pummel it into the ground with one blow, but he didn't think it was worth the effort, so he ignored him. Now Andy was acting like he wanted to be friendly.

"You were picking on me a little while ago. What changed?" Greg said, and turned away. He came to regret the encounter.

One of Andy's gifts that Christmas was a double-barreled shotgun. A few days into the new year, the lonely teenager went into his backyard and turned the gun on himself.

During his classes that January, Greg thought he could detect a change in the atmosphere. While one boy used the tragedy as cruel ammunition, suggesting that Greg should follow Andy's lead and kill himself, most of the students were shocked and chastened by the terrible intrusion of mortality into their world. Teenagers weren't supposed to die. The suicide of one of their own seemed to give the young people pause and leech out some of their spitefulness.

In the early weeks of 1965, Greg noticed that people didn't call him names nearly as often. The tripping and shoving stopped. There were no more physical attacks like there had been in the fall. Maybe he had outlasted his enemies and they had become bored. Maybe the seniors were looking ahead to graduation and preoccupied with life after high school. Whatever the reasons, Greg was happy for the reprieve. "I had been their favorite joke, and it seemed like the joke was over."

The new dynamics were apparent in Mrs. Bailey's government class, where the alleged insult that led to the confrontation with Thomas had been uttered. It was the final period of the day, a time that seemed to loosen inhibitions. During a discussion early that year, David Morgan told everyone that he had been thinking and that maybe they should stop bothering Greg, even if they disagreed with what he stood for. "I'm not saying that you have to be his friend. I just think we should leave him alone."

The outcry was immediate, as some of the boys razzed David for suggesting something so conciliatory. "What's the matter? Are you a nigger lover, too?" one of them taunted.

David didn't say another word. He didn't need to. A door had been cracked open. Greg had never heard anyone at school give voice to the proposition that an American citizen had the right to hold out-of-favor opinions, even in Sumter County. He looked around the room and wondered how many of the other students agreed, because most of them, he noticed, had remained silent and had not told David to shut up.

No one had ever talked with Greg in his classes if they didn't have to, but that also started to change. Mrs. Bailey let her students debate current events, and Greg, with his lightning-rod political views, was often at the center of the disputation. There was a lot to debate; during that winter and early spring, Malcolm X was assassinated in Harlem, the United States sent the first ground combat troops into Vietnam, and the battle for voting rights reached its epic climax in Selma and Montgomery, Alabama. Greg was the only person in class who spoke against the war and in favor of racial equality, which left him isolated, as usual, but he was heartened that other students were quizzing him about his beliefs instead of just ignoring or dismissing him. It felt good to explain himself instead of sleepwalking through the day like a zombie. It was refreshingly educational. "We had some hot discussions in there," David remembered. "Sometimes Mrs. Bailey lost control of the class."

The subject that came up repeatedly was, unsurprisingly, civil rights. Greg's classmates were still struggling to come to grips with integration and wanted to know why the federal government was trampling on their rights of free association.

"We don't want to be forced to do anything," one of the girls said. "We don't want anyone telling us who our friends should be."

"You're missing the point," Greg rebutted. "No one wants to dictate who you should be friends with. But you can't have two classes of citizens. We all have the same rights. Black people pay taxes just like white people, and they shouldn't have to stand in different lines or go to different schools. If you just want to judge people by the color of their skin, you're the one who's missing out."

In a way, Greg was judging his classmates through a similar oversimplification. He didn't know them any better than they knew him, and because of that, he tended to lump them together into one faceless mass of opposition. But there were distinct faces in that mass and an array of attitudes. While most of the students felt threatened by the changing rules of society, it was beginning to dawn on some of them that they were going to have to come to terms with the new day.

Greg got a preview of the coming accommodation that spring when one of the seniors who had been an outspoken hardliner on race told the government class about an interesting film he had seen. During a visit to the New York World's Fair, he watched a movie that was playing continuously at one of the pavilions there, the Protestant and Orthodox Center. It was a controversial short subject called *Parable,* which depicts a Christ-like clown dressed in white who rides into town on a donkey and takes up with a traveling circus. He comes to the aid of several performers but angers the show's autocratic impresario, who takes his revenge by leaving him lifeless and dangling from marionette strings like a lynching victim. The obvious religious allegory disquieted the senior and raised uncomfortable questions in his mind about persecution and inhumanity. He admitted to the class that he was reexamining some of his views about justice and civil rights, then quickly backtracked after some of the other boys swatted down his musings and wondered what the hell was getting into him.

Greg was astonished. This was one of the guys who used to call him "Greg Witt-nigger from Korn-a-nigger Farm." He never thought that he would hear him, of all people, express doubts like that.

Later that year, when a reporter from the Southern Conference Educational Fund interviewed Greg about his high school experiences for its monthly newspaper, the *Southern Patriot,* he put a positive spin on the discussions with his schoolmates. "If I had just had a little bit longer," he said, "I could have made believers out of some of them."

He didn't win any obvious converts in government class, but he may have made some of the students think about things they had never questioned, and that was a step in the right direction.

———————

EVERY WEEKDAY AFTER LUNCH, GREG LOOKED FORWARD TO STUDY HALL in Mrs. Crabb's room downstairs in the annex building. He left the cafeteria as soon as he had scarfed down his food so he could arrive early and have a few minutes to visit while she was getting ready for the next class. She was curious about Koinonia and wanted to know what it was like to live there. Greg told her about their communal system and their belief in pacifism and how they had remained nonviolent when they were bombed and shot at. Mrs. Crabb nodded approvingly, but there was one detail she did not like; as a good and proper English teacher, she was appalled by the way Greg referred to the Jordans by their first names. She urged him to show more respect for his elders and at least call them Uncle Clarence and Aunt Florence.

Greg and Mrs. Crabb talked about a wide range of topics: news events, drug abuse, civil rights. She suggested that just as the other students ought to tolerate his beliefs, he should make more of an effort to be sensitive to their traditions. "You have to remember that they were brought up a certain way, to have pride in their race."

"You can get carried away with racial pride," Greg replied.

One day Greg came to study hall and found Mrs. Crabb in a somewhat testy mood. She had heard a rumor and wanted to get to the bottom of it. "I heard that you've been seen walking around town with black girls, holding their hands? Is that true?"

Greg wasn't sure whether Mrs. Crabb disapproved of such behavior or merely thought it was foolish for him to openly flout one of the South's strictest taboos, interracial dating. She seemed placated when he denied the gossip. But Greg wasn't telling her the whole truth. While he wasn't so dumb as to swan around Americus with a black girl on his arm, he had dated them and more than a few times. He took them to dances and on outings to Koinonia and to basketball games at the black high school. He would later go to the prom there at the invitation of one of the students he knew, wearing his brother's old tuxedo vest and boogying the night away to Motown hits. Although Greg was usually honest with Mrs. Crabb, he didn't see the point in spelling out his predicament: he was a healthy American male who desired female companionship, and he certainly wasn't going to find it among his white schoolmates at Americus High. "There were girls in my classes who I thought were attractive, but I knew that making any advances was totally out of the question."

As if to confirm the point, one of the girls in government class asked Greg outright whether it was true that he went out with black girls.

"Sure," he answered. "I mean, none of you are going to go out with me."

"Eeeeew!" the questioner said, as if she had spied a rat. Greg laughed to himself. After all the bad names he'd been called—criticizing his

Greg and Collins going to the prom at the
black high school. *Courtesy of Faith Fuller*

religion, his politics, his manhood—none was more common than the
one about his love for black people. He got pleasure from confirming that
the slur was, in this case, true.

Among the young ladies Greg saw was a good friend of Jan Jordan's,
Lena Turner, a civil rights activist who was a couple of years older and
had already been married and divorced. His mother did not approve of
him spending time with such a *knowledgeable* woman; the racial aspect
was irrelevant to her. Greg also saw Rosie Rushin, another civil rights
protester, who was still in high school. She was the granddaughter of
Rosa Lee Ingram, a sharecropper who had become the focus of a case
that drew national attention when she was given the death penalty in
1948 for killing a white neighbor who she said had threatened her with a
shotgun.

Despite such a checkered history between the races, Greg always felt
accepted in the black community, even when he was going out with one
of their young women. He figured he was a novelty, an allowed exception. It helped that he was still hanging out with Collins McGee, who
knew everybody and every place. Greg sold his red MG that spring, and

the two of them tooled around in his latest import, a gray Volkswagen Beetle. "Collins saved my life," he said. "If he hadn't shown me around, I probably would have become a stark raving lunatic."

The local police took note of Greg and Collins and jerked them around on several occasions. One night, Sheriff Chappell himself tailed their car for a while, breaking off the surveillance by firing his revolver several times into the air. Another time, a city officer pulled over the twosome, checked their license and registration, and then told Greg to get out of town.

"But I live here," he protested.

"Well, you know what I mean," the officer said, glancing toward Collins. "Quit going to that side of town and quit carrying them around."

Fortunately for Greg, neither he nor Collins had been drinking excessively that night. That wasn't always the case. At times during his last two years of high school, Greg overindulged, returning to Koinonia with his pal in the wee hours when no one was awake to see them staggering to bed. One night, getting home around 3 A.M., they were startled to find Clarence and Will stirring in the barn. A cow was giving birth.

Will took a whiff of his son and went into stern father mode. "What's the meaning of this?" he demanded. "I know what you've been doing."

He wasn't talking about alcohol; Greg and Collins had been shooting pool in a dive, and Will was smelling the tobacco smoke on their clothes, which was as objectionable to him as booze. Greg didn't dispute his daddy. He gathered himself and got to work helping out with the birth. The calf didn't make it.

———

A FUNNY THING HAPPENED IN SENIOR ENGLISH THAT SPRING. ONE OF Greg's classmates wrote a paper about him titled "Four Years Without a Friend." The author, Donnie Smith, a good old boy who apparently had forgotten that his main character lived out of state for one of those years, had been antagonistic toward Greg like most of the fellows. Perhaps the coming end of their high school days put him in a more generous, reflective state of mind. Or perhaps he just needed a topic for his final English theme and knew that their teacher, Mrs. Crabb, was sympathetic to Greg. She didn't think much of the composition, but she gave Donnie a C for his choice of subject matter, which is pretty much what he had been angling for anyway.

As for Greg, his final English paper was a polemical essay calling for the US government to lift its ban against travel to Castro's Cuba. He had long since stopped caring what others thought about him and his ideas.

As the school year dwindled to its last month, Greg was more relaxed than he had ever been at Americus High. Except for the occasional wisecrack, the jocks and ruffians who had pestered him since the fall of 1961 had left him alone for most of the second half of the school year. The respite didn't last. A few weeks before the end of the term, Greg started to hear threats from some of the repeat offenders as he walked from building to building between classes: *Don't screw up our graduation . . . Why don't you stay away? . . . Don't bring any of your friends, or someone's going to hurt you . . . If we see any niggers, you're going to get killed.*

The menacing talk was rooted in the previous year's commencement, when Jan Jordan had invited Collins and other black friends to watch as she received her diploma. The superintendent, afraid that their presence would provoke some spectators in the otherwise white crowd, wouldn't let them into the reserved seating area. So much had changed since then—the outlawing of legal segregation, the arrival of black students at Americus High—but one thing had not: many white people in Sumter County simply did not want to sit with black people. As in 1964, the school authorities saw graduation as a potentially combustible situation.

They came up with a new plan to avert trouble. Seniors would be given a limited number of tickets for family members to sit in a roped-off area of the football grandstand. Other relatives and friends would have to sit farther away in unreserved seating. Given that there were no black graduates in the Class of '65, the restricted zone would remain white, just like the old days.

Principal McKinnon dispensed the tickets at the commencement rehearsal. When he asked whether anyone needed extras for friends, Greg sauntered up and said he could use a few. Mr. Mac could see what he was up to. This thorn-in-the-side was trying to inflict one last prick by slipping his black buddies into the roped-off area, where they would most decidedly be unwelcome.

"Greg," he said, "you wouldn't do that, would you? People are going to be coming from all over, and who knows what they'd think."

"If that's the way it's going to be, I don't want any of your tickets," Greg replied, handing them all back to the principal. He was so peeved that he forgot his own family needed to sit somewhere.

———————

ONE DAY THAT SPRING, GREG WAS PLEASANTLY SURPRISED TO SEE Robertiena Freeman in the hallway between classes. He had rarely glimpsed her around campus in the months since they rode together in the funeral home limousine and weathered the disturbances on the second day of school. As a sophomore, she took different courses and ate lunch on a different schedule from seniors and juniors. She was still coming to classes late and leaving early as part of the administration's plan to circumvent any disturbances. Hardly anyone spoke with her as Greg was doing now.

"How have you been doing?" he asked her.

That was a loaded question.

By the time Greg ran into her, Robertiena was the only black student left at Americus High. Dobbs Wiggins had departed during the fall because he didn't want to do constant battle with white boys. David Bell, who had pledged to stay at the school when the group received certificates of recognition from the Georgia Council on Human Relations, was the next to go. He grew weary of people shoving him and calling him "Martin Luther Coon," but the racial garbage was only part of his motivation for returning to the black school, Sumter County High. The plain truth was that he was flunking. He had always known that black classrooms received fewer resources than white ones—he could see that in the tattered, hand-me-down textbooks he had grown up with—and now he understood the consequences of that unequal education from his own experience. "Going from my old school to Americus was like going from sixth grade to college," he later reflected. "It was much more intense. I wasn't prepared for it." Jewel Wise left for the same mixture of reasons. While she hadn't been mistreated as much as David and Dobbs, she sensed that the odds were stacked against her. "I felt like the teachers were ignoring me. I didn't get the help I needed. I wanted to get a better education than I had been getting, and I felt like my purpose was totally defeated."

One night soon after their departures, Robertiena's father appeared in the doorway of her bedroom and told her that the other students had transferred. "You're going to be the only one left. I don't want to ask you to do anything you don't want to do. It's your decision. Whatever you decide, we'll support you."

Robertiena knew what her father wanted to hear—he was the head of the NAACP, after all—but she had to be sure that it was what she wanted. After a long silence, she told him, "You ain't raised no quitter. I'm going to stay." Her father seemed pleased.

Robertiena withstood the same sort of harassment that Dobbs, David, and Jewel had endured, but as the honor roll daughter of educators, she was better equipped to handle the course work at Americus High. As it happened, her biggest obstacle to finishing her first year didn't come at school. It came on the side of a road.

One Friday evening in late May, as darkness was falling, Robertiena and her boyfriend pulled their car off US 19 on the north side of Americus and started engaging in a little teenage necking. The smooching came to an abrupt halt when a police cruiser appeared, lights pulsing, and a state trooper scribbled out a ticket for illegal parking. At least that's what Robertiena thought it was. "All I could think was, 'Daddy's going to kill me.'" She did not tell him about the incident when she returned home.

On the following day, Warren Fortson, the attorney who had worked to desegregate the high school, phoned Mr. Freeman and told him that the police were on the way to Americus High to arrest his daughter. Mr. Freeman immediately sent a car for her. When she arrived at the middle school where he was employed, he asked her what had happened, and she handed him the citation. He read it and realized that she was being charged, not with illegal parking, but with fornication, an antiquated morals offense that carried a much harsher penalty. He had been through the movement wars and knew a trumped-up charge when he saw one. One way or another, he thought, they were trying to get his daughter out of that school.

Robertiena turned herself in, was booked and fingerprinted, and locked up. She spent three nights in jail, much of it crying, cowering in the corner of her cell, trying not to listen to the lewd comments of the male inmates. She found the jailing much more traumatic than the thirty days she had done in the Leesburg Stockade during the civil rights protests of 1963. The conditions had been horrible then, but she was part of a spirited group of girls standing up for justice. Now she was alone and scared, facing the kind of public embarrassment that could ruin a teenage girl.

Robertiena's mother brought some of her textbooks to the jail and suggested that she could occupy herself studying for her final exams, which were coming up soon. Back at the school, tongues were wagging about the scandal that had entangled the student body's one remaining black person, the sole survivor. "They thought it was funny," Greg said. "You'd hear people laughing about it. They thought she was going to get kicked out, and it'd be an all-white school again."

Robertiena did manage to take her exams that spring and pass. For all of her legal anguish, she was not finished with Americus High.

———————

WHEN GRADUATION DAY FINALLY CAME FOR THE CLASS OF 1965, THE weather did not cooperate. It was the first Monday in June, and a late afternoon thunderstorm boiled up in the early summer heat, forcing administrators to move the ceremony at the last minute from the football stadium to the much smaller gymnasium. In the process, the restricted seating scheme was forgotten, and the eighteen hundred spectators found space wherever they could in the roll-out wooden stands on either side of the basketball court. Hearing the first rumbles of thunder, Greg thought maybe God was looking down and clearing his throat.

As the seniors waited under the breezeway outside the gym, one of the few girls who had openly disparaged Greg all year confronted him with the rumor that he had invited black people to the ceremony. She had

David Morgan.

heard right; Greg had driven to town that afternoon with Collins and expected to see him and a couple of their civil rights friends in the stands. As far as this girl was concerned, that was tantamount to lighting a stink bomb during the alma mater.

"Greg Wittkamper," she whined, "you're ruining our graduation."

"This is my graduation, too," Greg corrected her.

A few minutes later, David Morgan walked up with a more amiable expression on his face. It had been an emotional day for David. Before he left home for the ceremony, he had burst into tears when an aunt told him how proud his father would have been. Mr. Morgan had died shortly before his son started high school. His memory hovered over the proceedings for David and put him into a state of nostalgia and heightened sensitivity. As he looked over the Class of '65, assembled for perhaps the last time, he noticed Greg standing there in his blue gown and mortarboard and felt something like admiration for the outcast he had once disdained. "I didn't think I'd ever see him again," David said later. "Even though I disagreed with him, he had always been honorable. He had endured against the odds, and I thought he deserved something from me. It felt good to put all that hatred to bed."

The "something" was a simple, sincere expression of congratulations. "I don't know how you made it," David told Greg outside the gymnasium, "but somehow you did." With that, he shook his hand in front of everybody.

Greg was dumbfounded. He had suspected David was different, especially after his comments in government class that winter, but he never would have anticipated such a public display of decency. In three years at Americus High School, it was the most considerate gesture any member of his class had ever made toward him—maybe the *only* considerate gesture. No wonder Ann Geeslin, the editor of the school newspaper, the *Paw Print*, wrote in David's annual: "May you always continue to have that virtue of thinking for yourself."

Many of the graduates did not possess that virtue, not yet. The commencement exercises provided one last opportunity for them to hiss at the kid from Koinonia. It was a typical program for 1965: an invocation, a few awards, a word from the valedictorian, some yawn-inducing speeches, a couple of inspirational anthems ("Climb Ev'ry Mountain," the showstopper from the hit movie *The Sound of Music,* and "You'll Never Walk Alone," which took on a certain irony for Greg under the circumstances).

Then came the roll call, in alphabetical order; almost the entire class of one-hundred-plus had collected their sheepskins by the time they reached the *W*'s and "Wittkamper," the next-to-last name, was announced. Spectators applauded at first, some of them no doubt out of repetition, but as the name sank in, a chorus of boos rose and drowned out the clapping. Most of it was coming from the seats directly facing the stage, from the graduate section—a final raspberry from some of the guys. Greg strode toward the lectern and accepted his diploma with a quick handshake. He smirked slightly, savoring his triumph of survival, and returned to his seat feeling drained and inexpressibly relieved.

THERE WAS ONE MORE HURDLE BEFORE GREG COULD LEAVE AMERICUS High School for good. Remembering the ominous threats he had received in the weeks leading up to graduation, he decided that it would be wise to make a quick getaway. Collins had dropped him off and knew where the car was. He scanned the stands to locate him—it wasn't hard; he was the only black man in sight—and as soon as the exercises were concluded, the two of them hurried out of the arena and started to cross the street in front of the gym.

They didn't get far before twenty or thirty adult men pursued them, shouting and cursing and throwing rocks and bottles that Greg could hear smashing into the wet pavement. It was a reprise of the beginning of the school year, a fitting bookend for a bad time. As the two continued toward the car, some of the men blocked their way, and one of them broke from the pack and smashed Collins in the head with a rolled-up umbrella. The amateur boxer instinctively raised his fists and coiled into a fighting crouch.

"Don't hit him, Collins!" Greg yelled.

Al Henry, a minister who was living at Koinonia with his family, witnessed the attack and rushed to Collins, throwing his arms around him to keep him away from the man with the umbrella. Collins collected himself and uncoiled from his fighting stance. Then he took off running for the car with Greg, the two of them dodging more rocks and bottles. They sped away in his Volkswagen Beetle, both of them shaken and laughing nervously about their close call.

That evening, many of the graduates went to a dance at the Americus Country Club, capping the celebration with a midnight breakfast. Greg was not among them. He and Collins were partying on the other side of town, bouncing around the black neighborhoods, getting blissfully wasted. Greg did not toast his alma mater.

PART 4

Continuing
Education

CHAPTER 10

The Next Selma

MARY KATE BELL DRESSED LIKE SHE WANTED TO MAKE AN IMPRESSION that day. On Tuesday, July 20, 1965, the twenty-four-year-old college student and mother of three donned her bright new sorority outfit—pink dress, green shoes, pink turban hat—and went to the Sumter County courthouse to vote in a special election for justice of the peace. She was a candidate for the office, the first black woman ever to run in a county-wide election, and she wanted to monitor the polls as well as cast her ballot. She never got the chance.

Bell saw two voting lines—one designated for white men, the other for white women—and then noticed a small sign reading "colored" that pointed to a third line in the back for black people of either sex. She couldn't believe it; she thought the civil rights act had ended segregation in public places, and here county authorities were still conducting elections as if nothing had changed. Her husband was home on leave from the US Army and would soon go back overseas, eventually to Vietnam. Was this what he was fighting for?

"Can I help you?" the lady behind the check-in table asked.

"I want to vote."

"You want the colored line. This one's for women."

"Last time I looked in the mirror, I *was* a woman."

By then, three of Bell's campaign workers had joined her at the doorway leading to the polling area. A sheriff's deputy told the four black women that if they wanted to vote, they'd have to go to the colored line. An onlooker cursed one of them and spat on her. When the women still didn't budge, the deputy arrested them on charges of obstruction. The bond was set at $1,000 apiece. Saying they'd rather go to jail than pay, the women were locked up, the candidate still in her assertive pink and green.

In the coming weeks, Americus found itself constantly in the news as residents took to the streets to express their resentments and grievances and were met, sometimes violently, by opposition. Hundreds of people carried picket signs and others wore white robes and tapped pistols in their holsters. Stores were boycotted, churches barricaded themselves, neighbors turned against each other, and the seat of Sumter County had neither justice nor peace.

Greg, who turned eighteen the week the disturbances started, would be pulled into the conflict along with a fellow member of the Class of '65, Joseph Logan, whose sentiments rested with the opposing side. It would prove to be a life-altering experience for one of them.

THE ARRESTS IN AMERICUS WERE JUST THE SORT OF OUTRAGE CIVIL rights leaders at the national level were looking for. The legislation that would become the Voting Rights Act was still making its way through Congress, and until the last compromises were struck and the final roll calls taken, another episode of white southerners behaving badly could be used to ratchet up political pressure.

The final stage in the battle for voting rights had opened that March in Alabama when state troopers kicked and clubbed demonstrators in a well-publicized melee at the Edmund Pettus Bridge in Selma—one of the news events students discussed in Greg's government class. If it hadn't been for Bloody Sunday, as the assault became known, President Johnson might not have pushed so swiftly for a bill to guarantee the ballot to all eligible Americans.

When he heard about the arrests in Sumter County, Hosea Williams, Martin Luther King Jr.'s pugnacious lieutenant at the SCLC, called a press briefing and vowed to make Americus the next Selma. Sitting next to him was John Lewis, chairman of SNCC, the student organization that had spearheaded the protests of 1963 in Sumter County. Both men had been beaten in Selma—Lewis bore a fresh scar on his head from a trooper's nightstick—but Williams also carried much older wounds that he had suffered in Americus.

Williams came from southwest Georgia, near the Florida line, and left home as a teenager to serve during World War II in an all-black army unit under General George S. Patton. Wounded and awarded the Purple Heart, he was returning home by Greyhound in 1945 when the bus stopped in Americus and he took a drink from a water fountain reserved for whites. A group of men attacked him so savagely that an undertaker was called to collect his body. On the way to the funeral home, the driver noticed that the corpse was still breathing; it took him five weeks to recover.

There was trouble in Americus? Williams eagerly led a cadre of organizers from Atlanta to whip up the protests. They joined a group of students who were already in Sumter County conducting a voter registration drive, part of an SCLC offensive across the South called SCOPE (the Summer Community Organization and Political Education project). They, in turn, coordinated with the SNCC field workers who had been there since '63. To many in Americus, it felt like an invasion.

During the next few weeks, anywhere from a hundred to a thousand demonstrators marched almost daily from the black side of town to the courthouse and the jail. People filled the pews for mass meetings at two of the stalwart black churches, Friendship Baptist and Allen Chapel AME, where they sang hymns and freedom songs and heard speakers exhort them to stand up for their rights as American citizens. Paramount among them was the right to vote. Sumter County did not make it easy for black people to exercise the franchise; while they made up 53 percent of the population, they accounted for fewer than 13 percent of the registered voters.

The white response to the protests, at least initially, was more measured than it had been in 1963. The police didn't arrest everyone in sight,

Protest march in Americus, 1965. The Reverend Robert L. Freeman is second from left. *Courtesy of the Americus–Sumter County Movement Remembered Committee*

as they had then. A handful of white moderates saw the demonstrations as an opportunity to deal with an issue that had to be faced whether people liked it or not. Warren Fortson, the school board member who was also county attorney, had been trying for some time to get white and black representatives to sit down and discuss their differences. Once, when he thought he was getting somewhere, the effort foundered after a couple of white participants backed out because they couldn't imagine calling Mabel Barnum, the matriarch of the black funeral home, by her last name. Such was the fear of violating racial customs.

Two days after the arrests, Fortson persuaded a delegation of twenty-five white businessmen to accompany him to a mass meeting so they could hear for themselves what the other side wanted. He warned that the rhetoric might get rough, and it did. "They were just pouring it on," he recounted. "One of the businessmen said he was going to leave, and I told him, 'No, we've got to sit here and take it.'"

Greg was in the sanctuary that night and was surprised to see Fortson's party. Considering the brutal response to protests two summers before, the presence of white men in a black church was a promising development. The Americus Merchants Association even passed a resolution opposing the segregated voting lines and offered to bail the women out of jail. Movement leaders declined, saying that freeing them didn't go far enough; the charges were illegitimate and had to be dropped.

On the day after the church meeting, Fortson's idea for a biracial committee disintegrated as word of the initiative spread and men who had been open to the possibility a few hours before retreated in the harsh light of a July afternoon. He blamed the John Birch Society, which had replaced the White Citizens Council as the center of reactionary opinion in Americus. As the dog days wore on, he noticed that people who had once been friendly to him ducked into stores or crossed the street when they saw him coming. Sometimes they'd phone and offer a weaselly apology: "Warren, you know I love you, honey, but I just can't afford to be seen with you."

The time for moderation was running out.

JOSEPH LOGAN KEPT HIMSELF BUSY THAT SUMMER. AFTER GRADUATING with Greg, he spent most of his time working in a cabinetry shop and getting ready to leave home to start classes at Auburn University. He probably should have stayed away from the racial brawls in Americus, as most of his former schoolmates were doing, but he couldn't help himself. It was like a car wreck on US 19. He had to look.

Joseph could see an aspect of the conflict in the church he had attended his whole life. First Methodist stood across Lee Street from First Baptist, forming the twin pillars of Protestantism in Americus. Several times that year, interracial groups of worshippers showed up at the churches to test their dedication to Christian brotherhood. The churches always failed, most notably when John Lewis of SNCC was barred entry at First Baptist and arrested after he staged a "pray-in" with others in front of the sanctuary.

The leadership of First Methodist had decided to keep out civil rights testers by informing them that this was a white congregation and that they should go back to *their* congregations. In case the polite approach didn't work, the church recruited its most imposing male specimens to stand at the doors of the sanctuary like God's own bouncers. As a recent cocaptain of the Americus High football team, Joseph was among the recruits. One of the others advised him to bring a pair of brass knuckles in the event of trouble, and if he didn't own any, to at least place a couple of rolls of pennies inside his clenched hands to turn them into fists of steel. "Brass knuckles?" Joseph thought. He didn't know exactly what brass knuckles looked like. He certainly didn't know anyone who owned a pair. In his whole life, Joseph had never been in a fight. He wondered what would happen if he hit someone with a fistful of pennies. Would the coins go flying? Would he hurt his hands?

If there was any doubt about how seriously some people in the congregation took the threat of unwanted visitors, a regular usher laid it out for Joseph. "The only way they're coming in this church," he told him, "is if they step over my cold, dead body."

The anticipated showdown came one Sunday morning when cars pulled up in front of First Methodist and several well-dressed people of both races climbed out. The minister met them on the sidewalk.

"We've come to worship with you," one of them said.

"No, you haven't. You've just come to stir up trouble."

The visitors asked if they could kneel and pray, and the minister said yes, as long as they weren't on church property. They knelt and departed without further incident. Joseph watched it all from the top of the steps in front of the sanctuary, standing shoulder to shoulder with the others, looking like the defensive line of a football team. He was fingering two rolls of pennies in his pockets, ready to hit someone if he had to. He was relieved it hadn't come to that.

On several occasions that summer, Joseph drove to Americus to watch protest marches with the white men who stood on the sidewalks heckling. Late one afternoon, as a double file of demonstrators passed by, some of the onlookers peppered them with rocks and bottles. Joseph didn't like the protests any more than the hecklers did, but he didn't throw anything, and when he saw others doing it, he cringed and found himself wondering whether anyone had been hurt.

He hung around after the march. As twilight fell, his better instincts almost failed him, and he did something he would regret for the rest of his life.

A black man was walking up the street by himself. "Here comes one!" shouted a white fellow in cutoff jeans and a shirt tied at the waist, like the comic strip character Li'l Abner. "Let's get him."

An impromptu pack of young men formed, some of them picking up whatever rocks or bottles they could find. Joseph didn't recognize any of them and had no good reason to join the group. But in the tingle of the moment, in the ambiguity of the dying light, he grabbed a jagged chunk of concrete and followed their lead as they confronted the black man. He looked to be about forty and seemed more weary than frightened.

"Look, guys, I don't have anything to do with these protests. I just got off work and I'm walking home . . ."

Before the man could say anything else, someone threw a rock and struck him under the eye. He covered his face with his hands and let out a woeful moan. Blood moistened his cheek. As the pack scattered, Joseph dropped his chunk of concrete and backed away in revulsion. He ran several blocks to the courthouse, to his car, as if he could reverse the last few minutes with his feet, and drove straight home.

———————

A WEEK AFTER THE VOTING LINE ARRESTS, CIVIL RIGHTS LEADERS called for an all-night vigil to pressure authorities into dropping the charges against the four women. Greg had attended most of the mass meetings in the company of Collins McGee, who was still living at Koinonia but was spending more time in town working with the movement. Collins had been at the courthouse on the day of the election acting as a poll watcher and had complained about white intimidation of black voters. As he later testified, a sheriff's deputy told him, "If you don't get your black ass out of this goddamned building, I'll kick it out," and then followed him outside and punched him in the face. As he had at Greg's graduation, Collins resisted the urge to take a swing at the lawman. He found other ways to fight; he wasn't about to miss this nocturnal vigil. On the afternoon of Wednesday, July 28, he joined Greg in his VW bug and they drove to Americus for the day's preliminary event, a march from Friendship Baptist Church to the courthouse.

It was hot in more ways than one. As the protesters wound their way through the business district, Greg noticed that many of the white spectators were carrying guns openly, some of them in holsters. They looked like cowboys in a western movie. Greg was used to being menaced, but not like this. This was dangerous.

The marchers arrived at the courthouse two hundred strong and found the grounds already occupied by a hundred white counterprotesters. The police ushered the civil rights crowd to a nearby parking lot, where they settled in for a long night of speeches, singing, and intermittent tedium.

Late that evening, a young white man named Andy Whatley got off work at the Sunset Drive-In out on US 280, where he was a projectionist, and headed into town to see what was going on. He was twenty-one and had just enlisted in the Marine Corps. He stopped at the Sing gas station three blocks from the courthouse and fell in with a cluster of guys who were standing around talking. An hour before, reported Gene Roberts of the *New York Times*, a group of about twenty had been loitering at the same corner yelling "nigger" at passersby and throwing rocks and bottles at them. There had been a number of such incidents since the protests began; a few nights before, a black teenager returning home from a mass meeting had been shot and wounded by a white man in a pickup truck.

Now came the terrible retaliation.

At midnight, a car sped by the gas station. Shots were fired. Whatley collapsed, bleeding from his head. Men darted into the street discharging their pistols toward the car. A police cruiser gave chase. The assailants' vehicle overturned, and the driver was taken into custody. A few hours later, the alleged shooter was caught. Both men were black.

News of the incident quickly spread to the vigil, where it had begun to rain and the crowd was hunkered under umbrellas and tarps. Around

3 A.M., someone announced that Whatley had died. Given the circumstances, the vigil was canceled and the protesters trudged back to Friendship Baptist under a wary police escort. It was a solemn procession: no freedom songs, no picket signs, precious little talk. As they retraced their steps across town, Greg and Collins peered into the shadows beyond the sidewalks and wondered if someone might be lurking, bent on revenge.

The church offered to let the marchers stay the rest of the night in the sanctuary, where they would be safer from vigilantes. Greg and Collins didn't want to drive back to Koinonia in the dark—a white guy and a black guy in a small foreign car might make a tempting target—so they stretched out on the pews with dozens of others and nodded off. They awoke near sunrise, slipped out of the sanctuary, and left Americus as quickly as they could, passing the Sunset Drive-In on their way back to the farm.

———

THE KILLING OF ANDY WHATLEY CRIPPLED ANY CHANCE FOR RACIAL reconciliation in Sumter County that summer. Both sides dug in. The mayor tabled plans to form a biracial committee. After a brief moratorium, protest leaders resumed their marches. Georgia Governor Carl Sanders ordered one hundred state troopers into the city to keep the peace, a task that was complicated by the proliferation of firearms. Retailers said guns were selling like never before, mostly to white people. "You wouldn't believe the fear you meet in these streets," a future Americus mayor, Russell Thomas, told a correspondent for *Newsweek* magazine.

Among the journalists who rushed in to cover the unrest was a young reporter from WSB-TV in Atlanta, Tom Brokaw. He arrived to find Americus clogged with pickup trucks full of gun-toting Klansmen threatening to punish any blacks who got out of line. He visited Whatley's mother, who told him that further violence wouldn't bring back her son. Then he went to a church meeting and asked a black teenager if she was scared to march with so many armed white supremacists wandering around.

"I'm absolutely terrified," she said.

"So what are you going to do?"

"March. We have no other choice."

The unrest in Americus during the summer of 1965 made front-page headlines. *Time* magazine called the town "Americus the Violent."

Brokaw's footage made *The Huntley-Brinkley Report* and helped land him a network job. Years later, near the end of his long tenure as anchorman of the *NBC Nightly News*, he would say that the most memorable interview he ever did wasn't with a president or a prime minister, but with that teenager in Americus. He never got her name.

Two days after the killing, a federal judge issued an injunction prohibiting segregated elections in Sumter County and ordering Mary Kate Bell and the other women freed. Such a decision might have calmed the protesters a week earlier, but there had been too much rancor. "It's too late to talk now, boss man," said one of the SCLC organizers, Willie Bolden. "You bought a whole lot of hog, and now you've got to eat a whole lot of hog."

The next couple of weeks were as bizarre as that statement. On the last Saturday in July, as Whatley's funeral was about to begin at First Baptist Church, a group of whites attacked picketers who were protesting employment discrimination at the Kwik Chek grocery store a few blocks away, injuring five of them. At another demonstration that day, police arrested a white man dressed in a Santa Claus suit and an army helmet, who had been delivering an extended segregationist rant with a Bible in

one hand and a bayonet in the other. Lester Maddox, the Atlanta restau-
rateur who had closed his fried chicken joint rather than serve blacks,
came to town to speak at a states-rights rally, a rehearsal for the campaign
that would win him the governorship the next year. Robed Klansmen led
a silent parade of six hundred to the courthouse, stopping to pay their
respects at the gas station where the young white man had been slain.

Of all the demonstrations that summer, the most significant one occurred on Friday, August 7, when the movement achieved its national goal
as President Johnson signed the Voting Rights Act in Washington, with
Martin Luther King Jr. and Rosa Parks looking on. In Americus that day,
the comedian and civil rights activist Dick Gregory led a voter registration
march to the courthouse. "Let's get everyone registered," he said. "If your
grandma won't come, hide her snuff and tear up her pension check." Some
three hundred black voters signed up. To everyone's astonishment, the
Sumter County board of registrars, yielding before the new law, appointed
three black clerks to help with the rush, which continued for days. By
summer's end, more than seventeen hundred black voters had been added
to the rolls. Fortson went to the courthouse to witness the spectacle and
was moved by the sight of people lined up to participate in representative
democracy for the first time. He never forgot the young woman who kept
repeating "beautiful, beautiful," as tears streamed down her face.

Things weren't so beautiful for Fortson. His efforts to foster a racial
dialogue irritated many townspeople and made him, like Greg at the
high school, a scapegoat for all the changes they resented. His enemies
collected two thousand names on a petition demanding that he be fired
as county attorney, while his defenders (including Jimmy Carter) mus-
tered only a hundred. While the Sumter commission did not discharge
him, it did bypass him by hiring another county attorney. Fortson's law
practice dwindled. Clients who owed him money didn't pay. A neighbor's
child pointed a rifle at his son. There were threatening phone calls and
suspicious cars stopping in the night outside the big house his family had
recently moved to in the historic district. Fortson kept watch from the
living room, a revolver in a nearby desk drawer.

His church provided no refuge. When the interracial group of worshippers were turned away at First Methodist, he walked out of the

sanctuary in protest. He was a member of the congregation's governing committee, the board of stewards, and taught a men's Bible study class named for one of the other teachers, Lloyd Moll, the retired president of Georgia Southwestern College, who was also suspect for his conciliatory views on race relations. (Moll was the one who suggested to his friend Clarence Jordan that Greg might be able to tame his enemies by fighting one of them.) The church was in no mood for dissent and sent word to both of the members that they were no longer welcome.

Fortson had had enough. In September, he left with his family for Atlanta—Moll departed a few weeks later for Pennsylvania—and journalists from *Newsweek*'s Marshall Frady to the *Atlanta Constitution*'s Ralph McGill composed sermons about the price of conscience in the small-town South. "The Devil," McGill wrote, quoting an unnamed minister, "has made Jesus look bad in Americus."

Fortson took a more measured view. He soon went to Mississippi to offer his legal services to the movement, gaining some perspective on his summer of discontent in Georgia. "I found out there was nothing really exceptional about Americus," he told Frady. "The whole white South— maybe all of white America—was Americus."

———

ON THE MORNING AFTER HE RAN WITH A PACK OF ROCK THROWERS, Joseph drove a hundred miles west to acquaint himself with Auburn University. The unsettling events of the night before receded in his mind as he toured the campus, met other students, and learned some of the school's customs, such as the way Auburn people greet each other by saying "War Eagle," not hello. But the unpleasantness all came back the next day in the dining hall when one of the other incoming freshmen asked, "Aren't you from Americus, Georgia?"

Joseph nodded.

"Well, I think somebody got killed over there last night."

Although he hadn't known Andy Whatley, Joseph felt a little queasy when he heard of the shooting. On his last evening in Americus, he had been standing across the street from the gas station where the killing had occurred. If that car had sped past a day or two earlier, he thought, that could have been him.

After the campus visit, Joseph returned home and worked until classes began at Auburn in September. He stayed away from the demonstrations, which continued off and on the rest of the summer and then petered out with little to show in the way of progress except for the voter registrations. He didn't tell anyone—not even his mother—about what had happened that night in July when he picked up a chunk of concrete and started to threaten another man. But he couldn't forget that pitiful moan, that pained face, that patch of blood. Even though he had not struck the man himself, he had watched it happen. He felt like the driver of a getaway car in a robbery. He was ashamed.

Joseph later came to realize that his attitudes about black people started to change the moment he almost assaulted one.

CHAPTER 11

Breaking Away

THAT FALL, AS JOSEPH AND OTHER MEMBERS OF THE CLASS OF 1965 LEFT for college, Greg stayed behind and worked on the farm. He had no plans for higher education, a lack of ambition that worried his mother. "It seemed like all Greg wanted to do was travel," she said, and she was right. Greg wanted to earn some spending money and see the world. He had no intention of living at Koinonia indefinitely. Nothing against the community; he was just sick of Georgia.

He certainly didn't want to leave courtesy of Uncle Sam. Greg turned eighteen a few weeks after graduation at a perilous time when the Vietnam War was escalating and the US troop deployment was rising by the tens of thousands. He registered for the draft as a conscientious objector, choosing not to take up arms as his father had done decades before. He knew he would have to perform some kind of alternative service unless he changed his mind and decided to go to college.

Then, abruptly, he changed his mind. Greg's ticket out of the South turned up when a white Cadillac pulled into the farm followed by several Volkswagen vans full of young people. They were from Friends World Institute, an experimental new school based in New York and conceived by America's best-known pacifists, the Religious Society of Friends—the Quakers. As part of their program, they had come to tour Koinonia, this semifamous outpost of dissent and courage.

Talking with the students, Greg learned they were part of the first class at Friends World and would soon be departing for Mexico to begin months of foreign travel and study. The man in the Caddy was the director of the school, Morris Mitchell, an old friend of Clarence's, who said the institute needed recruits for its second year. Greg raised his hand. This was exactly what his wanderlust was craving. The only problem was money; the Wittkampers had lived in a commune for twelve years and had shared everything, saving nothing for college. How were they supposed to pay $2,625 a year in tuition?

Mitchell had an idea. The school needed to stock its library; if Koinonia could ask its supporters to send books to Friends World, he agreed to credit it against tuition. Greg tried to write a solicitation letter, but when he recounted some of his experiences in high school, he thought he came off sounding like a pathetic victim. He asked Clarence to find the words, and his letter was sent out to hundreds of people on the farm's mailing list.

While Greg was waiting to see whether the appeal would bring results, Koinonia received a couple of visitors who would have a profound effect on the community. Millard and Linda Fuller didn't intend to stay long when they stopped by in November. They were on a driving trip and remembered that a minister friend of theirs was living in a religious fellowship near Americus, some place with an odd-sounding name that started with a *K*. They decided to look him up, just briefly—two hours tops. They stayed for a month.

Millard was a tall, lanky lawyer from Alabama who had defended Klansmen and had made a fortune selling mail-order cookbooks and other products. In his rush to amass a million dollars, he had neglected his marriage and was crushed to learn that his attractive young wife had been having an affair. They tearfully reconciled and resolved to give away their wealth and commit their lives to some kind of Christian service. On the day they arrived, they listened as a reporter interviewed Clarence and were so enraptured by his answers that they couldn't bring themselves to leave.

When the Fullers shared their story at the farm, Greg's eyes lit up at the part about them giving away their money. Maybe, he suggested, they could direct some of it toward his tuition. Millard stared blankly at Greg.

Fortunately, no such help was required. Friends World went ahead and enrolled Greg, anticipating that the books would come. And they did—fifty thousand of them. It was enough to cover all four years of his tuition. In a letter to donors, Mitchell attributed the overwhelming response to the story of Greg's "plucky struggle" in high school. His tribulations had been good for something after all.

That Christmas season, as he prepared for college, Greg had one last encounter in Americus that served as a reminder of everything he wanted to leave behind. The father of a Koinonia resident was speaking at First Baptist Church and invited her friends from the farm to go hear him. Greg was part of the group that night, along with the Jordans, the Fullers, and his pal Collins McGee. First Baptist had been one of the churches that turned away black worshippers earlier that year. Clarence hoped things were changing in Americus but cautioned everyone to stay calm, whatever happened.

The Koinonia party was met at the door of the sanctuary by an usher whose eyes widened with alarm at the sight of a black hand reaching for a bulletin. He looked at Greg and asked, "Who's he?"

"Why, that's Collins McGee," Greg answered and kept going.

A few people moved away as the group settled into a pew and turned its hymnals to "It Came upon a Midnight Clear." Just as the carol reached the line about "peace on Earth, goodwill to men," the usher hurried over and grabbed Collins by the collar.

"You gotta get out of here."

No one stirred. The usher got more excited.

"Am I going to have to drag you out of here?"

The Koinonians left peacefully. Outside the sanctuary, Clarence was struck by the way the white-columned church and its floodlit steeple stood out against the vast night sky. "I want you to notice," he told everyone, "how much darkness there is."

———————————

A FEW DAYS INTO THE NEW YEAR, GREG LEFT GEORGIA AND BEGAN ONE of the damnedest educations imaginable. Friends World wasn't a school as much as an extended, enlightened field trip. The idea was to send students from different countries to a series of educational centers around the globe, where they would explore humanity's biggest problems—poverty, racism, war, environmental degradation—while they immersed themselves in local cultures. Experience would be stressed over traditional classroom time. "Our stated mission," Greg said dryly, "was to save the world."

The campus was located, of all places, on a mothballed military installation on Long Island, the decommissioned Mitchel Air Force Base. There were only sixteen or so students in his class, most from alternative communities like Koinonia or from wealthy liberal families in the Northeast. Greg settled into his new digs, which had been officers' quarters for flyers training for war, and quickly learned a valuable lesson in 1960s student life: he smoked pot for the first time.

The group spent the first few weeks listening to lectures and taking short excursions to see organic farms and other exemplars of counter-cultural living. In the spring, the students boarded a couple of VW vans and took a swing through the South, visiting Berea College in Kentucky, the region's first interracial institution of higher education, and the High-lander Center in Tennessee, where the Browne family had gone after it left Koinonia. By June 1966, the class was in Selma, Alabama, scene of the great voting rights battle of the year before, when news came of another outbreak of violence. James Meredith, the man who desegregated Ole Miss, had been shot and wounded in Mississippi during an odd solitary walk he was undertaking to protest racism.

The students voted to suspend their tour and join a motley army of civil rights supporters who were assembling in Mississippi to continue the march in Meredith's name. Once they arrived, Greg spotted a black activist he knew from Americus and went over to say hello. The man didn't seem happy to see him. "We can handle this ourselves," he said. "We don't need whitey." Greg, feeling a bit stung, had innocently wandered into a fault zone, a growing break between establishment black leaders like Martin Luther King Jr. and younger firebrands like Stokely Carmichael, of SNCC, who were less patient and less willing to enlist white allies. Both were at the Meredith march, where Carmichael attracted attention by exhorting protestors with a new rallying cry—"Black power!"—a phrase King preferred not to use.

On June 23, as the marchers reached Canton, a few miles north of their ultimate destination in Jackson, Greg and the other students were getting ready to pitch tents for the night on the grounds of an elementary school. The authorities said they didn't have the necessary permits to stay there. A phalanx of state troopers ordered them to disperse, fired tear gas, and waded into the marchers, striking some of them with rifle butts. Mitchell, the Friends World director, witnessed an officer beating a medical student and scolded him, "You should be ashamed of yourself."

"You get back or I'll put it into you," the trooper warned.

Greg spent the night sleeping on the floor of a black family's home. In the confusion after the ruckus, one of the school's vans—the one carrying his luggage—drove off without him. He continued with the march, which grew into a throng of fourteen thousand as it entered Jackson, and then hitchhiked home to Koinonia, his clothes still reeking of tear gas. He recuperated for a few days and returned to school in New York.

His education was just beginning.

———————

IN THE FALL OF 1966, FRIENDS WORLD SENT GREG OVERSEAS TO BEGIN his international studies. His first stop was Sweden. The college had arranged for him to attend a folk school near the Arctic Circle, part of a continuing education system that welcomed foreign students. Unfortunately for Greg, the programs were in Swedish. He had picked up little of the language, making the classes fairly pointless, so he stopped attending them and started hanging out with a group of musicians. He told them he was an American folk singer like Bob Dylan and pulled out his guitar, and they let him play some gigs with their band. The Swedes appreciated his rustic voice; kids asked for his autograph, and girls found him intriguing. For a nineteen-year-old who had been so detested in high school, popularity was novel and intoxicating.

Even so, Greg became homesick for his family and Koinonia. During the interminable hours of darkness and cold that winter, he was alone

Greg as a troubadour on the Spanish coast
during his travels with Friends World Institute, 1967. *Courtesy of Greg Wittkamper*

with his thoughts and sometimes brooded about his turbulent school days. One night he dreamed he was back at Americus High facing down the usual suspects. In the waking world, he had turned the other cheek. Not in Dreamland. He calmly leveled a machine gun at his tormentors and cut them down. Waking in a panic, Greg was relieved that it had only been a nightmare. Clearly, he was sorting through some posttraumatic stress. It might have helped if he had talked it out with someone, but the language barrier would have made that difficult. Besides, he didn't want his new friends to know that this cool American folk singer had once been thoroughly loathed.

Greg left Sweden in the spring of 1967 and reported to the Friends World coordinator in Vienna, Ernst Florian Winter, who ran a school of diplomacy and was married to one of the von Trapp daughters of *The Sound of Music* fame. Winter laid out his options: Greg could stay with the other students in Austria or begin an independent study program that would let him travel as widely as his daily allowance of $8 would permit. Greg wanted to ramble.

He spent the next few months bumming around Europe. He went to Geneva and fell in with some Canadians he met at a youth hostel, and they decided to have an adventure. They reconditioned an old canoe and lit out for France, where they paddled past the castles and cliffs of the Rhone River. Near Lyon, their vessel capsized in a discharge of water from a dam, and they lost all their money and passports, although Greg was able to salvage his guitar. As soon as he could replace his passport and scrape together some dollars, he left by himself and hitchhiked to Spain for the summer.

In the United States, that was the Summer of Love, the high season of hippies and flower power. For Greg, it was skid-row time in Barcelona. The stipend payments stopped coming, despite his pleas to Friends World. Nearly out of funds, he slept on park benches and the beach, playing music for tips in the tourist areas or selling his blood for cash. He survived on food the markets were throwing out and learned to ply the shoreline and catch small octopuses, pulling out their entrails and boiling the tentacles in a tin can. He looked like a tramp, his beard scraggly, his hair long and greasy, his jeans riddled with holes. "I was like Jesus in rags," he said. For weeks, he forgot to send his parents the occasional postcard he had been mailing them. They grew increasingly concerned, not knowing where their son was or whether he was still alive. He eventually dropped them another card.

After the college finally wired him some money, Greg backpacked down the Mediterranean coast to Gibraltar and then across the strait to Morocco. He traded his leather vest for a djellaba, the hooded robe worn by the Berbers of northern Africa, and passed several weeks in Tangiers and Marrakesh sipping tea and puffing dope with the local artisans. When he made his way back to Austria that fall, it occurred to him that he hadn't been inside a classroom for months. "We learned by living," he said.

Greg stayed in Vienna long enough to clean up and collect $300 in back stipends. Then he was off to Africa, where Friends World had scheduled classes at an educational center in Nairobi, Kenya. The seminars on African history were interesting, but as usual, Greg was more enthusiastic about educational opportunities outside the lecture hall.

He tried LSD and enjoyed it so much he was afraid to try it again. He climbed Kilimanjaro, reaching the summit on Christmas Day and witnessing a full-circle rainbow that was more spectacular than anything he had experienced on acid. He walked through the slums of Nairobi and realized for the first time how poor much of the world was—the frugal life at Koinonia seemed lush by comparison. "The kids would befriend us and try to get us drunk on the local brew," he said. "It tasted like piss, but we drank it in the interest of world peace."

While he was in Kenya, Greg received a letter from the draft board in Americus ordering him to report for alternative service at a mental hospital in Kansas. He wrote back saying that he was in college overseas and couldn't come. This displeased the board, which responded that he shouldn't have left the country without notifying it and that his college wasn't accredited anyway. If he didn't show up in Kansas on the appointed date, he could be arrested the next time he set foot in the United States. So much for going home, Greg thought.

The correspondence with the draft board must have triggered something in his mind, because while he was in Nairobi, he had that nightmare again, the one where he was slaughtering his high school classmates with a machine gun. Only this time it was more vivid than it had been in Sweden. He woke in the predawn darkness, half expecting to find himself in a bloody classroom in Americus, and realized that he was in Africa and had only been sleeping. He was more than relieved; the anger and desire for vengeance that had followed him from Georgia seemed to lift in one cathartic moment.

After half a year in Kenya, Greg told Friends World that he wanted to see the Middle East. The college forwarded $500 and instructed him to rejoin the class three months later in India. He flew to Khartoum, took a riverboat down the Nile, and hitchhiked into Egypt through the Valley of the Kings and past the tombs of the pharaohs. It had been less than a year since Israel humiliated the Egyptian military in the Six-Day War, and feelings were still raw. Thumbing a ride outside Cairo, Greg was surrounded by a group of teenagers who heckled him and threw rocks. For a moment, he felt like he was back in Americus. A kindly young man in a suit and tie took him by the arm and led him to a police station, where an officer explained the reason for his predicament: "They thought you were an Israeli spy." The constables allowed him to sleep overnight in the station and brought him breakfast the next morning.

Greg pressed on to Alexandria, Cyprus, and Beirut, where he befriended a Dutch couple who had a Mercedes and invited him to ride with them to India. Border guards wouldn't let him into Syria, where Americans were considered suspect after the war with Israel, so he flew to Turkey and rejoined the couple, and they made their way into Iran and Afghanistan, sampling the native hashish as they went. They sold the car in Kabul and hitched across the Khyber Pass into Pakistan, where four Frenchmen in a VW van picked them up and let them sit on the roof rack as they drove into Kashmir. It was the most enchanted place Greg had ever seen. The snowy mountains and deep valleys were so extravagantly scenic that you didn't need to get stoned to enjoy it, but they did anyway.

As he entered India, Greg realized that he had taken so much time wandering that he was in danger of missing the rendezvous with his Friends World class in Bombay. Running low on money, he thumbed a ride on a watermelon truck and then bought a third-class ticket on a train where he shared space with goats, sheep, and pigs. It was hot and stuffy, so he followed the lead of other passengers and climbed atop a railcar, ducking whenever they passed through a tunnel. He arrived in Bombay just in time and found the address of the Friends World contact, where a woman answered and gaped at the sight of the unwashed vagrant in the doorway. Greg understood her reaction after she showed him to the bathroom and he saw in the mirror that coal soot from the train had completely darkened his complexion. He looked like Al Jolson in blackface.

It was the spring of 1968, and as Greg reconnected with his fellow students, he caught up on the news from home. The war in Vietnam wasn't going well, with American casualties reaching their highest level during the recent Tet Offensive. Greg didn't think the United States should even be there. The most upsetting news came in April when he heard that Martin Luther King Jr. had been shot to death in Memphis. Greg was not surprised, knowing his country's racial demons as intimately as he did. He remembered seeing King speak in Albany, being swept up by the excitement and possibility swirling through the church that day. Now that voice was silent.

In a nod to conventional higher education, Friends World students were required to choose a theme for their studies. Greg elected an appropriate topic for a minister's son: a comparative investigation of world religions. He had already seen a broad swath of Islamic culture; now he wanted to explore Hinduism. He spent six months in India visiting Hindu ashrams, learning yoga, and taking field trips to Nepal and the Himalayas. Buddhism was next on his agenda. He left for Bangkok, Hong Kong, and Japan, where his class reconvened in Hiroshima, which had become a mecca for peace activists in the years since the atomic bomb annihilated the city. As part of his study of religions, Greg stayed for a month at a Zen Buddhist monastery, where he practiced meditation and experienced the excruciating liberation of mind over body that comes from holding a cross-legged position for hours. Whenever his form was lacking, a monk would whack him with a long stick like a stern schoolmarm. No one spoke English. Meals consisted of a rice and vegetable porridge. It was like a graduate course in endurance. When he wasn't meditating, he had ample hours to himself and filled some of them by reading the Bible for the first time from beginning to end. He thought it was pretty good, although not to be taken literally.

During his stay in Japan, Greg received another letter from the draft board in Americus. It was good news. The board had recognized Friends World as an accredited educational institution and had given Greg a student deferment. He was no longer AWOL and could finally go home without fear of arrest.

———

HE TOOK HIS TIME. IN THE SPRING OF 1969, GREG LEFT JAPAN FOR VLADivostok and boarded the trans-Siberian railroad for a weeklong trek across the Soviet Union to Moscow. Then he traveled to Leningrad, Helsinki, Stockholm, Luxembourg, and London, where he tarried for a month. He didn't return to the United States until midsummer, around the time of the moon landing, and like the Apollo astronauts, he felt like he was entering an alien atmosphere. It had been almost three years since he left the country. Everything seemed foreign to him after he touched down at JFK airport and checked in at Friends World on Long Island. The cars looked so big. The people sounded so boisterous (and he could actually understand what they were saying). The food seemed so excessive, especially after the rice and vegetable regimen at the monastery.

The years abroad had altered Greg. He was no longer the reticent farm boy who hid inside a hard shell to protect himself from the emotional battering at school. He had opened himself up to the world and learned firsthand that there was much more out there than the claustrophobic black-and-white obsessions of southwest Georgia. With distance and perspective, he now regarded Americus as a blip in the bigger scheme, a receding image in the rearview mirror.

Margaret Wittkamper noticed the changes in her son when he arrived at Koinonia in late July. It wasn't so much his appearance, although he was twenty-two now and wore his hair longer than he had when he left as a teenager. It was more his way of being. Greg seemed more assured, more inquisitive. "He grew in a lot of ways," she said. "He never was much for reading before he went."

Koinonia had changed as well. For one thing, there were more residents. Communes were becoming fashionable, and the farm was beginning to draw young people who recognized its version of Christian life as countercultural. "It was starting to look like a hippie commune," Greg said. Among the newcomers were a family who had been there before, Millard and Linda Fuller and their children. After visiting that first time in 1965, the couple had indeed redirected their lives away from the pursuit of material success. They gave their wealth to charities and moved to Mississippi, where Millard raised money for Tougaloo College, a small, historically black school near Jackson. He never forgot those soul-searching conversations with Clarence, and after a couple of years, he contacted him and asked what was going on.

The two of them got together and imagined a new vision for Koinonia, something they called the Fund for Humanity, an ambitious plan to help poor people with no-interest loans for farming, business development, and better housing. It was that last idea that lifted off. A few months before Greg returned, Koinonia started building houses on its property in partnership with local families. In the coming years, the Fullers would refine the concept and expand it in Americus and beyond. Habitat for Humanity, the organization that grew out of Millard and Clarence's brainstorming, went on to build hundreds of thousands of homes in a hundred countries around the world. In the summer of 1969, Greg could see the first four of them under construction at Koinonia. David Wittkamper, who had graduated from high school that spring, was among the volunteers working on them.

Greg's younger brothers had taken a winding path through secondary education, trying to avoid replicating his struggles. Danny, the youngest, refused to consider Americus High and started eighth grade in Tallahassee, Florida, where he lived with a family that had spent time at Koinonia. David's odyssey was more convoluted; it took him six years, three schools, and two states to earn a diploma. Like the oldest Wittkamper son, Billy, David couldn't stomach the treatment in Americus and left the high school after one year. He moved in with an uncle and aunt in Indiana, where he repeated a grade, and returned to Georgia two years later to finish at Sumter County High, the black school on the north side of town, where he and Lenny Jordan, Clarence and Florence's youngest, integrated the student body. The white kids got a much better reception than the first black students at Americus. "We were treated like kings," said David, who went out for the football team and joined an interracial rock band called the Knockouts. Sometimes he rode to school on a Harley-Davidson Sportster, long hair flowing, arriving with the honk of a horn that sounded like a braying ass, and the students would laugh and say, "Here comes Jesus on his donkey."

Greg noticed another thing that had changed at Koinonia: his running buddy Collins McGee was gone. During the farm's lean period, Clarence had considered putting him in charge of operations but thought better of it, probably because Collins, always a hard worker, was also a hard drinker. He had married and moved to Atlanta. In place of Collins and his hooch, Greg found that a new recreational substance had roosted at the farm. While he was there, his mother dug through one of David's drawers and found a stash of pot.

"Is this marijuana?" she asked. "Now, David, you shouldn't be doing this. It's addictive, and it leads to other things."

Greg, now seasoned in herbs, came to his brother's defense. "Mom, let's get serious," he said. "Coffee is a drug, too. If you're really that concerned about our health, we'll make a deal with you: if you give up coffee, we'll give up pot."

Margaret thought that sounded fair. The next morning, when the boys awoke to the aroma of brewing Maxwell House, she conceded the point.

Greg stayed at the farm a couple of weeks. One day he rode into Americus and thought everything seemed about the same, down to the hulking form of Sheriff Chappell, a sight that still made him tense up involuntarily. Beyond appearances, though, the town was finally beginning to evolve. More blacks were voting and two had been appointed to the city school board. Americus had even hired a black police officer, which would have been unthinkable a few years before.

Greg was most startled by his alma mater. When he drove by campus, he couldn't believe that at least half of the students he saw were black. In the four years since he had graduated, many white families had fled the city system and were sending their children to a private school started after Americus High had desegregated, the aptly named Southland Academy. All across the region, academies like Southland were popping up like dandelions after a downpour. Greg wasn't the least bit surprised that some people were going to such trouble and expense to avoid having their children rub elbows with black children. Still, it was surreal to see so many black kids walking the grounds where, not that long ago, the presence of just four of them had caused a small riot.

———————

ONE AFTERNOON TOWARD THE END OF HIS STAY, GREG WAS LISTENING to Clarence and some of the other adults debate some point of religion. It was a typical Koinonia discourse, preacher talk. As a teenager, Greg had never joined such discussions because they seemed over his head. But now that he was an adult himself and had seen something of the world and its many faiths, he spoke up and volunteered his conviction that affiliations didn't count for much, that you didn't have to call yourself Hindu or Muslim or Christian to be religious.

Clarence looked displeased. "Well, you have to be something."

"Why?" Greg challenged him. "I think labels can divide as much as they can unite."

Greg had been rethinking his religion for some time. He no longer believed in a traditional deity who ruled creation like a monarch from a throne. He no longer prayed because he thought any God worth praying to already knew what was in everyone's mind. Nevertheless, like countless young people of the time, he felt a yearning for spirituality. That yearning didn't necessarily lead to a pew looking up at a pulpit; it could just as easily lead to a Buddhist monastery or a Hindu ashram. Greg still shared Koinonia's beliefs in brotherhood and living for the collective good, and he definitely shared its distaste for materialism and violence. But he wasn't persuaded about the core of the faith, the beliefs that meant everything to his parents. Christianity, for him, had become more of a starting point than a conclusion.

Not that he articulated all that to Clarence as they sat on a porch at Koinonia. If the opportunity ever arose, they could talk about it later.

Greg soon left for New York and Friends World accompanied by David. They worked at the college late that summer repairing roofs, passing up an opportunity to attend a rock festival near the upstate village of Woodstock so they could earn some money. In autumn, they set out on a cross-country driving trip to California, where they sold their car, bought a motorcycle, and headed south toward Mexico. They took the Pan-American Highway into Central America, looking a little ridiculous in World War I helmets they purchased on the fly so they wouldn't violate local riding laws. They camped and found itinerant work along the way. They were in Nicaragua, helping fishermen throw nets and sleeping in a cabana on the beach, when David had the strangest vision one night. He saw Clarence standing before him crying what appeared to be tears of joy. "Keep it up, boys," he said. "Keep it up."

Greg told him he had been dreaming.

"It wasn't a dream," David said, "Clarence was standing right here."

A week later, a letter from home found the brothers in Panama. Their mother broke the news: Clarence was dead. On a brisk October afternoon in 1969—perhaps on the day David had his vision—he was holed up in the shack he used as his study, working on his "Cotton Patch" translation of the Gospel of John, when a young woman who was living at Koinonia stopped by to visit. After chatting for a short time, Clarence reached out to give her a parting hug. She felt his body shudder and his head fall limp. A heart attack. He was just fifty-seven.

Will Wittkamper took it hard, throwing himself over the body and praying, "Please, Lord, take me. Don't take Clarence. He's a young man. I'm old. Please, take me."

Americus treated Clarence no better in death than it had in life. Millard Fuller couldn't get the coroner to come to the farm to certify the death, so he and another man loaded the body into a station wagon and drove it to the hospital in town, where an autopsy was performed. Once the remains were released, they were taken back to Koinonia, laid in a cedar crate, and buried beside the pines on Picnic Hill, a spot Greg and David knew well from so many outings during their childhoods. Clarence Jordan had returned to the soil he loved, to the land he refused to leave.

A plaque memorializing Clarence and Florence Jordan and their oldest daughter was erected years after his death.

CHAPTER 12

Growing Up

WHILE GREG TREKKED THE WORLD BUMMING ON BEACHES AND MEDI-
tating with Buddhists, several of his former schoolmates who would
one day write to him were taking journeys of their own. Their travels may not have been as exotic—they involved other states, not other
countries and cultures—but they were enlightening in their own ways.
There was so much to learn, and unlearn. They were proud sons and
daughters of Americus who had grown up in a system that suddenly
and tumultuously became anachronistic as they were entering their final
years of high school. Navigating adolescence is tricky under normal circumstances. Doing it in the midst of a social revolution was even more
confounding.

FOR JOSEPH LOGAN, THE KEY TO THE JOURNEY WAS DISCOVERING WHICH
parts of his heritage were worth honoring and which deserved to be left
behind. Joseph came from one of Sumter County's oldest families and
esteemed his connections to its past. One of his grandfathers was mayor
of Americus, and a great uncle was a prominent physician and mayor
of Plains. He was also related to the most tragic chapter in local history;
his great-grandfather, Alonzo Josephus Logan, was a Confederate clerk

at Camp Sumter, as the POW stockade at Andersonville was officially designated.

Joseph knew the site well from summers he spent with an aunt who was postmistress in the nearby village. He would wander the grounds of the park that commemorated the thousands who had perished and catch crawfish in Providence Spring. According to legend, the spring was miraculously created when a lightning bolt struck the ground and water gushed forth in answer to the prayers of the desperately thirsty Union prisoners. One of Joseph's uncles thought that was hooey. "You mean to tell me that God sent lightning to bring fresh water to a bunch of Yankees?" he told his nephew. "That ain't so." Joseph, in his youth, viewed the prison camp differently from the Koinonia children who were visiting on day trips around the same time.

When he looked back years later, Joseph cherished his small-town upbringing: the neighborliness, the easy pace, the Protestant assuredness everyone seemed to share. He was the second of two children born to an insurance salesman who taught Sunday school at First Methodist Church and his wife who stayed at home with the kids. "All the Logans were Methodists and drove Chevrolets," Joseph remembered, chuckling at the insularity of it all. "I was in my twenties before I realized Catholics were Christians."

His cozy world was upended when he was in the third grade and his father, only thirty-nine, abruptly died of kidney failure. His mother went back to school to earn an insurance license and remarried a year later to a former beau who lived thirteen miles away in the little town of Ellaville.

Joseph's stepfather, Sherman Walters, was a dogged man who had contracted polio as an adult and been told that if he ever got out of his wheelchair, he would never walk without crutches. When he did learn to walk again, with great difficulty, he was so sensitive about his awkward gait that he refused to go to church or school activities with his new family because he didn't want people staring. Joseph resented him at first and couldn't understand why he didn't attend his football games, but he came to respect his stepfather's determination, and they eventually grew close.

Mr. Walters ran a small business making office cabinetry and store displays in a woodworking shop behind his home. Joseph often worked with him and absorbed many of his opinions and attitudes, which were typical for that time and place. Mr. Walters believed completely in white supremacy and the separation of the races. "I hate to say it, but we thought black was dirty, so a black person had to be dirty," Joseph explained. "You've seen those Westerns where the good guys wear white hats and the bad guys wear black hats? That was pretty much our mentality. You grow up believing the things that the people around you believe. You're going to believe what your daddy says and what your uncle who takes you fishing and baits your hook says." Joseph went so far as to root for the New York Yankees—the Yankees!—when they faced the Brooklyn Dodgers in the World Series, simply because Jackie Robinson played for the Dodgers. Most of his teammates in youth baseball felt the same way.

Mr. Walters employed several black men in his wood shop and was capable of paternal acts of kindness toward them. When one of his charges, a brawny fellow named Dallas, was shot in a domestic dispute, Mr. Walters was enraged to hear that the emergency room had stopped the bleeding but refused further treatment unless payment was guaranteed. He told the hospital that they'd better treat Dallas or they'd hear from his lawyer. "He had no use for black people, but that was *our* nigger—and that's what he called them," Joseph said. Another time, when a doctor was summoned to look after one of their workers, Joseph was startled to hear that the physician was not white. "I didn't know how that could be. You have to go to college to become a doctor, and I didn't know any black people who had gone to college." It had never occurred to him that they might aspire to something more in life than being maids or manual laborers.

After his brush with racial violence on the streets of Americus, Joseph left for college in the fall of 1965 and became preoccupied with his studies. He rarely thought about the issues that had turned his hometown into a battleground and only later recognized that the night he had joined the rock throwers was a moment of epiphany. While Auburn had integrated a few months before Americus High, Joseph never noticed a black student in his classes. One of the few times he saw one on campus was at a football game, and he was lining up with the opponents.

The Auburn Tigers were still an all-white football team in those years, as almost every major-college squad in the Deep South was. During the kickoff game of the 1968 season, Joseph watched as Southern Methodist University, energized by its first black player, wide receiver Jerry LeVias, upset the home team. Joseph had never competed against black players when he was in Americus, but he was curious about them and used to park his '65 Chevelle near the practice field at the black high school to scout them secretly. Now that he was sitting in the stands at Auburn watching LeVias blow past defenders, he was amused by the way some of the fans changed their tune in a matter of minutes. "At the start of the game, people were saying, 'Kill that . . . *black guy!*' By the end, it was: 'We got to get us one of those.'"

While he was at Auburn, Joseph married the girlfriend he had been seeing in high school, and before long they had a son and daughter. Mindful of supporting his young family, he signed up for a state fellowship that allowed him to stay in school and pursue a master's degree in teaching in exchange for working as an instructor in an Alabama junior college. He was assigned to Enterprise State Community College in the southeastern corner of Alabama and began teaching business and economics. Given the demographics of the area, many of his students were minorities taking advantage of educational opportunities that would have been closed to them a decade before.

"They really wanted to learn," Joseph said. "They'd come and ask me questions before and after class, and we'd talk. And I began to see through some of the darkness that had been around me at home, where there were so many people who made ugly jokes about blacks. I thought less and less about color with every term I taught."

When Joseph returned to Georgia to visit his family, his stepfather would ask how many blacks he had in his classes, peeved that there would be any. "I couldn't tell you," Joseph would answer. "I don't count them."

He found his stepfather's attitude off-putting. They weren't talking about racial politics; they were talking about students—*his* students— and they had as much right to better themselves as any of the white kids at the community college. For the first time, Joseph found himself siding with the changes he had once reflexively opposed. He loved his stepfather and admired many things about him—especially his work ethic and his tenacity in overcoming his disability—but he did not admire his stubbornness on race. Joseph thought he was moving on; his old man was not.

Their exchanges reminded him of the highest-rated TV show in America during those years, Norman Lear's *All in the Family*. His stepfather obviously bore some resemblance to the bigoted Archie Bunker, although he hadn't been around enough ethnic groups to spout Bunkerisms like "spic" and "wop." The surprise for Joseph was that he found himself identifying with Archie's bleeding-heart son-in-law, Michael "Meathead" Stivik. "Here I was starting a career and dealing with blacks like I never had in Americus, and my dad was saying things that made me realize that bigotry was stupid and deserved to be made fun of."

Norman Lear couldn't have said it better himself.

JUST BECAUSE DAVID MORGAN FELT BAD FOR GREG DIDN'T MEAN THAT he was pleased with the way their world was changing. He wasn't. He was particularly sore about the integration of his high school. "I sure didn't like seeing Robertiena Freeman walking down the halls of our school, but there she was. That was the law, and we couldn't do anything about it. We had to accept it."

David was keenly aware that he was witnessing the passing of something. He liked to brag that he was a member of what would probably be the last all-white graduating class of Americus High School. At the time, it seemed like something worth bragging about. His perspective would mature.

The Morgans were a solidly middle-class family who lived in a modest frame house in a postwar subdivision near the school. David was the middle of three children—bracketed by sisters—and knew Joseph from an early age. They went to the same kindergarten, the same grade school, the same church, and belonged to the same Scout troop. David's family, on his mother's side, went back as far in Americus as Joseph's. When he rode his bicycle through the historic district, David might pass half a dozen fine old homes where his kin lived or once had dwelled. "By the time I got to town, three or four ladies had called my mother and told her that they had seen me ride by. Everyone looked out for you. Growing up in Americus was just the sweetest time imaginable for me. I realize it wasn't that way for other people sometimes."

His father, Dave Morgan, taught aircraft mechanics in the vocational school at Souther Field, an airstrip north of town where aviation history had been made. Built during the Great War to train pilots, the field was abandoned by 1923 when Charles Lindbergh arrived to acquire a surplus Curtiss biplane. He slept in a hangar for two weeks while the craft was being assembled and then took to the skies over Sumter County in his first solo flights. Mr. Morgan, who was from neighboring Dawson, came during World War II as a flight instructor.

David learned a softer style of prejudice from his parents. They didn't mind colored people—their preferred term—as long as they knew their place and stayed in it. Mr. Morgan would get ticked off when they were watching TV and Ed Sullivan would embrace a black performer like Nat King Cole. Later, at a church youth program, David was similarly annoyed when a visiting speaker prayed that God would remind everyone that Jesus was not a blue-eyed, auburn-tressed Caucasian but a dark-skinned, black-haired Jew. "You could hear a lot of stirring and grumbling in the room," he recalled. "We all talked about it later and thought that was a cheap shot. But it did make me go off and think, and I could see that the man was probably right, even if I didn't like it."

When David was thirteen, his happy-go-lucky childhood changed as his father fell ill and died of a strangulated hernia. He became the man of the house, taking on more responsibilities, working part-time jobs. While his mother was able to support the family through veterans benefits, Social Security, and stock dividends, she never got over the loss of her husband and cried herself to sleep for years. When David shook Greg's hand at their graduation, his generosity of spirit had a lot to do with his emotional state of mind and his memories of who was not there.

After high school, David bounced between Auburn and Georgia Southwestern College, where he earned a degree in math and physics. He enlisted in the navy and entered the aviation officer candidate school, wanting to be a pilot like his father. He finished the program but left the service soon afterward, a decision he later regretted. He was newly married and expected that he could find good-paying employment with a navy commission on his résumé. "I thought people were going to be lined up to hire my sweet ass. Nuh-uh." He had trouble finding a job and ended up applying with the Americus school system, using the teaching certificate he had gotten in college. His first position was rather ironic. He taught at Staley Middle School, formerly all black, where he worked with a black principal and a black assistant principal: Robert L. Freeman, Robertiena's father.

David had driven by the school but had never set foot inside. By the time he started teaching there in the fall of 1970, the student body was split evenly between the races, a situation that he could not have imagined when he was a senior five years before.

"That's where the changes really hit me in the face," he said. "It helped that I had been in the navy. The navy doesn't care about black and white. They don't stand for that crap. I didn't know many black men in the navy, but there were a couple of guys I worked with who were wired up good and did their job. I didn't think anything about it. When I grew up, I tried to put all my learned prejudice behind me."

David taught social studies, industrial arts, and physical education, focusing much of his attention on keeping order, not instruction. Teenagers, he found, do not obey like military personnel. He got to know and like several of the black faculty members, including Robertiena's father ("a straight-up guy") and a peppery young woman who was a civil rights activist and later became a member of the Americus city council. "She was pretty militant," he said. "I'm not sure I would have liked her when I was in high school."

David remained at Staley for two years and then moved on to a school thirty miles away in the town of Cordele. He and his wife were starting a family. Wanting to earn more money, he soon left teaching and began a long career as a loan officer with the Farm Credit System.

Years later, David was reading a book by a best-selling Georgia writer, Ferrol Sams, called *The Whisper of the River*. The autobiographical novel follows a young man who wants to be a doctor as he goes away to college in Macon and finds himself challenged by new ideas. During the student's senior year, Clarence Jordan comes to campus during Christian Focus Week to speak about the experimental farming community he wants to establish outside Americus, Koinonia. Clergymen from miles around come to listen and quiz him about his controversial beliefs. One of them wants to know whether he's a Marxist. Another asks, "Dr. Jordan, how would you like your daughter or sister to marry a nigra?"

As David read the novel, a rush of recognition came over him. He realized that Dr. Jordan was one of the founders of the commune people in Americus had wanted to run out of the county, the farm whose market he had seen in smoking ruins as a boy, the place his classmate Greg had come from.

Greg Wittkamper—David had to smile. He wondered what had happened to him since they last saw each other at commencement. And then his mind moved on to something else.

CELIA HARVEY HAD NEVER THOUGHT OF HERSELF AS PARTICULARLY bigoted. Growing up in Americus, she found racial slurs crude and cringed when she heard them spew from the mouths of others, which happened all the time—sometimes within her home. She was the youngest of three daughters in an upper-middle-class family. Her father, James Harvey, was a conservative man of his time, a bank vice president who joined the John Birch Society and was chairman of the Americus school board when it voted to exclude the three students from Koinonia. He was one of the first witnesses called in the federal lawsuit brought by the Brownes, Jordans, and Wittkampers. "Daddy was a very strong figure in our household," Celia remembered. "If he didn't agree with something in the news, he'd let us know. He did not want integration at all. He wanted blacks to stay on their side of town and in their schools."

Celia Harvey.

Celia believed she took more after her mother, who never used racial vulgarities and who made a point of being considerate with the domestics they hired. When Mrs. Harvey drove their maid home, the maid rode in the front of their car, as if she were a member of the family; her father had her sit in the back. It was one of the little behaviors that suggested how kindly someone felt toward the Negro race. Celia's mother once took her along to attend a birthday party for one of their maids at a black church, giving her a closer look at a part of her hometown that she usually saw only glancingly.

Even so, Celia never seriously questioned segregation or the subservience of one class of people. It was just part of the scenery of her youth. "I felt it was wrong," she said, "but I didn't know what to do about it." When civil rights protests arose in Americus, however, she reacted with a low-grade defensiveness, like many of her well-raised friends—especially when it came to integrating their high school. "We felt like people were trying to push it down our throats. This system was something that had been going on for generations and generations. People weren't going to be changed quickly just because others wanted it to happen."

After graduation and a short stint at Georgia Southwestern College, Celia's life veered away from Americus. Through the boyfriend of a cousin, she met a soldier from New York and married him, which did not go over well with some of her kin. They moved several times in the mid-Atlantic states and then settled outside Charleston, South Carolina, after he left the army in the early seventies. To bring in extra money, Celia started selling Tupperware. The area was thick with military families, many of them black, and some became her customers. She visited their homes, ate their food, used their kitchens and bathrooms. This was different from dropping in on a maid's birthday party in Americus; now *she* was the working woman, meeting her clients in social settings where everyone was equal.

There was one moment that knitted everything together for her. At one of her Tupperware demonstrations, Celia couldn't take her eyes off the young hostess's toddler. "I fell in love with that little girl. She was all over me, kissing me, wanting me to hold her. That baby just melted me."

It occurred to Celia that she had never touched a black person like that before. When she was a girl, she had loved her family's maid, Christine, but that was no different from the warm regard thousands of southern children had for their mammies. Holding a dark-skinned baby girl humanized a people for Celia as never before. "I just hadn't been around black families that much," she reflected. "Almost everything we heard about black people in Americus was negative. If you talked about them at all, it was because something bad had happened. Now I was going into their homes and working, getting friendly with them. It really changed my attitude. It made me realize that there's no difference here."

As farfetched as it sounds, Celia began to see the light at Tupperware parties.

<hr />

If Americus High School had chosen a Miss Congeniality, Celia's best friend, Deanie Dudley, would have been a leading candidate. Not only was she a cheerleader and the homecoming queen, but she styled herself as a sort of goodwill ambassador for the senior class. It was a running joke that you couldn't pass Deanie in the hall without her saying hello. Sometimes she even nodded to the black students. The sole exception to this outpouring of hospitality was Greg. Her aloofness toward him wasn't so much selective meanness as a defense strategy; it grew out of a mind churning with fear and insecurity, the result of a racial drama that had shaken her family when she was sixteen. More than with any of Greg's classmates, Deanie's experience suggested how threatened and confused many white people in Americus and elsewhere felt during the civil rights reformation.

Deanie was the oldest of four children in a family that had been in Americus since its founding in the 1830s. There was an Andersonville guard somewhere in her ancestry, but she didn't pay much attention to such things until years later. Like many white children in that era and setting, she first learned about racial barriers through her family's relationship with "the help." Once, when she was little, she insisted that their maid, Pearl, sit down beside her and eat with everyone else. "It bothered

me that she was going to have to sit by herself. I didn't realize until later
what the deal was. And then I didn't think about it much. It was just part
of our lives."

Later, when the protests started in Americus during her high school
years, Deanie tried to stay away from the controversies. "Our father kept
us sheltered from all that, so we were kind of ignorant about things," she
remembered. "I was more interested in when I
was going to get my hair done for Friday night."

Then the troubles spread to her congregation, and she could ignore them no more.
Deanie's family attended First Presbyterian
Church on Jackson Street, where her father,
Crawford Dudley, served as an elder and Sunday school superintendent. In those days of
flux and unrest, every white church in town
knew that black worshippers would soon ap-
pear at their sanctuary doors to gauge their
commitment to Christian brotherhood. The

Deanie Dudley.

largest congregations—First Baptist and First Methodist, where Joseph, David, and Celia went—were dead set against even token integration. First Presbyterian was smaller and more undecided on the
issue. At first Mr. Dudley was inclined to keep out any civil rights testers. He believed that they would be coming for political reasons, not
spiritual ones, and didn't see any reason to accommodate them and
provoke dissension within the congregation. But he kept thinking and
praying about it.

One day he called his family into the living room—a sure sign that he
had something important to say—and told them that the Lord had spoken to him and said that the church belonged to him, not to the people in
the pews, and that if worshippers of a different race wanted to enter the
sanctuary, no one had the right to bar them. He intended to say as much
at a congregational meeting. He warned that the issue was contentious
and that his statement would probably anger some people. It might get
to the point where he could lose his job. "We're probably going to have to
move from Americus," he said.

Her father's words alarmed Deanie. It wasn't that she disagreed; the whole family was behind him. But having to leave town? She dearly loved Americus—her friends, her church, her school—and the thought of up-rooting the only life she had ever known frightened her terribly.

On the day of the congregational meeting, the church was jammed. Deanie was proud of her father as he stood up and spoke his mind. Mr. Dudley was well read, a lover of poetry and literature, and could be un-commonly eloquent for a man who sold Chevys for a living. As a mem-ber of the church's governing session, he voted for an open-door policy, but the panel split evenly over the question. The minister, C. W. Right-myer, broke the tie in favor of admitting all worshippers, making First Presbyterian one of the earliest churches in Americus not to exclude black people. Soon afterward, a small party of them showed up and were seated without incident.

On the afternoon of the congregational meeting, Deanie answered the front doorbell at their house and found a church member who wanted to speak with her father. She couldn't help but overhear part of their conversation, as the man told her dad that he wished he had had the guts to speak out in public about what he knew was right, as Mr. Dudley had done, but he didn't. He broke down sobbing.

A few days later, another man widely respected in Americus told Deanie's father that he really ought to resign his job because his stand on church integration was costing James Chevrolet customers. The man was right; some people had taken their trade elsewhere because of what had happened. Mr. Dudley felt bad about the lost business and offered to re-sign, but his employer, Woodrow James, wouldn't hear of it. "Crawford," he said, "a man's got to do what he's got to do. As long as you want to work here, you have a job." Mr. Dudley stayed at the dealership until he retired, and his family did not have to leave Americus after all.

The church integration trauma deeply affected Deanie. Thinking back on it years later, she realized that she had drawn the wrong lessons from her father's courage. He had resolved to speak out, regardless of the consequences. Without really articulating it, she had decided to do the opposite. The controversy so agitated her that she decided not to do or say anything that might complicate matters for her family. That included speaking to any classmate from Koinonia. At times she felt a hidden sympathy for Greg, Lora Browne, and Jan Jordan because of the way they were being treated, but she couldn't say so out loud. It was safer to shun them. So that's what Deanie did when she saw Greg in the hallway: she suppressed her gregarious nature and ignored him.

"I was a coward," she said.

———————

AFTER SHE GRADUATED, DEANIE STAYED AT HOME FOR A YEAR TO ATTEND Georgia Southwestern College and then married her high school sweetheart, Bill Fricks, the son of an Americus pharmacist who was several years older and had already finished at Auburn. They moved to Newport News, Virginia, where he went to work for a shipbuilding company. She was nineteen and had never lived away from her family, and she had a hard time adjusting to being alone for so many hours. "I went into shock when I realized that my husband wasn't going to come home in the middle of the day and eat lunch with me. That would have been unheard of in Americus."

It wasn't her biggest shock. Not long after the newlyweds settled in Virginia, Deanie was walking to the laundry at their apartment complex when she came upon a young maintenance man wearing a work uniform. As he passed her on the walkway, he looked at her and said, "Good morning. How are you?"

Deanie was taken aback. As innocent as the greeting may have seemed, it was a breach of etiquette to her. The young man was black. On the sidewalks back home, at least in her experience, a black man would usually look down or away when he passed a white woman he didn't know personally; he certainly wouldn't lock eyes with her and speak in such a familiar manner. Maybe things were different in the Tidewater of Virginia, with all its bases and naval personnel, but she did not like it one bit.

When she considered it later, Deanie had to admit that she had expected deference from the young man simply because he was black and she was white. "I guess it came out of the sense that I was better than him. That's what I was used to."

There was another dimension to her visceral reaction, one that was rooted in perhaps the deepest American phobia about race. Many of the rules of segregation had to do with prohibiting interracial contact between the sexes. Flouting those rules could be dangerous. People had been beaten and lynched for such offenses, real or imagined. That's what the Emmett Till case was all about; the black teenager from Chicago was showing off to friends and got a little fresh with a white woman in Mississippi, and it cost him his life. Deanie certainly wasn't thinking about such horrors when the maintenance man greeted her, but she did feel an involuntary and irrational fear, and it disturbed her.

When her husband returned from work that evening, Deanie told him about the incident, expecting that he would commiserate with her.

"Bill, he looked right in my face and said good morning."

"Deanie, he was just being friendly. Get over it."

"Don't you understand?" she said. "He can't do that to me."

Her husband understood. He was from Americus, too, and knew the racial customs as well as anyone. But he had formed a relationship during his youth that had broadened his outlook. He took golf lessons from an employee at the Americus Country Club who happened to be black. The employee was a fledgling golf pro who was allowed to play the course only during the early morning hours and was expected to show proper respect to the white members and their sons by not calling them by their first names. He and Bill became good friends during their sunrise sessions. Some people around town told his father that they were becoming too close.

"I think you need to deal with this," he told his wife.

Deanie took his words to heart and began to examine the attitudes she had been raised with: the assumption of superiority, the habit of fear. The next time she saw the maintenance man, she spoke to him first. It was a start.

PART 5

Reunion

CHAPTER 13

Almost Heaven

IN THE FALL OF 1969, GREG AND HIS BROTHER DAVID MADE IT AS FAR AS Panama before the road ran out and they decided to end their ramble through Central America. They shipped their motorcycle home, flew to Miami, and hitchhiked to Koinonia, arriving a few days before Christmas. It was less than two months since Clarence Jordan had died, and they could see the freshly turned soil on his unmarked grave on Picnic Hill. The brothers had been looking forward to letting Clarence try out the cycle they had ridden on their trip, a powerful, new four-cylinder model from Honda. He may have been a minister and a man of letters, but Clarence enjoyed motorcycles and engines and loved getting his hands dirty. "When we got there," Greg remembered, "the mood was different. Everyone was still in shock that he was gone."

While they were home, Greg and David had to attend to a potentially troublesome piece of unfinished business: the draft. Both of them had been granted conscientious objector status, but they had yet to perform their alternative service. They didn't know what to expect as they walked into the federal building in Americus and reported for assignment—after all, this was the draft board that had threatened Greg with arrest while he was in Africa. He proposed that they fulfill their obligation by working at Friends World College, and a day later, much to his relief, the authorities approved the request.

After the first of the year, the two of them rumbled into New York on their Honda, their faces frosted in the middle of a snowstorm, and settled back in at the college on Long Island. Greg wasn't technically a student anymore. He never received a degree because he didn't want to write his final thesis about what he had learned during his round-the-world exploration of faith: namely, that there are as many religions as there are people. Now he was an employee. He and David spent the next two years doing general maintenance and helping the college relocate from the old air force barracks it had occupied to a new home on a North Shore estate—Great Gatsby country. They lived there for months with other workers, camping out in a colonial mansion as they retrofitted it for students.

Greg fell for one of those students, a tall, vivacious young woman who came from a prosperous family in New York. Judy was curious about communal living and was fascinated to hear about Greg's upbringing at Koinonia and his ordeal in school. He hadn't told many people about his tribulations at Americus High—just talking about it usually made him well up with tears—but it helped him to relate the story to Judy. It was a way of organizing the bad memories, of finding meaning in the pain. Greg had always exhibited a reticent personality, and his adolescent experience as a social pariah only reinforced his nature. His new girlfriend helped him make sense of his emotions. "She warmed me up," he said. They were soon living together, beginning a relationship that would last five years.

When he finished his alternative service at the end of 1971, Greg joined Judy in Europe as she toured communes for her Friends World studies. It was the heyday of intentional communities, a flowering of spiritual enclaves and agricultural collectives that liberally mingled strains of religion, mysticism, environmentalism, and occasionally pharmacology. Although he didn't want to return to Koinonia as a resident, Greg was partial to communal life and wondered whether some other version of it might suit him.

The couple's first stop was the Community of the Ark, an isolated farming commune in the mountains of southern France that mixed Christianity, Hinduism, and an Amish aversion to modernity. They met

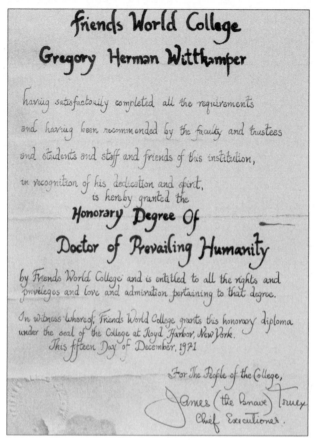

An honorary "doctor of prevailing humanity" from Friends World. *Courtesy of Greg Wittkamper*

the founder, an Italian priest who had traveled to India to become a disciple of Gandhi, and worked beside the "companions," as the inhabitants called themselves. They were all pacifists who believed in simple living and the sanctity of hard physical labor. They spun their own cloth, grew their own food, and used almost no electricity or mechanical devices. It was like a monastery; Greg thought his father would love it.

After two months at the Ark, he and Judy moved on to a spiritualist community in the north of Scotland called Findhorn. It was a nexus of New Age thought, the kind of place where they heard people discussing fairies, nature spirits, and the power of crystals. Greg listened with an open mind, but he was dubious about the way the community's leaders claimed to relay orders from God. One of them had heard of Koinonia and asked him to tell everyone what it was like.

"Well, we were founded on the principles of nonviolence and racial equality, and we own everything in common," Greg said, "but we don't really have anyone who communicates directly with God." He suspected that last part offended the man. He and Judy departed after a few days.

They drove across Europe to Turkey and then sailed to Cyprus and Israel, where they took up residence at a kibbutz in the Jordan River Valley. Sha'ar HaGolan was a traditional agricultural collective enjoying a respite between wars with the Arabs. It was harvest season, and Greg woke at four every morning to cut and haul bananas, strenuous work that was harder than anything he had done at Koinonia. He loved it. Sweating in the Middle Eastern heat, alone with his thoughts, he found the exertion cleansing, like a good session of meditation. When the picking was done, there was time for fun and dancing with the other young people. Greg and Judy lived there for five months. As their sojourn drew to a close, he again found himself the outsider, in a good-natured way. "Everyone wanted Judy to stay because she was Jewish. Nobody asked me to stay. It was like: 'What are you doing with that goy anyway?'"

AFTER A YEAR ABROAD, GREG AND JUDY RETURNED TO THE UNITED States in early 1973 and found an unlikely new setting to pursue their longing for communal living: West Virginia.

It was his brother's doing. The head of Friends World had asked David whether he would like to fix up a rustic home he owned in Monroe County, tucked in the low, green mountains at the bottom of the state along the Virginia border. David was married now, with a child on the way, and he leapt at the chance to put down roots in an unspoiled place that seemed cut off from the cares of the materialistic, war-mongering outside world. Greg and Judy moved in with them, and they were joined for

David and Greg Wittkamper getting ready to hit the road by motorcycle. *Courtesy of Greg Wittkamper*

a time by his younger brother Dan and one of their childhood friends from Koinonia, Charles Browne.

They tried to create a community, pooling their resources, growing their food, living the life organic. It didn't take. Some of their spouses weren't keen on sharing and bickered about money and trivial matters like one of them using too much toothpaste for another one's liking. Judy wanted out, so she and Greg moved to a house down the road while he split the communal property with David, a process that consisted of "You take this screwdriver, I'll take that hammer."

The brothers continued to work together, supporting themselves by putting up hay, digging septic tanks, roofing houses, and doing other manual labor for chicken-feed wages. Greg used much of his earnings to buy a milk cow, and he and Judy made artisanal cheese and butter to sell—that is, until the cow got into some bad fodder, bloated, and died. "That was a $500 cow," he said. "After that, we had nothing left. That's when I thought it might be time to stop this hide-in-the-wilderness thing and rejoin the world."

Judy's father agreed. He was a lawyer and developer in Manhattan and had been warning his daughter that she and his man had better make some money or they would be paupers for the rest of their lives. Greg told him that land was cheap in West Virginia and that people were starting to buy sites for retirement homes in their part of the state, which had never been ravaged by coal mining. The New Yorker proposed they go into business together. He would find investors and arrange financing if Greg and Charles Browne, who was in on the deal, would scout tracts of land to purchase, subdivide, and market. They'd draw a salary to manage the operation and wouldn't have to put up any funds, which was just as well because Greg didn't have any.

They started with four hundred acres and expanded from there. Soon Greg was roaring around the country roads on his motorcycle, meeting prospective customers and showing them to their slice of mountain heaven. The boy from the commune was becoming a capitalist. He was also becoming single again. Greg and Judy broke up not long after he went into the land trade, but he continued the business arrangement with her father. "She always joked that her dad stole me from her," he said.

Greg met another woman who worked in their real estate office and married her a couple of years later. He and Sharon settled into a late-1800s farmhouse he was able to afford with his new earnings. Soon they had a daughter, Stephanie, followed a few years later by a son, Stephen.

As he was starting a family, Greg faced two crises that threatened everything he was building in West Virginia. First, the land business caved in during the hyperinflation of the early '80s, bringing down the company Judy's father had formed. Then Greg almost got prosecuted for growing marijuana. In the suspicious eyes of the law, the two misfortunes were linked.

While the real estate venture was teetering, Greg briefly cultivated pot, as many countercultural types were doing in the secluded hill country. He was a small operator compared to his neighbor, Charles Browne, who was eventually busted and served time in a federal prison. Charles didn't miss a beat after his release; he converted his cannabis fields into vineyards and started making wine. "I went into a different branch of the mood-altering business," he explained.

Greg narrowly escaped becoming a criminal defendant. The Drug Enforcement Agency was cracking down on pot growers in the back-country, and he expected to see government helicopters hovering over his property at any time. He prepared for them by digging post holes throughout his marijuana patch, cutting down some small trees, and sticking them in the ground like beach umbrellas to keep the illegal crop out of sight. It worked for a while, but then the grand jury investigating Charles began asking questions about Greg. "They thought the land business was a front for pot," he said. "I think they just wanted me to testify against Charlie." Greg stopped growing the stuff, and the inquiries ceased after someone else turned on his friend and he was convicted.

The real estate collapse took much longer to resolve. When the business went into bankruptcy in 1984, a lawyer counseled Greg to offer his services as a property manager to the trustee who was handling the liquidation. It was solid advice; the trustee took him up on the offer and put him on salary. As interest rates declined and the market recovered, Greg began dealing land again and by 1992 was able to purchase almost three thousand acres from the liquidation at a bargain price. "I thought I was going to lose my house when all this came down," he said, "but I ended up with a golden egg."

David said it was long overdue divine intervention.

GREG VISITED KOINONIA REGULARLY OVER THE YEARS, USUALLY TO PICK up or drop off his parents, who were spending more time with him in West Virginia. He would linger at the farm for a week or so and then drive back to the high country, relieved to be leaving the bugs and humidity behind. Despite the sticky climate, he enjoyed his stays. "They always treated me special." He was touched when the community rechristened the modest frame home his family had once occupied as the Wittkamper House.

In the years after Clarence Jordan died, Koinonia flourished as never before under the leadership of Millard Fuller and others after he and his wife, Linda, left to devote their energies to promoting Habitat for

Humanity. The commune reached its peak population of about one hundred during the 1970s and then tailed off as the counterculture era faded and the enthusiasm for collective living subsided. Greg's parents never lost their enthusiasm. They stayed on the farm for the rest of their lives, becoming beloved reminders of Koinonia's early years.

Will Wittkamper grew even more eccentric in his old age. In the spirit of the times, he let his hair grow long and frizzy and featured a scraggly white beard that would have made him look like an Old Testament prophet if it weren't for the ball cap and baggy secondhand clothes he wore. He didn't care whether anything matched; Greg once saw him with a size-11, blue high-top sneaker on one foot and a size-10, red low-top on the other. His zeal for recycling, organic farming, and natural living knew no bounds. Sometimes, in the predawn darkness, he greeted the day by trotting around the house naked, taking what he called an "air bath." During one visit, Greg and David took their parents out to eat in Albany and watched as Will, ever the faithful steward of God's resources, plucked the lemons off everyone's seafood plates and collected them in his cap to take home and add to his health-shake blender. "People were staring at us," Greg said. "We all had long hair and must have looked like the family Jesus."

Greg's father never shed his distaste for money or material goods. When his sons sent him a flannel shirt for Christmas or some cash to buy something nice for Margaret, he would invariably give it all away to a poor family. Greg inherited some of his father's uneasiness about the almighty dollar. As the value of his acreage began to climb, he couldn't help but feel pangs of guilt. His mother, who had never been quite as committed to the ascetic life as her husband, tried to reassure Greg that a reasonable degree of success was not a character flaw. "You shouldn't worry that you're a little bit of a tycoon," she told him.

In the summer of 1980, not long after Greg and Sharon had their first child, his father died of a heart attack during a visit to West Virginia. He was eighty-seven and perfectly at peace with death, which he saw as merely the closing of a chapter. During his dad's last full day among the living, Greg had taken him along to pick up some lumber he had gotten milled from trees on the property. Will admired the pine boards, so they used them to build his coffin. They buried him on a gentle slope within view of Greg's living-room window. When they tried to excavate his grave with a backhoe, they struck rock and had to dig in a perpendicular line, meaning that the Reverend Will Wittkamper was laid to rest, appropriately, in a cross-shaped incision in the earth. Sixteen years later, in 1996, Margaret Wittkamper died of cancer while she was staying with Greg and was interred next to her husband—actually, he's at her feet.

By the time Greg's mother died, five Koinonians were living within a few miles of his home in Monroe County, including his brother David and three of the Brownes: Charles, his sister Carol, and their brother, John. They made an odd little expatriate community. Some of them had money; others had little. Some of them struggled with substance abuse; others were clean. Even though they were the children of ministers, most of them no longer believed in God, and only one even gave lip service to being a conventional Christian. What joined them at the heart was their unique background, their shared history of joy and terror. All of them— the ones in West Virginia and elsewhere—carried happy memories of growing up on the farm and of belonging to a large, loving extended family. But those memories were counterbalanced by other scenes none of them could forget. They had been shot at, spit on, called names—all at a tender age. It left a psychic scar.

"I wrote Daddy about how I was feeling after I had gone off to college," recalled Jan Jordan, who went to a Mennonite school in Indiana after graduating from Americus High in 1964. "I was very restless. I couldn't focus on anything. I'd get angry about something instantly. He said, 'Jan, you're just like a soldier home from war.' And I was. We were all suffering different degrees of posttraumatic stress syndrome."

A few of the children who had grown up at Koinonia during the violence saw therapists. Charles consulted one after he went into a rage and destroyed a couple of chairs, and his wife told him that he'd better deal with his temper. "I found out that I have this Christian self-righteousness where I believe I'm a warrior of God and I'm just waiting to punish someone," he said. "You know: I made it through Koinonia, bullets flying, and God's chosen me to beat the crap out of someone who deserves it. I'd get blood in my eyes. I think it all goes back to being that little kid who felt like all the other schoolkids had done him wrong. I've done a lot of transference."

Bill Wittkamper saw a therapist as well. He had always blamed the adults at Koinonia for letting their children be cannon fodder in a battle they had not volunteered for, and it took years to untangle the knots of resentment. Greg could see the value in that kind of counseling, but he never pursued it. Therapy wasn't his style. When he thought about high school and the terror attacks on the farm, he didn't feel anger or resentment as much as sadness.

———————

WHEN HIS PAST CAME CALLING IN THE SPRING OF 2006, GREG WAS A contented man. He had done so well buying and selling mountain property that he didn't have to work full-time anymore and considered himself, at fifty-eight, semiretired. He had another reason to relax and smell the wildflowers; he had a new spouse, Anne Gardner, and they had a four-year-old daughter, Sallie.

Greg and Sharon had grown unhappy together after nineteen years of marriage and divorced in 1999. He met Anne at a cookout soon afterward. She was an occupational therapist from Roanoke, Virginia, and was as intense and talkative as he was easygoing and reserved. She wasn't sure they would click at first. "He looked like a typical West Virginia guy—most likely very conservative," she said. But she was curious and accepted an invitation to have dinner at his house—although she wondered what she was getting into when it took her forever to find the place and she hit a deer on the way.

Greg's children, Stephanie and Stephen, were at the dinner and kept prodding him to tell Anne about his upbringing at Koinonia and his miseries in high school. "They were really drawing it out of him," she said. "It was like: 'Tell her about the day at the baseball field. Tell her about this, tell her about that. . . .'" Anne phoned her sister afterward and described this intriguing man she had met, and her sister reminded her that their aunt and uncle used to buy candy from Koinonia and had sent books to help one of their young men go to some Quaker college. The young man was Greg.

Anne and Greg married in 2001 and led a pleasant, bucolic life in the farmhouse he had bought in the Greenbrier River Valley. It was half an hour but light years away from the exclusive Greenbrier resort, on a hill overlooking a pond where they sometimes went skinny-dipping. She learned much more about his days at Koinonia and about his trials in high school, and she came to understand that her husband, as well adjusted as he seemed, was still carrying a burden. She heard his voice crack. She saw him tear up. She knew there was unresolved pain.

Then, on that cool spring morning in May 2006, it all came back when Greg drove to the post office and found an invitation to his high school reunion and the first letter of apology from his long-ago classmate David Morgan. It was like breaking a seal on his emotions. The past was present.

While the letter was unexpected, the name on the return address was not. David was the only one of his classmates Greg had ever considered contacting in the four decades since they had graduated. He'd come close to doing it once before, when he returned from overseas in 1969. During his brief stopover that summer, he and his mother went to lunch at the house of his senior English teacher, Gladys Crabb. The two ladies had become friendly at the Episcopal church in Americus, where Mrs. Wittkamper occasionally visited. After everyone chatted about his travels and his unorthodox college education, the conversation inevitably turned to high school. Greg mentioned that David had approached him before the commencement ceremony and shaken his hand.

The teacher smiled. "You really ought to get in touch with him. I'm sure he'd love to hear from you."

Greg said he might just do that. And then he left for New York and Central America and alternative service and more travels, and he forgot about it. Now, thirty-seven years later, David was taking the initiative, reaching out the same way he had stuck out his hand in the Americus High gymnasium.

David's letter—and the ones that soon followed from other members of the Class of 1965—prompted much discussion among Greg's friends and loved ones. Anne had no doubt that the writers were sincere. But some of the Koinonia expats in West Virginia and elsewhere weren't as certain about what it all meant.

Bill, who had been living outside Chicago for years, told his brother that he didn't know whether he could forgive and forget, however well intentioned the words seemed to be. "You could open up a lot of stuff by going back down there."

Charles Browne wept when he read the letters. "It made me think about how much I still hate those guys who tormented us in school and how much of that anger I still carry with me. Those poor bastards might have changed and they might have repented, and here I still want to kill them. They might be Justice Department lawyers prosecuting Klansmen for all I know. Isn't that the way it works? When we change, we put on a little act to convince ourselves, and eventually we start believing it. The ones who harassed me, some of them are probably still racist assholes. But I imagine some of them *have* changed."

The most skeptical of the Koinonia kids was the one who always seemed the most damaged: Carol Browne. Carol was only eight when she was visiting the Jordans one night and Jan slammed her to the floor after a rifle shot intended for her father pierced the house. She spent two years at Americus High, jawing back whenever she was provoked, and then moved away with her family. She never got over the sense of injury. Years later, she remained skittish, suspicious, ornery.

Carol couldn't imagine anyone going back to Americus, not after what had happened to her the one time she went back in 1983. She stayed a single night at Koinonia but couldn't sleep because she kept thinking about bombings and gunshots and some thug roughing up her father. "I'm sorry," she told Margaret Wittkamper the next morning. "I can't handle this. I've got to leave."

On her way out of town, Carol stopped for gas in Americus, her nerves still frayed, and got into a tiff with a convenience store clerk who muttered something rude about the way her son looked. Carol had lived with a black musician and had a mixed-race child. "I gave this clerk a piece of my mind, and I thought: 'Yeah, nothing has changed around here.'" She swore she would never return to Americus. When Koinonia held a fiftieth anniversary celebration in 1992, one of the planners tried to allay her fears, telling her that Sheriff Chappell was dead and they'd buried him extra deep. The dark humor did not sway her. Carol refused to go, and she didn't think Greg should go now.

After he showed her the first letters, she conceded that his classmates might have learned to tolerate some things because society had changed and they couldn't afford to look like bigots, but underneath it all, they were the same people. "Leopards don't change their spots," she said. "If you go back down there, you'd better take every gun you've got."

Greg thought Carol was being unnecessarily dramatic, as she was wont to do, but he understood why she and some of the others harbored misgivings. He had questions himself. He picked up the phone and started calling his former classmates. He wanted to know why, after all these years, they were finally being kind to him.

CHAPTER 14

Guilt and Grace

THE CLASS OF 1965 HAD HELD AT LEAST THREE OTHER REUNIONS, BUT no one bothered to tell Greg about them. The graduates who had loathed him would not have wanted to see him, and the others, if they thought of him at all, might have found his presence an awkward reminder of an embarrassing part of their high school years. Since Greg was living in another state and had no friends in the class, he was easily ignored when reunion rolls were drawn up and invitations mailed. If anyone had contacted him, he would have attended—he had thought about it—but he wasn't going to go without being asked.

The fortieth reunion promised to be different if only because of the person who was coordinating it: David Morgan. David volunteered for the job because he had time on his hands. He had retired from his position as a loan officer with the Farm Credit System and was taking a break while he considered what to do next. The reunion was scheduled for June 2006—a year past the actual anniversary, but better late than never. David began by e-mailing fellow graduates and scouring the Internet to assemble a roster of class members. Ninety-eight of the 107 he listed were still living, two-thirds of them in Georgia and most of the rest in neighboring states. Greg was unaccounted for. David had no idea where he was living, or *whether* he was living, but he aimed to find out. "You don't forget someone who was as center stage as Greg was," he said.

David lived in Perry, fifty miles northeast of Americus, but he still had family in his hometown and kept in touch with friends there. One of them was his English teacher, Mrs. Crabb. Years before, she had mailed him a page from the Koinonia newsletter in which Greg had written a short reminiscence about his graduation day and the student who congratulated him in front of everyone. "I thought you'd like to know that you had an impact on Greg's life," she wrote. David had no idea that his handshake and words of encouragement had meant so much. Looking back, he was proud of what he had done. He wasn't as proud of some other things.

As he thought about the reunion, David pulled out his high school yearbooks and lingered over the portraits of his classmates. There was a surprise in his freshman annual: he had scratched out Greg's picture with a ballpoint pen. When the yearbooks arrived for the 1961–1962 term, some of his friends started scribbling on the picture for laughs, and David went along to show that he was one of them. "I guess I thought it messed up my whole annual to have him in there," he reflected. "It was stupid. I was ashamed of doing it just a few years later."

David had long regretted the way Greg was maligned in high school. "It kind of gnawed at me." In his conversations about the reunion with other class members, he floated the idea of reaching out to Greg in some way and making sure he was included this time. A couple of people advised against it, speculating that the gesture might not be well received, but everyone else thought it was justified and long overdue. When he phoned Deanie Dudley Fricks, she brought up the subject without prompting. "Have you ever been sorry for what we did to Greg?" she asked.

DEANIE AND HER HUSBAND HAD DONE WELL FOR THEMSELVES IN VIR-ginia. Bill worked his way up to CEO of the company that recruited him out of college, Newport News Shipbuilding, which makes aircraft carriers and submarines for the US Navy. His wife, who was so lonely and dislocated after she moved from Americus as a newlywed, regained her equilibrium largely through religion. As her Christian faith deepened, she questioned the way so many people from her background had been raised to believe that white people were better than black people. It took years, but she eventually came to accept that everyone was equal in God's eyes. "I wish I could say that I decided one day that I was done with prejudice, but it doesn't go away that easily. It evolved. It wasn't fast. I had to wrestle with it. And you're never done wrestling with it." She was gratified that their three children were remarkably more tolerant than she and her friends had been at their age. When their son went to the College of William & Mary, he had a black roommate for all four years, something his mom never would have imagined when she left Georgia.

By the year of the reunion, Deanie's husband had retired, and they were splitting their time between homes in Naples, Florida, and Albany, Georgia, a few miles down the road from Americus, where her elderly parents still resided. Over the years, Deanie had thought of high school occasionally and grieved about the way the students from Koinonia had been ostracized—not only Greg, but Lora Browne and Jan Jordan as well. She was sorry for any hurt she had caused them and their families and wondered whether their parents were still around. "Greg had been in my heart for some time," she said. "It had gotten more intense. My conscience was really bothering me, and I wanted to make things right."

She and David agreed to approach a handful of other class members to ask whether they would be willing to write letters of apology. Deanie called her friend Celia, who was working for an insurance company outside Charleston, South Carolina, while David called Joseph, who was still teaching at the community college in Enterprise, Alabama.

David spoke to a few other classmates who said they would participate, and then he sent a general e-mail to most of the names on his reunion roster, telling them that an effort to reconcile with Greg was in the works. He did not copy the e-mail to a small number of graduates whom he suspected would not approve. "We knew a few of our class-mates wouldn't like it," he said, "but I didn't care what they thought. We were all grown-ups now. I told everyone I was going to do what I thought was right."

David and the core group debated whether to compose a single letter with multiple signatures on the bottom, but decided not to because that might smack of a committee undertaking. They wanted this to be more personal. They elected to write separate letters and mail them at the same time for greater effect.

But first they had to find Greg. David assumed Mrs. Crabb would know where he was, or how to locate him, so he phoned her and filled her in on their plans. She was in her eighties and had long since retired from the classroom, but she remained every inch the teacher and was over-joyed to hear that her former pupils were finally tackling this last piece of difficult homework. She contacted Koinonia and got Greg's address in West Virginia.

That was the easy part. Now they had to write the letters.

———

TEENAGERS MAKE FUN OF PEOPLE AND SOMETIMES, INTENTIONALLY OR not, cross the line between kidding and cruelty. Learning the difference between needling and genuinely hurting someone is a passage of ado-lescence, like dealing with acne or anxiety. Few people who went too far ever get the chance as adults to say they are sorry. Were they to have the opportunity, what, exactly, would they say without it sounding strange or self-pitying? Just because someone wants to make amends doesn't mean that it will turn out well.

David was mindful of the pitfalls; that's why he labored over his letter for two days. "It was very tough. I wanted to get it right. Words are im-portant. I didn't want to be misunderstood." He drafted the message on his computer, editing and refining, and then wrote it out in flowing blue cursive so it would seem more intimate. It ran five hundred words, two and a half pages:

> May 01, 2006
>
> Dear Greg,
>
> I expect you will be quite surprised to hear from me. If you remember me at all, it will likely be for unpleasant reasons. I was a classmate of youre at Americus High School, and graduated with you in 1965.
>
> I don't recall ever directly assaulting you, but I probably did, to gain acceptance and accolades of my peers. In any case, I surely participated as part of an enabling audience, and tacitly supported and encouraged those who did. For that I am deeply sorry and regretful.

The first letter came from David.

Dear Greg,

I expect you will be quite surprised to hear from me. If you remember me at all, it will likely be for unpleasant reasons. I was a classmate of yours at Americus High School, and graduated with you in 1965.

I don't recall ever directly assaulting you, but I probably did, to gain acceptance and accolades of my peers. In any case, I surely participated as part of an enabling audience, and tacitly supported and encouraged those who did. For that I am deeply sorry and regretful.

Throughout the last 40-plus years, I have occasionally thought of you and those dark days that you endured at our hands. As I matured, I became more and more ashamed, and wished that I had taken a different stand back then. I knew, even then, that it was all wrong, yet I did nothing to stop it, or even to discourage it. I secretly admired your ability to take such abuse without retaliating.

I knew that you were physically stronger than most of those who taunted you. Indeed, you had an impressive physique. Sometimes I wished you would "clean the clock" of your tormentors. I realize, of course, that it took greater courage to hold back. In any case, had you fought back, you would have been besieged by a "mob" of bystanders, who were encouraging your tormentors. It hurts me to say that I was sometimes part of that "mob" of bystanders. Did you ever notice that you were seldom confronted unless there was a gaggle of supporters giving courage to your attackers?

As an adult, I have read more about the origins, philosophy, and mission of Koinonia Farm. I now see that it was a noble experiment, based on sound Christian principles. Mr. Jordan was years ahead of his time, but the rural south just wasn't ready for blacks and whites to co-exist as equals, much less live, work and commune closely together. Anything so contrary to old southern culture was quickly and easily labeled as "subversive" and "communist" in those crazy days.

All I can do now is say that I am sorry, acknowledge the good principles behind Koinonia's existence, and commend you for your courage. I hope that the hatred and hardship you endured at our hands has made you stronger and more resolute in your character and faith. You were right! I hope God has smiled on you for holding fast and suffering in His Name. God bless you for your pacifist courage, and God forgive me for participating in your torment.

Your old friend, Mrs. Gladys Crabb, has remained dear to many of us. Then, as now, she was a quiet conscience, gently reminding us (without scolding) that we were wrong. She still serves as a bridge for healing the chasm between us. God bless her for many good things she taught us: by her example, as well as her valuable academic instruction.

God bless you, too, Greg, and I wish a good life for you.
David Morgan

> May 1, 2006
>
> Dear Greg,
>   I write to you from Naples, Florida
> where my husband Bill and I live — as
> I read the book of I Peter, I see you
> there throughout the chapters, the Christian
> who has suffered unjustly, and I am
> grieved.
>   As a fellow Christian I caused you
> pain and suffering — How could that have
> happened? I can only answer, "guilty."
> It did happen, and I am ashamed and
> deeply sorry that it did.

The second letter came from Deanie.

Deanie's letter—also handwritten—was longer than David's by one hundred and fifty words. She sprinkled it with biblical allusions, saying that Greg's plight in high school reminded her of the first book of Peter, in the New Testament, an epistle to early Christian churches that were being persecuted. But there was another book, by a man of another faith, that informed her thinking just as deeply when she sat down to write Greg.

His name was Samuel Althaus, and he ran a delicatessen and catering business in Newport News that handled the receptions after a launching at her husband's shipyard. They got to know him and his wife through work. "I was very fond of Sam," she said. "He was so gentle."

Althaus was a Holocaust survivor, although he didn't talk about it much. Deanie didn't learn the disturbing details of his young life until she was leaving a diner in Virginia and noticed her friend's name on a slender book for sale at the counter. It was his memoir: *Where Is God? Auschwitz-Birkenau to Dachau, 1942–1945*. She bought a copy and read about how his family, who were poultry suppliers in Poland, lost

everything after the Nazis invaded in 1939: their livelihood, their syna-
gogue, their friends, their freedom. The family was eventually deported to
concentration camps; by the time the war ended, both of Althaus's parents,
three brothers, and two sisters had been gassed or otherwise murdered.

"As I was reading it, I was stunned," Deanie recalled. "It was just too
much like what happened in Georgia. I'm not saying that what happened
in Americus ever came close to the Holocaust. But we were on the same
road and didn't know it. I'm talking about the dehumanizing of certain
segments of mankind. I'm thinking about the names African Americans
used to be called, the way people treated them like they were less than
human, like we were so superior to them. That's the thing that tied it
together for me. When I read Sam's book, I saw that connection. It upset
me terribly."

That sense of distress overflowed in Deanie's letter:

> Greg, you have shared the sufferings of Christ as few have.
> "He was despised and rejected of men." I did not despise you. You
> were a young man girded with courage. I have not personally
> witnessed that kind of courage before or since. I don't know how
> you endured, but what an example of godliness with humility you
> have been to me.
>
> I have only recently discovered what Koinonia was truly about.
> It broke my heart that I never took the time before to discover the
> truth, but allowed prejudice and fear, and the things that I was
> told by people I thought knew the truth, to affect my thoughts and
> actions.
>
> I will never again say, "How could the Holocaust have
> happened—how could all those Christian people in Poland and
> Germany have stood by and allowed it to happen?" I'll never need
> to ask that again. . . .
>
> I can't say now, "Well, that didn't happen in my time," or, "I
> wasn't a part of something terrible," or, "I never lynched anybody,"
> or, "I wasn't in Germany." No, but I was present with you over a
> long period of time, and I never once did one thing to comfort you
> or reach out to you. It was cruelty.

Celia had a hard time beginning her note, but when she finished it, she felt a sense of relief, as if she had finally said things that she wished she had said decades before. She mentioned her second husband, Ron Gonzalez, a man of Spanish extraction who had grown up in New York and counted blacks among his closest friends. When she told him about Greg and Koinonia and those rocky days at Americus High, he wondered whether, with his ethnicity, he would have faced the same abuse. More than likely, Celia had to admit. She asked Greg to come back:

> I do hope that you will consider coming to the class reunion in June. My husband, Ron, and I would love to see you. Ron is a little younger than us and he is having a hard time understanding why we let this happen to you—as do I. After trying to explain it to him, I realized that there is no excuse. God has helped me deal with this, and I am grateful for the opportunity to write you.

Joseph's letter was different; it was essentially reportage. He wrote a two-page sketch about the confrontation behind the baseball stands after school, when a crowd of boys cheered as his football teammate Thomas slugged Greg in the face—and then fell silent as he refused to strike back. In Sunday school as a boy, Joseph had heard about Jesus teaching his followers to turn the other cheek if someone attacked them, and he thought it sounded like a dumb thing to do. But as an adult teaching his own Sunday school class, he understood the wisdom behind nonviolence and told the story of Greg and T.J. as a real-life illustration. In his sketch, he narrated the scene vividly, down to the way Greg staggered after Thomas hit him and then stuck out his chin awaiting another swing:

> The inevitable did not happen. A coach came and the crowd dispersed. Greg whipped all fifty of us that afternoon without throwing a punch! I did not realize it until years later, though.
> I saw a sermon that afternoon. Because I did, I understand the Scriptures better today—one verse in particular.
> As a boy, I, that day, went home feeling embittered about life and a missed opportunity to get even with someone I violently

disagreed with. As a man, I admire a young man whose actions matched his words. I want to thank him for what he taught me.

"Who would have ever thought I would offer you as a role model?" Joseph marveled in his cover note.

———————

THOMAS'S BLOW WAS NOTHING COMPARED TO THE ONE-TWO PUNCH that came in the mail during the first week of May 2006. When Greg opened his P.O. box on the first morning, he found the reunion invitation and the letter from David and read them outside the post office in Sinks Grove. Those got his attention, straightened him up. On the next day, Joseph, Celia, and Deanie's letters arrived in a flurry and practically knocked him out. He read them on the way home, pulling over to the side of the road, and was so overcome with emotion that it took him fifteen minutes to compose himself and continue.

On the night he received David's message, Greg looked him up in the directory and called him at home. Hearing his voice after so many years sent chills down David's spine. He asked how Greg was doing, a nice way of trying to find out whether he hated everyone in the class; Greg picked up on the unspoken question and assured him that he had put his bitterness away years ago. After that, the conversation grew more relaxed, and they were soon laughing about the terrible names Greg had been called in high school. "Maybe we'll write one of those on your name sticker at the reunion," David joked.

In the coming days, Greg phoned the other letter writers and thanked them for their thoughtful messages. He spoke with Joseph for more than two hours in a sort of therapy session for both of them. By the end of May, four more classmates had written him: Mary Ellen Smith Daniels and Shelby Jean Bradley Bowen from Americus; Linda Mitchell Thomas from Fort Meade, Florida; and Joan Rogers from Savannah. A fifth one, Jeannie Fletcher, called him from Georgia. "It was an answer to a prayer to find your address," Linda Thomas told him. "I've wanted to do this for many years but didn't know how to find you!"

After such an outpouring of remedial concern, he couldn't imagine not attending the reunion. He made plans to travel back to Georgia with his wife and their daughter. His brother David volunteered to come along and drive them in his roomy old Mercedes. He regarded his time at Americus High as the worst year of his life and said he could use some healing himself.

Despite the gracious letters and the warm phone conversations, Greg was nervous about how he would be received in Americus. After all, nine-tenths of the class had not written him. Joseph warned him about one man—a friend who had played football with him—whom he believed still harbored his old biases. (It wasn't Thomas; T.J. had died many years before.) David also mentioned the possibility that there would be people who would be unhappy to see him. Even Mrs. Crabb, when he called her, seemed a bit cautious about him returning to Georgia and facing his former classmates. All it would take to undo much of the good would be for one tongue to lash out at him. "Greg," she said, "don't be surprised if there are some diehards."

It all gave him pause, but it didn't change his mind. Greg was going, and he didn't think it would be necessary to pack guns and ammo, as Carol Browne had suggested.

As they drove the six hundred miles from West Virginia to Americus, Greg and the others talked off and on about what to expect.

"What do you think your father would think of all this?" Anne asked her husband.

"He'd say, 'Hallelujah! The Lord works in mysterious ways.'"

"How about your mother?"

"She'd say, 'Well, this should be interesting. You boys behave yourselves.'"

Greg certainly didn't want to cause a scene by showing up. He just wanted to close the circle and find some redemption. He hoped that would be the way it played out, but if it didn't, he had been through worse. Turning off Interstate 75 for the last leg of the journey through the peach groves of middle Georgia, he looked at the others and cracked a little joke: "You know, it's not too late. We can still turn around."

CHAPTER 15
———

Back to Americus

THE LONG DRIVE FROM WEST VIRGINIA ENDED IN FRONT OF A REDBRICK house with white shutters on West Glessner Street, three blocks from Americus High School. It was Mrs. Crabb's residence, the same place she had lived when she was the faculty advisor for the Class of 1965. Greg and some of the schoolmates who had written him were meeting for a Friday lunch at their teacher's home before the reunion weekend got under way that evening with a reception. It seemed like an appropriate setting for them to get together and sift through their emotions before they gathered with the rest of the graduates.

Greg climbed out of his brother's Mercedes, still feeling edgy about what awaited, and reached for Anne's hand as he made his way up the front walk. David followed with Sallie, who was carrying a gift bag for their hostess and waving an old-time fan they had picked up at the Americus visitors center. Greg paused at the front door, which was decked out with an American flag, and took a deep breath. Anne pressed the bell.

The door opened, and an elderly woman with glasses and white bangs appeared. "Goodness gracious alive, you look wonderful!" Mrs. Crabb exclaimed when she saw Greg. The two embraced. "I think I'm going to spend the day crying."

There was another familiar face in the entry hall. "I recognize this man," Greg said, and shook hands again, after forty-one years, with

David Morgan. Deanie stood behind him with her husband, Bill, beaming as she hugged Greg. The doorbell rang and another classmate, Mary Ellen Smith Daniels, walked in with a yearbook tucked under her arm, and there were more hugs and handshakes.

Everyone settled into the living room, a grandmotherly sanctuary with rockers, curio cabinets, and family photos staring from the walls and tables. Greg tried to break the ice. "So," he began, "after all these years . . ."

It was awkward at first. Greg had never been friends with these people when they were students. Other than their letters and their recent phone conversations, they hardly knew each other. The last time they had been together was at their graduation, when he was booed and chased off the campus by rock throwers. It wasn't like they could reminisce about the prom or the homecoming game; most of their shared memories were not pleasant ones. Seeing him for the first time in more than four decades, his classmates looked him over for signs of mental bruising. They hadn't expected him to walk in twitching or wearing a straitjacket, but they wouldn't have been shocked if he had seemed haunted in some way—a Boo Radley they had all helped create.

Greg put them at ease. He joked about being so nervous that he had almost asked his brother to turn the car around and go home. He told them about his real estate business in West Virginia and made the requisite crack about the suspected commie growing up to become a capitalist. Everyone fussed over his doe-eyed four-year-old, who climbed into his lap and then joined her mother on the oriental rug to play with some toys Mrs. Crabb had found for her.

His classmates were relieved to see that Greg was not haunted. He seemed happy. He seemed to be at peace.

It was time for lunch. Mrs. Crabb asked everyone to stand up, link hands, and go around the circle saying a prayer. "Father," Deanie offered in her hushed, earnest tone, "you have softened hearts and changed our minds about different things, and we are very thankful."

The group moved into the dining room for chicken salad sandwiches, chips, and iced tea, Greg sitting at the right hand of his teacher. He said that the scene reminded him of all the days when no one would come near him in the cafeteria, and the others nodded knowingly. Soon they

Deanie, David, and Greg at Mrs. Crabb's house before the reunion. *Courtesy of Faith Fuller*

were talking about all the things they wouldn't talk about in high school: Koinonia and the Klan, bombings and boycotts, all the shunning and abuse Greg put up with. They stayed at the table talking for more than ninety minutes, the conversation becoming so animated at one point that Mrs. Crabb had to resort to an old teacher's ploy to get everyone's attention. "Y'all aren't listening to me," she said, and then clapped her hands and shouted, "Class!"

Mary Ellen admitted that much of what she was hearing came as news to her. Although she attended grades one through twelve with Greg, she said she hadn't realized it was so bad for him because the boys were behind most of the harassment and they didn't usually brag about it to the girls. A male friend had recently told her about some of the things they did, she said, "and it just made me ill."

Greg assured her that he had never thought most of the students truly hated him. They just went along with what their parents believed and bent to the will of the most opinionated among their peers. "I'd say maybe 10 percent had that racist attitude of white supremacy. But they're the ones who set the tone, who put their ideas ahead of everyone else's. Everyone kowtowed to the outspoken ones."

Deanie, who had been listening intently, felt compelled to weigh in on the psychology of bigotry, something she had thought about over the years. "It's hard to fathom prejudice. It's hard to understand where it comes from and how it develops. Growing up, I knew—and nobody sat me down and told me this stuff; you just absorb it—I believed that blacks were not clean and that morally they were corrupt. Y'all understand that's not true, but I thought it was. That was the mind-set I had."

She turned to Greg with a pained expression. "I don't know who told me this, but I heard that someone had gone out to Koinonia and seen a black woman, and she was in a slip, like it was an immoral atmosphere. There was a tremendous fear of intermarriage in those days. We thought that if you brought black people into our lives as equals, intermarriage was bound to occur, and our people were proud of their heritage and their bloodlines."

As if on cue, the doorbell rang, and in walked Deanie's friend Celia, accompanied by her Hispanic husband, Ron Gonzalez. The two women gave each other hello kisses, and the couple sat down at the table and joined the discussion, which had moved on to their graduation day.

"We figured you were going to be killed," Mary Ellen told Greg.

"I did get death threats," he said.

Celia glanced at her husband, who looked like he was staring into headlights, and explained that he was younger and came from a very different background that made it hard for him to comprehend the way people behaved toward Greg. "I grew up in the North," he said, "and most of my friends were black. When she told me about all this, I said, 'What do you mean? Call the man up.'"

Celia wrote instead. As the lunch was drawing to a close, Greg thanked everyone again for their letters and told them how touched he had been as he read them.

Deanie said they were so relieved. "We didn't know how you were going to respond—or if you were going to respond. We were concerned that we had really done some damage to you. I'm so thankful you've been able to forgive us."

"But not all of us have," Greg answered. "Carol Browne is still very resentful. She said, 'If I saw any of those kids from high school, I'd smack them in the face.'"

While it was true that Greg had forgiven them, he wanted these most understanding of his classmates to know that there had been damage, that it had taken time for him to disarm his resentment. He described the nightmares he had experienced when he was overseas with Friends World, the ones where he retaliated in a bloody high school revenge fantasy that could have come out of a Stephen King novel. "I was standing there with a Thompson machine gun mowing down the bunch of you," Greg said, his voice even and calm. "I was so relieved it was a dream. I guess I had to work it out subconsciously."

The table was quiet for a moment.

"When you think about it," Greg continued, "if my parents hadn't been nonviolent, if we really had been Russian Communist atheists who thought that you settle things with military might, I could have reached a flashpoint. I could have walked into that school and shot everyone. Gone down in a blaze of glory. The way I was treated, we could have had a Columbine on our hands."

Anne was surprised that her husband had been willing to talk about his nightmares. He was confessing that some part of him had once wanted to kill them all—not your typical luncheon chitchat. But when she thought about it later, she was glad he had done it. They needed to know exactly what they had been forgiven for.

THE RECEPTION THAT NIGHT WAS HELD IN A CLASS MEMBER'S HOME IN the Americus historic district, a picturesque two-story traditional with a wraparound porch that exuded southern charm. It was the kind of neighborhood Greg rarely visited as a teenager because he was usually hanging out on the other side of the tracks when he came to town on a social call. He thought the luncheon had gone well—he had been impressed with everyone's candor and sincerity—but he was more apprehensive about this event and the reunion on Saturday night. Only four classmates had been at Mrs. Crabb's. He was about to see many more of them, including ones who had not wanted to write him and some who had bedeviled him in high school.

"Don't worry about it," David Morgan reassured him. "There are going to be just as many people there who don't like me. You'll be among friends."

When Greg and Anne arrived at the reception, they saw Joseph Logan standing out front with Deanie and several others. "Greg?" he said, sticking out his hand. "How are you doing? Do you remember me? Was I ugly to you?"

Greg hugging Joseph outside the reception, with Deanie and his brother David looking on. *Courtesy of Faith Fuller*

Joseph apologized for missing the lunch—he hadn't been able to leave Alabama early enough—and was genuinely moved to see Greg for the first time in forty-one years. "The character this guy has . . ." he said, and then choked up and couldn't finish the thought. He regained his footing by making a pointed joke.

"I was just telling folks that I ain't out to get you, but I don't know who's in there"—he motioned toward the house—"and what they might do."

"We'll find out," Greg said.

"Well, you haven't changed. You haven't run from anything."

If Joseph seemed a little overwrought, it was because of what he had been doing before Greg walked up. He had been sitting in a wicker chair on the porch doing an interview with a documentary filmmaker, Faith Fuller. Greg had phoned her after he received the letters and invited her to come to the reunion with a camera. Faith was one of Millard and Linda Fuller's daughters and spent much of her childhood at Koinonia before her parents left the community to devote themselves full-time to Habitat for Humanity. She had known the Wittkampers her whole life and had been baptized by Greg's father, whom she requested for the job because she thought Will looked like Moses. A few years before the reunion, she made a film about Koinonia called *Briars in the Cotton Patch*, which aired on public television across the nation; she saw Greg's reconciliation with his classmates as a continuation of the story.

Joseph readily agreed to speak with Faith, but he was uneasy about doing the interview in front of the arriving guests. "Other people might come up and think something," he said, his eyes scanning the street. He went ahead and did it anyway, talking at length about the boy nobody wanted to be around. When he retold the tale of Thomas striking Greg beside the baseball stands, he misted up and had to pause several times to recompose himself.

"He went to some Quaker college and went around the world to broaden his mind—like he was the one who needed that," he told Faith. "We were the ones who needed it. We were narrow-minded jerks. We had blinders on. I really struggled with whether I needed to apologize to him. Did I hit him? Did I do anything? What he said hurt him the worst was being ignored. If somebody were to ignore me, that would hurt. We were doing the worst thing in the world by ignoring him."

Joseph had been right to wonder what some of his classmates would think of him holding forth about Greg in a taped interview. Faith went to every event over the weekend—the luncheon and reception on Friday, the reunion on Saturday—and some people at the larger functions did not like seeing her there with a camera. They expected their reunion to be lighthearted and nostalgic, not soul searching. It rankled them to hear class members like Don Smith, the one who had written a senior English paper about Greg, telling Faith about the time he had aimed a pistol behind Greg's neck and fired a blank. "She was asking questions about the bad things, and it made some of the people mad," David said. "They were going, 'She don't need to be here. Listen to what they're saying over there.'"

It was a complicated weekend for Joseph. As much as he had matured over the years, part of him was still a teenager longing to be liked, concerned about appearances. He was trying to make things right with Greg at the same time he was reconnecting with people he didn't see very often anymore, especially his old football teammates. He suspected they would not look kindly on him chumming around with Greg and getting all weepy as he told some filmmaker about the way people used to gang up on him. "My classmates are going to see that, and they're going to resent what I had to say," he said later, "and that bothers me. I cherish their friendships. I hope they don't hold it against me, but I'm just telling the truth."

On the day after the reception, Joseph and David visited Greg at the Hampton Inn where he was staying in Americus. Greg and David got out their guitars and picked a few tunes, and then they talked for much of the afternoon. Joseph told Greg that what had happened to him in high school was wrong. They embraced, and then he left to drop by a team-mate's house for another get-together. He seemed sorry to go.

THE CLASS OF 1965 CONVENED IN THE OLD CARNEGIE LIBRARY ON Jackson Street, long since cleared of books and converted into an elegant event facility. Soon after Greg got there, one of the classmates who had phoned him, Jeannie Fletcher, reintroduced herself with a surprising ad-mission. "I don't want to upset you," she told Anne, "but I had the biggest crush on your husband all through high school."

Greg had no idea. "Why didn't you tell me?"

"I actually thought about asking you to the prom."

"I would have gone," he replied. There was a deejay playing oldies, so he did the next best thing and asked Jeannie to dance.

As the evening progressed, Greg began to feel something like a guest of honor. People who had been secretly sympathetic to him in school thanked him for coming and told him how nice it was to see him. Some of the guys who had made his life miserable came over to pay their respects; once menacing, they looked rather harmless with their middle-aged paunches pressing against their Polo shirts. They were friendly enough, if not quite confessional. Greg saw one of the hardest cases standing across the room and made a point of introducing himself first and shaking his hand—still loving his enemy; Clarence Jordan would have been proud. Their meeting was as polite as could be. A casual onlooker would not have known that this particular fellow once tried to kick Greg down a stairwell.

After they helped themselves to the buffet, many of the class mem-bers lingered over a table where yearbooks, photos, and yellowed copies of the *Paw Print* student newspaper were displayed. David had brought his annuals, including the one with Greg's portrait scratched out. Some people laughed when they saw the page. David later cut a small patch of white paper and glued it over what was left of the picture so no one would have to confront his youthful foray into vandalism again.

Anne overheard some of the laughter at the table and was not amused. Several times during the evening, she had to fight the urge to reprimand the adults milling around her having a good time for what they had done to her husband as adolescents. "I was getting angry. I wanted to blurt out things like: 'Did you ever think what it was like to stand in his shoes?' I thought they all should have been torn up emotionally. I didn't want them to minimize what had happened. This wasn't a bad week for Greg. It was his life."

Anne was having a tough time of it. Her lower back had been hurting—she would soon require surgery—and she was moving slowly and stiffly. She probably should have been at home resting, but the weekend meant so much to Greg that she wanted to be there with him, even if she had to do it on prescription painkillers. Knowing few people at the reunion, she spent much of the night on guard, tense, observing. As far as she could tell, there was only one black person in the room, a young man who was tending bar. She sidled up to him and sketched out the narrative between the lines.

"You have no reason to know this and you may not be interested, but there's a significant story unfolding at this reunion," she said. As he continued to pour drinks, she gave him a five-minute synopsis of the tale so far: about Koinonia, the terror campaign, the ordeal Greg went through in high school, and now this scene. As busy as he was, the young man appeared to listen and seemed taken aback.

"That happened here? In Americus? Well, I've got just one question: Why did your husband want to come?"

The answer came a few minutes later when the music stopped and the president of the senior class stepped up to make a few announcements. He recognized David Morgan, thanked him for planning the reunion, and handed him the microphone. David made some routine remarks and then, in a matter-of-fact fashion, mentioned that one of their classmates had rejoined the fold.

"It's significant that Greg Wittkamper is here," he said. "I think everybody has heard the whisperings of this story, and it's a wonderful story." He stopped as applause swept through the gathering. Faith's camera located Greg across the room and zeroed in on his face, which was flushing and turning several shades of pink.

"It's remarkable what he endured," David continued, "and how he dealt with it and put it behind him even before we contacted him. It's a sweet story and an appropriate story, and I'm glad it turned out this way."

He paused and cleared his throat. "I'm starting to get emotional."

Later in the evening, there was an open mic for class members to tell stories and share reminiscences. A few of the women urged Greg to get up and do a song or two. Others weren't so eager. "Do we have to go there?" one of the men groused. Greg's brother went out to the car to fetch his guitar, the same Gibson he had bought in high school and taken around the world in college. During his worst days as a student, Greg had daydreamed of becoming a famous folk singer and imagined how sorry his classmates would be that they had treated him so shabbily. In his fantasy, he would put them down by singing the caustic lyrics of Bob Dylan's "Positively 4th Street":

> You got a lotta nerve
> To say you are my friend.
> When I was down,
> You just stood there grinning.

Now that he actually found himself facing his class with a guitar and a harmonica, the circumstances had changed and the cutting message he had imagined was out of the question. Needing something more conciliatory, he settled on two other Dylan songs: a reunion evergreen, "Forever Young," and one of the anthems of the civil rights era, "Blowin' in the Wind."

"I hope you enjoy this," he said, and then added with a sly expression: "Please, no one boo. I have a fragile ego."

Perhaps a fourth of the people in the library congregated in front of him as he performed the songs in his raspy, countrified voice. Elsewhere in the room, Joseph noticed others standing quietly and waiting for the impromptu concert to pass. "I could almost hear them grumbling under their breath," he said. But the grumbles were not spoken for general consumption. Greg's fragile ego was safe. When he finished singing, there was no booing, as there had been at his graduation; there was only applause.

GREG STAYED AT THE REUNION UNTIL THE PARTY WAS BREAKING UP. That night in their motel room, Anne was aware of her husband tossing and turning in bed as his mind replayed what had happened the past two days and sorted through what it all meant. The next morning, they visited Koinonia and then started for home later that Sunday.

Back in West Virginia, Greg decided that he needed to say something to his schoolmates—even the ones who were unenthusiastic about him showing up. He sat down at his computer and wrote a thank you note and mailed copies to everyone in the class directory, almost a hundred names:

> OPEN LETTER TO THE AHS CLASS OF 1965
> *Thank you all for the overwhelmingly warm and friendly reception of me and my family at the reunion. It was an occasion that I had decided would never happen. I am moved by all of your words of acceptance and your smiling faces.*
>
> *Please forgive me for not recognizing more of you. The lack of constructive communication in high school kept us from getting to know each other very well. I hope this turn of events will change things. I would be open to corresponding with any of you who would want. Special thanks to those of you who have been moved to write or call me so far.*
>
> *I believe the story about what happened at AHS is a story that should be told, not to find fault, but to give hope to all who hear it. If you have any memories or insights, I would love to hear them.*
>
> *I have free long distance and am better at talking than writing. If you would like to talk, let me know and I will call you. Also, I would love to read anything you might like to write.*
>
> *May You Stay Young Forever*
> *Your friend,*
> *Gregory Wittkamper*

As Greg reread the letter, he lingered on the line above his signature: "Your friend." He never dreamed he would be writing those words to these people.

But he still wasn't finished. He had one more thing to do before he could turn the page on high school.

Epilogue

On a sweltering afternoon in August 2013, Greg Wittkamper walked inside his old high school for the first time in forty-eight years. He hardly recognized the place. Much of the complex had been rebuilt after he left—construction necessitated by the fire during his junior year—and little remained as it existed in his imagination. There was a new main building, the cafeteria wasn't where it used to be, and the structure that had housed the government class where he "insulted" Thomas was no longer standing. The biggest difference was the student body; an administrator who took him on a tour around campus estimated that almost 90 percent of the children enrolled at Americus–Sumter County High School South, as the institution had been rechristened, were black. They looked neat in their school uniforms of blue and khaki and barely paid attention to the older white man peering down the hallways as if he were trying to see something that was no longer visible.

Greg had come to Americus to take part in a panel discussion at Georgia Southwestern State University about the civil rights movement in Sumter County. He made several such trips in the years after his class reunion, but this visit stood out because the program included an event at the scene of his stormy exit from high school. The weekend was going to culminate with a Saturday night banquet in the gymnasium where he received his diploma to a round of catcalls. That building, at least, had survived, although it had been updated, mercifully, with air-conditioning.

As Greg approached the gym on Harrold Avenue, a wry look came over his face. "This is about where they started throwing bricks at us after the ceremony," he said. He motioned up the hill to a side street. "And that's where the car was. You should have seen us running; we couldn't get out of here fast enough."

Inside the arena, the basketball goals were raised, dinner tables covered the court, and a buffet was being readied along one of the sidelines. Large blue letters on a wall proclaimed it "The Panther Den," with matching blue paw prints. As Greg was taking it all in, a heavyset man with a long, gnomish beard came over to say hello. It was Tommy Bass, the classmate who had welcomed Greg to Americus High as a freshman by firing paper clips into his back with a rubber band. He had changed, too; he was wearing an Obama T-shirt.

Greg wandered around the room speaking with other guests, many of whom he vaguely recognized from the protests and mass meetings of the 1960s. The banquet was sponsored by the Americus–Sumter County Movement Remembered Committee, a group that believes the local civil rights struggle has not received its due and has been unfairly relegated to near obscurity in comparison to Selma. "What happened in Americus is an untold story," Congressman John Lewis, who saw action in both campaigns, said at one of the committee's earlier functions. Its members dream of a museum or some kind of permanent exhibition and have begun collecting artifacts like the door of the cell where Martin Luther King Jr. was jailed in Americus. But on this evening, they just wanted to celebrate, raise money, and honor a handful of leaders who were instrumental to the cause.

One of them was the Reverend Robert L. Freeman, the late father of Greg's classmate Robertiena. In accepting the award, his son, Robert Jr., told a story about the desegregation of Americus High that Greg had never heard. It happened on the day he, Robertiena, and two others rode to classes in the funeral home limousine and found themselves in the center of a howling mob.

Robert was home from school that afternoon when his father charged into the house, disappeared into a back room, and then left without a word. He returned a few minutes later and departed again hastily. Some time afterward, he told his son what the comings and goings had been about: at the end of the school day, Robertiena had gone to the principal's office and couldn't leave because another angry rabble had formed outside. Someone phoned Freeman at the middle school where he worked, and he rushed home with a grim determination to defend his daughter at any cost. "Son," he said, "I came home to get my gun. And then I thought about it and decided I didn't want to do something I would regret. So I brought the gun back home and put the situation in the hands of the Lord."

Greg had no idea that the day he remembered so vividly had come so close to ending in disaster. If Robertiena's father had waved a gun in front of those people at the school, something horrible might have happened. It had taken courage for him to overcome his anger and remember what he stood for.

GREG NEVER FORGOT ABOUT THE OTHERS. FROM THE WEEK HE RECEIVED the first letters from his fellow class members, he thought about the four who had desegregated Americus High—Robertiena, Jewel, David, Dobbs—and wondered whether anyone had ever apologized to them. He hoped so; reconciliation, he had discovered, was a wonderful thing.

When Greg returned to West Virginia after the class reunion in 2006, he glowed for weeks with the warmth of a healing he had not fully realized that he needed. More letters and phone calls helped prolong the feeling. Richard Crutchfield, whom Greg recalled as a studious boy with kind-looking eyes, wrote from north Georgia to thank him for coming "as I believe it meant so much to everyone to finally accept you as a classmate . . . something we all should have done so many years ago." Ellen Marshall Beard, who had been head cheerleader and one of the most popular girls in school, sent him a card from Atlanta with a picture of a thickly fleeced sheep. "Saw this card and it reminded me of the Class of '65 in 1965," she wrote. "Hopefully we are not so sheepish anymore." She went on to say that Greg's coming was the highlight of the reunion. "Maybe love does conquer all!"

The most unusual communication was a call from another class member who lived in Oklahoma and had not been able to make it to the reunion. He told Greg that he had felt bad for him in school and thought, in another setting, they might have become friends, if only because they both played the guitar. Then he dropped a stunner; he confided that his father had been a Klansman, something he didn't discover until he saw him marching in his white KKK regalia. "That's strange to think that your dad was in the Klan, and they were the ones shooting into the houses where we lived," Greg said. "Yes," his classmate agreed, "that is strange."

In all, a dozen members of the Class of '65 took the trouble to write or call Greg—one out of eight—and many more spoke to him at the reunion. The whole experience had been gratifying beyond all his hopes. It had also proved beneficial for his mental well-being. After they returned from Americus, Anne noticed that her husband was able to talk about things in a way he had seldom been able to in the five years they had been together. "He really opened up," she said, then added with a laugh: "This saved us a lot of money on counseling."

The reconciliation wasn't limited to Greg. The sense of remorse that led Deanie to square things with him also drove her to track down two other students from Koinonia who had been in the class ahead of them. She phoned Jan Jordan in Highlands, North Carolina, where she and her husband were running a bed-and-breakfast, and Lora Browne in Fort Lauderdale, Florida, where she had settled with her husband. When Deanie heard that Lora occasionally visited her mother-in-law near her home in Naples, she invited her to drop by, and she did, the two of them talking for four hours. More tears fell.

In the midst of all this apologizing and forgiving, Greg felt compelled to reconnect with the black students who had braved Americus High in 1964. He hadn't spoken with any of them since he left town a few months after graduation. He wondered how the rest of their schooling had gone, what had become of them, how they dealt with the traumatic

Greg Wittkamper today.
Courtesy of Sallie Wittkamper

memories they must carry. His journey would not be complete until he talked with them.

————————

A LITTLE MORE THAN A YEAR AFTER THE CLASS REUNION, GREG RETURNED to Americus for a Labor Day weekend of events celebrating the activists who had participated in the Sumter County movement. He used the occasion to get together with three of the people who had broken the color line at the high school—Jewel Wise, Dobbs Wiggins, and David Bell—taking them to dinner at one of the chain restaurants that had sprouted along the highways on the fringes of town, Ruby Tuesday. As the party took its seats at a table by the windows, David looked around and chuckled. "You know, we couldn't have done something like this in the old days. Stewart's and all those other places downtown didn't serve black people."

"I guess we could have gone to Koinonia," Greg said.

For the next hour, they talked mostly about what daring kids they had been: the church rallies, the street protests, the truculent cops, the resulting arrests. "All my friends were in jail," David remembered. "If you weren't locked up, you were out of it." The three of them didn't dwell as much on Americus High. They were proud of their part in ushering the school into the future, but the details of the day-to-day hazing seemed less stirring than the memory of marching through Americus with a crowd of teenagers singing freedom songs. Going to the white high school seemed like a grinding battle without glory that ended in a tactical retreat, because none of these three had stayed. "That's not my alma mater," Jewel said. "I just happened to go there for a while. I have no happy memories of that place."

David told a story about an unlikely person who knew about his role. After he finished at the black high school, he served in the army for twenty-two years and then came back to southwest Georgia to work as a corrections officer. One day an inmate asked him whether he was the David Bell who had helped integrate Americus High School. David said yes and wondered how he knew about it. His mother had told him. "He seemed impressed to meet me. That made me feel good."

All three of Greg's dinner mates had spent years away from Americus. Two of them had returned to the area to live, and Dobbs, who had retired from a business career, would soon move back into the house where he grew up. They all agreed that the civil rights revolution they had fought for had changed the town for the better in so many ways. "But then you see something that makes you realize that some things haven't changed much at all," Jewel said. "Did you see those photos in the paper today?"

She was referring to a special section in the *Times-Recorder* previewing the football season. Most of the front page was taken up by two photos of the local high school teams. They made quite a contrast. The Americus–Sumter High Panthers suited up seventy-six players, all but four of whom appeared to be black (with a few white coaches around the edges). The Southland Academy Raiders dressed forty-seven players, all of whom appeared to be white. The two teams don't play each other. Less than three miles apart, the schools might as well be in different towns.

The photos were a topic of discussion at the civil rights commemoration that weekend. While some conceded that Americus wasn't that different from hundreds of other communities where parents had taken their children out of the public schools, others pointed out that Southland was founded specifically because those public schools began to admit blacks. It moved beyond its origins as a "seggie" academy and evolved into a well-regarded institution that stresses religious instruction and advertises a nondiscrimination policy—and does indeed have a small percentage of minority students. Greg couldn't see any of them on the newspaper page. To him and Jewel and many others at the civil rights gathering, the football photos looked like a disturbing reminder of a time they had hoped was past.

IN THE FALL OF 2012, GREG TRAVELED BACK TO AMERICUS TWICE FOR A symposium marking the centennial of Clarence Jordan's birth and then a reunion of more than a hundred people who had lived at Koinonia over the years. As he listened to the speakers at Georgia Southwestern and strolled the grounds of the farm during the pecan harvest, he was struck by how much local feelings toward his onetime communal home had shifted.

Greg could remember when some of the gray-headed elders at the reunion were children and tried to hide where they lived from outsiders. If a student who didn't know him asked his brother David where he was from, he'd mumble something about the north end of the county—anything but admit that he came from that strange place on the opposite end. In the years after Greg left, attitudes toward Koinonia softened as more people realized that it was not an outpost of Soviet Communism and really did spring from a fundamentalist reading of early Christianity. He noticed that the Americus visitors center was even displaying brochures about Koinonia. "People are curious about it. There's almost a caché attached to being from there now."

The fact that Habitat for Humanity traces its birth to Koinonia helped immeasurably. During Habitat's fledgling years, some people advised Millard Fuller to distance himself from the commune in order to make his housing ministry more acceptable to the community. He refused, telling them, "I'm not going to disown my mother." Those lingering sentiments against Koinonia faded as Habitat grew and became a cornerstone

of Sumter County's identity. Even after the organization moved many of
its operations to Atlanta a few years ago, Habitat has remained one of the
county's largest employers, occupying one of the most prominent structures in Americus, the handsome old Rylander Building on Lamar Street.
It isn't the only housing ministry of its kind in town; after Millard parted
ways with the nonprofit he founded, he and his wife, Linda, established
the Fuller Center for Housing, which has similar ambitions to alleviate
poverty housing around the world. Millard died unexpectedly in 2009,
but his latest endeavor has continued to spread. Both ministries grew
from the seedling of an idea that he and Clarence planted at Koinonia
during the late 1960s. The two are buried near each other on Picnic Hill.

As Greg saw during the reunion, Koinonia is thriving. Around two
dozen members and interns live there, although it usually seems more
crowded because so many people visit for retreats and sabbaticals. The
fellowship still professes brotherhood and peacemaking, along with a
newer emphasis on sustainable farming practices—permaculture, in the
argot of its devotees—which would no doubt please Koinonia's original
Mr. Natural, Will Wittkamper. They still ring the dinner bell for a communal lunch at noon, and the questers and pilgrims still wander in. In
front of the property on Highway 49, there's a history marker bearing
testimony to the community's complicated past.

When Greg goes back to Americus now, he can drive down Habitat
Street, turn left onto Millard Fuller Boulevard, and continue until it runs
into Martin Luther King Jr. Boulevard. On the sidewalk in front of the
Rylander Theatre, he can look down at a plaque memorializing Clarence
Jordan, part of a Walk of Fame display honoring notable people from
Sumter County.

One of those notables was among the first speakers at the Clarence
Jordan Symposium. Before he took the stage inside the Rylander Theatre,
Jimmy Carter lingered over the sidewalk and noticed something interesting about the company Clarence was keeping. "I looked at some of the
other names, and it was kind of ironic because I remember that some of
those other names who are inscribed in front are partially responsible for
the bombs and the bullets and the fires that tried to destroy what Clarence Jordan did at Koinonia."

With a flash of his grin, Carter mentioned the farm's mail-order slogan during the boycott years, the quip about shipping the nuts out of Georgia. "A lot of the nuts who tried to burn out Koinonia have been converted into supporters of what Clarence Jordan stood for. And I'm very grateful for that."

Clarence himself foresaw the day when Koinonia would be accepted. During an interview in 1965, he predicted that it would happen as naturally as the hatching of a chicken egg. "You watch, and you think it will never hatch. Then one day you look at it, and what was a lifeless object yesterday is a warm, living, and beautiful thing. But you know all that change didn't happen since you looked at it yesterday; the change had been going on all the time, but you couldn't see it.

"Who knows?" he continued. "Maybe in twenty years the white people in Americus will be willing to speak to us."

———————

GREG FOUND ROBERTIENA FREEMAN AT THE HOUSTON MEDICAL CENTER in Warner Robins, an hour northeast of her hometown, where she worked as director of the pharmacy. Distracted in the middle of a busy workday, she didn't recognize his name over the phone at first. Then he mentioned riding to school in the funeral home limousine, and it all came back: the crowd, the hollering, the rock throwing. "I thought we were going to get killed," she said.

Robertiena (or Tiena Fletcher, as she was now known) had come a long way since the end of Greg's senior year. She spent three nights in jail that spring after police found her necking with her boyfriend and charged her with fornication—a transparent attempt to oust her from the white high school, in the view of her parents. The case was eventually dismissed, but while it was being adjudicated, the court and her family agreed that it would be a good idea if she got out of town for a while. That summer, while Americus erupted in its worst racial violence, she was in Berkeley, California, attending an enrichment program called the Encampment for Citizenship, where she learned about hippies and lefties and peaceniks.

When Robertiena returned to Americus High that fall for her junior year, she was no longer alone. Forty black students were entering the city's once all-white schools. By November, fourteen of them had dropped out because of widespread abuse, physical bullying, and threatening phone calls to their homes. The US Commission on Civil Rights examined the Americus system, interviewing many of the students and administrators, and reported that "a pattern of harassment and violence in the secondary schools had developed, accompanied by a lack of supervision and enforcement of discipline by the high school officials." Greg could have told them that.

It never got easy for Robertiena. During her final two years at the school, some kids continued to spit on her, shove her into the lockers, call her "that smart little nigger." The longer it went on, the more outspoken she became. She remembered one day in senior English when Mrs. Crabb encouraged the white students to ask Robertiena anything they wanted, as long as they remained civil, and one of the girls said, "Why do you want to go to a school where you're not wanted?"

"Because it's my right to go to this school," Robertiena replied. "I don't have to go to a black school just because you want to put me there. I don't have to sit in the balcony at the movie theater just because you want me to stay up there where it's dirty and dingy. You shouldn't get the best of everything, and we get whatever's left over. We're human beings, too."

As Robertiena recalled it, the classroom fell quiet. Some of the students, she believed, were beginning to listen.

Robertiena graduated from Americus High in 1967 along with Emmarene Kaigler and Bessie Walton—the first black students to earn diplomas from the school. The inscription under her portrait in the senior annual was, oddly, the same one that ran next to Greg's, with only the pronouns changed: "She shows her true nature in what she does." Robertiena went to Mercer University in Macon on a scholarship, launched a career in pharmacy, got married, and started a family. She served on the county school board, the chamber of commerce, and was eventually appointed by the governor to the state board of human resources, which she would later lead. She was, by any measure, an accomplished alumna.

When Greg reached her on the phone in 2006, he told her about the reunion and how heartening it had been to get the invitation and to read the expressions of regret from members of his class.

"That's great, Greg," she said. Robertiena herself had not been offered those same kind of apologies.

"Have you ever been to a class reunion?" he asked.

"No," she said. "I've never been invited."

She had been to reunions of classes at the black schools, but she had never been to one at the formerly white high school where she received her diploma. If she were invited, she admitted, she wasn't sure she would want to go.

She was tethered to Americus High in another way, though. More than twenty years after Robertiena graduated, her older sister, Juanita Wilson, became principal of the school. One day she asked Robertiena to speak during Black History Month. "I begged her not to make me do it," she said. "I'd never been back inside that school, and I didn't want to go then."

After Robertiena spoke, a white teacher named Susan Parker made her way to the stage and asked if she could say a few words. "You probably don't remember me," she began, "but I went to school with you. I didn't do anything to you, but I stood by while others did, and I am so sorry for that. I'd like to welcome you back to Americus High School." With that, the teacher reached for Robertiena's hand and asked her to join in singing their alma mater.

As he listened to her story, Greg only wished he could have been there.

ACKNOWLEDGMENTS

THIS BOOK BEGAN FOR ME DURING A VACATION TO ROCKY MOUNTAIN National Park when I did something that's not a very healthy thing to do if you're trying to get away from the office and commune with nature: I checked my voice mail at work. There was an intriguing message.

"Jim, this is Ann Morris. I just got together with some people who told me the most wonderful story, and it made me think of you."

Ann had been my editor at the *Atlanta Journal-Constitution* and had gone on to become managing editor of the *News & Record* in Greensboro, North Carolina. The voice mail was a little hard to follow, but it seemed that a friend of hers had a sister who was married to a guy in West Virginia who had just gone back to Georgia for a high school class reunion that had something to do with the civil rights era and a farming commune called Koinonia, and she thought it sounded like my kind of tale. Her paper couldn't do anything with it because it was set in Georgia, not North Carolina, so she passed along the contact information. Thanks for the tip, Ann.

As soon as I returned to Atlanta, I contacted the guy in West Virginia, Greg Wittkamper, who filled me in on the backstory and sent me copies of the letters his classmates had written to him apologizing for the way people treated him in high school. Over the next few years, I interviewed Greg at least thirty times at his mountain home, during trips to Georgia and elsewhere, and over the telephone. I couldn't have wished for a better protagonist; I am deeply grateful for the opportunity to tell his story. Thanks also to his wife, Anne, who was always supportive and usually patient.

Greg introduced me to the people he had grown up with at Koinonia, a rich supporting cast that included Brownes (Conrad and his children Carol, Charles, John, and Lora), Jordans (Jan and Lenny), and Wittkampers (Bill, Dan, and David). Thanks to all of them for sharing their time, and special thanks to Conrad Browne, Lora Browne, and Lenny Jordan for sharing their archival materials.

Greg's classmates were helpful and forthcoming in reflecting on parts of their past that weren't always easy to talk about. Many thanks to Deanie Dudley Fricks, Celia Harvey Gonzalez, Joseph Logan, and David Morgan for going there—and to their teacher, Gladys Crabb, for preparing the way. I'd also like to thank Robertiena Freeman Fletcher and the other students who desegregated Americus High—David Bell, Dobbs Wiggins, and Jewel Wise—for revisiting some tough times with me. And I should mention Sam Mahone, one of the young activists who worked for change in Americus and is now trying to preserve that history.

I'm especially indebted to Faith Fuller, a filmmaker who recorded the reunion weekend and made a copy of her video for me.

I already knew about Koinonia when I met Greg. During my first job out of college, as associate editor of *Presbyterian Survey,* the denominational magazine of the southern Presbyterian church, a colleague of mine, Lynn Donham, told me about the farm and its history of persecution and wrote an article about it for me. A couple of years later, when I went to work for the Atlanta newspaper, one of the first out-of-town assignments I received was to drive to Americus and do a feature about how Koinonia was faring. It had been almost exactly eleven years since its cofounder and guiding spirit, Clarence Jordan, had died, but I was able to speak with his widow, Florence, and feel the soul of the place.

I returned to Sumter County many times to write about Jimmy and Rosalynn Carter; the Andersonville POW camp; and Habitat for Humanity, whose founders, Millard and Linda Fuller, had lived at Koinonia and recognized it as the birthplace of the nonprofit housing ministry. Americus is one of the most interesting towns in America, and I've always felt welcome there. That's especially true at Koinonia, where I've stayed several times and spent hours trying to imagine the ways things were. I'd like to thank Bren Dubay, the fellowship's director; Amanda Moore, who set me up in the archives; Kat Mournighan, who assigned me to bunk in the Martin Luther King Jr. Room; and everyone who had a hand in cooking the communal meals that are an enduring part of life at the farm.

Several former colleagues at the *Atlanta Journal-Constitution* deserve recognition. Valerie Boyd, an arts editor who went on to become a journalism professor and successful author, long urged me to write a book and read an early version of my proposal for this one. Her biography of Zora Neale Hurston, *Wrapped in Rainbows,* was an inspiration. Fellow reporters Drew Jubera, Cameron McWhirter, and Gary Pomerantz have all published books and encouraged me directly and by example. Other staffers, past and present, who have acted as sounding boards and morale officers include Howard Pousner, Susan Puckett, Ralph Ellis, Michelle Hiskey, and Eileen Drennen.

The newspaper story that contained the kernel of this book was edited by Diane Lore and Jan Winburn. I'll never forget walking around Centennial Olympic Park in downtown Atlanta one sunny September afternoon as Jan and I talked out the narrative structure. She's pretty good. Our managing editor, Hank Klibanoff, who did a final read on my piece, set a lofty standard for aspiring authors in his newsroom as coauthor of *The Race Beat,* a Pulitzer Prize–winning history of media coverage of the civil rights movement.

I'd like to thank a couple of my historian friends: Clifford Kuhn of Georgia State University, who knows volumes about Sumter County and conducted some of the oral histories I consulted; and Steve Oney, author of *And the Dead Shall Rise,* about the Leo Frank case, who listened to my outpourings and said, "You have a book there."

Several archives and libraries were essential to my work. Thanks to Kathy Shoemaker at Emory University's Manuscript, Archives, and Rare Book Library; to the staffs at the University of Georgia's Hargrett Rare Book and Manuscript Library, the University of Tennessee's Hodges Library, and the National Archives in Morrow, Georgia; to Ru Story-Huffman at the James Earl Carter Library at Georgia Southwestern State University;

and to Jill Dalton Kloberdanz at the Lake Blackshear Regional Library in Americus.

I'd also like to thank my agent, David Black, who helped me learn the difference between long-form newspaper writing and doing a book. David's reputation for ushering journalists through that transition is well deserved. My editor at PublicAffairs, Benjamin Adams, took it from there. Ben even stopped by Atlanta on his way back from a family trip in Florida and spent two days hashing out the book with me, at a time when I really needed that kind of interaction. We talked a little baseball, too.

Finally, I'd like to thank my wife, Pamela Brown Auchmutey, a fine editor and writer herself, who kept her day job at Emory University so I could leave the newspaper after twenty-nine years to undertake projects such as this one. That's love.

Jim Auchmutey
September 2014

NOTES

THE PRINCIPAL SOURCE FOR THIS BOOK IS ITS MAIN CHARACTER, GREG Wittkamper, whom I have interviewed for many hours at his home in West Virginia and during visits to see other Koinonia alumni in Florida, Illinois, North Carolina, Rhode Island, and, of course, Georgia. We've gone back to Americus together five times. The story is much broader than Greg's experiences, however, and there were many other sources of information that helped fill in the narrative.

PROLOGUE

"Negroes Quietly Enter AHS Today," read the small headline at the bottom of the front page of the *Americus Times-Recorder* on August 31, 1964. A more accurate picture of the desegregation of Americus High came from interviews with Greg and the first black students: David Bell, Robertiena Freeman, Dobbs Wiggins, and Jewel Wise. Greg kept the letters he received from his former classmates before their 2006 reunion and cherishes them. Some of them are so eloquent they make *me* want to cry.

CHAPTER 1: FARMING FOR JESUS

The Wittkamper family's story is based on interviews with Greg and his brothers Bill, Dan, and David and on an oral history that their mother, Margaret, did in 1987. I learned much about the family's background from Ferrill Wittkamper, a cousin of Greg's who lives in Indiana near the farm where Greg's father grew up. He still had the letters Will Wittkamper had written him during World War II, trying to persuade him to become a conscientious objector.

There have been half a dozen books and at least that many dissertations done about Koinonia and Clarence Jordan. The most comprehensive ones are Tracy Elaine K'Meyer's *The Story of Koinonia Farm* and Dallas Lee's *The Cotton Patch Evidence*. K'Meyer is an academic historian whose book started as a dissertation and is particularly detailed about the inner workings of the commune. Lee was a journalist and had the advantage of living at the farm and interviewing Jordan before his death in 1969—hence his colorful portrait of the man. Jordan told Koinonia's story in numerous speeches, articles, and interviews, and I read as many of them as I could run down at the farm's archives and in the Clarence Jordan Papers at the University of Georgia's Hargrett Library. Conrad Browne, whose family lived at the farm from 1949 to 1963, described Koinonia's early days in our interviews. He also started a memoir and shared what he had finished of that manuscript.

For context about intentional communities such as Koinonia, I consulted Timothy Miller's *The Quest for Utopia in Twentieth-Century America* and William Hedgepeth and Dennis Stock's *The Alternative: Communal Life in New America,* for which they visited Koinonia shortly before Jordan died. They must have been impressed; they dedicated the book to him.

CHAPTER 2: "WE MADE OUR REALITY"

Americus was founded in 1832, a few years after the Muscogee Creeks ceded the territory to the state of Georgia. (That was the tribe that left the arrowheads Greg collected as a boy.) The town fathers literally pulled the name out of a hat full of suggestions. Americus is the male form of America, itself a feminized tribute to the Italian explorer Amerigo Vespucci.

My main sources for learning about Americus were William Bailey Williford's *Americus Through the Years,* a 1975 history that deals forthrightly with Koinonia and the civil rights traumas; and several books by Alan Anderson, an Americus historian who has written a history column in the *Times-Recorder* for years. Thanks to Anderson, I learned that "Shoeless Joe" Jackson played minor league baseball in Americus not long after he had been banned from the majors for his part in the conspiracy to fix the 1919 World Series—a different sort of outcast.

My understanding of what it was like to grow up at Koinonia during the 1950s and early '60s was based on my interviews with members of the Browne, Jordan, and Wittkamper families, and on the Lee and K'Meyer histories of the farm. I also consulted oral histories Koinonia has posted on its website. Another useful source of information came in the mail when Lora Browne sent me seven cassette tapes of reminiscences her parents had recorded in the early 1970s. I wish I could have met her mother, Ora—she sounds like a pistol. It was Lora who related the details of the visit to her friend's house and of the ensuing debate over what the Bible says about black people.

The section about Koinonia and its pacifist convictions was informed by my conversations with Conrad Browne and the Browne and Jordan offspring. Greg and his brothers described their father's devotion to nonviolence—and how it didn't extend to the unwanted farm animals that he coolly dispatched. It's worth noting that the denomination that ordained him, the Christian Church (Disciples of

Christ), gives a Will Wittkamper Peace Award every two years to a person who has worked for peace and justice.

CHAPTER 3: TERROR IN THE NIGHT

Ralph McGill's column anticipating the Supreme Court decision on public school segregation appeared in the *Atlanta Constitution* on April 9, 1953—more than a year before *Brown v. Board of Education of Topeka*. He prophesied that the court would outlaw racially separate schools, but that it would be years before the changes would actually come to pass. Wise man. The *Times-Recorder* published several pieces reacting to the ruling during the week of May 17, 1954.

The event that provoked the terror campaign against Koinonia—Clarence Jordan's endorsement of black students attempting to enroll at the Georgia State College of Business—made the front page of the *Times-Recorder* on March 24, 1956. An accompanying box showed his photo and pointed out that the commune was on the Dawson road. More than a year of vandalism and violence followed, much of it covered in the local newspaper, all of it recorded in great detail in the monthly (more or less) newsletter Koinonia sent to its supporters across the country. Jordan spoke and wrote about the farm's persecution many times. I found two examples very useful: "Christian Community in the South," an article he did for *The Journal of Religious Thought* in its autumn–winter 1956–1957 issue; and a talk he gave in November 1956 at the Fellowship House in Cincinnati. I found the 46-minute audio on YouTube under the title "Clarence Jordan Tells the Koinonia Story." It provides a vivid example of his humor and heartfelt emotion—and his accent. If the man sounded any more southern, you could pour it over pecan waffles.

Sumter County's efforts to shut down the interracial summer camp for children at Koinonia are detailed in Lee's and K'Meyer's books. The farm took out three ads in the *Times-Recorder* during the summer of 1956, responding to the first bombing of its roadside market and trying to explain the community to its neighbors (July 24, July 31, and August 8). The economic boycott against Koinonia is documented in its archives and in the Jordan Papers at the University of Georgia. In December 1959, the commune made one last effort to reach out to local businesses, sending them letters asking to meet about their differences. One of the few replies came from an executive with the Citizens Bank: "On July 6, 1957, we wrote you as follows: 'We prefer not to accept any further deposits from your Corporation and if tendered, they will be declined.' That is still our attitude, and we do not see where any change could come from any conference with you." Conrad Browne, who was in charge of the farm's egg marketing, gave me an eyewitness view of the way that business and others dried up.

The relationship between Koinonia and Jimmy and Rosalynn Carter was examined several times after he rose to political prominence, most memorably in an article that accompanied the November 1976 *Playboy* interview that became infamous for Carter's admission that he had "lusted" in his heart for other women ("Jimmy, We Hardly Know Y'all," by Robert Scheer). In my interviews with the Carters, they were mystified as to why Florence Jordan told Scheer that she had never met them. When I interviewed Mrs. Jordan during my first visit to Koinonia, a couple of weeks before Carter lost his reelection bid in the fall of 1980, she had softened her tone toward the first couple. Carter's White House chief of staff, Hamilton Jordan, devoted twenty-five pages to his Uncle Clarence in his book *No Such Thing as a Bad Day,* holding him and Koinonia up as profiles in courage.

The violence against Koinonia was widely publicized. One of the best overviews ran in *Redbook,* which was more of a general-interest magazine in those days ("The Conflict of a Southern Town," October 1957). The five-page spread featured a haunting photo of Florence Jordan peering into an oval mirror that had been cracked by one of the bullets intended for her husband, which just missed their oldest daughter. When I visited Koinonia more than twenty years later, you could still see bullet holes in some of the wood-frame buildings.

Koinonia's plight drew comment from several prominent Americans. Reinhold Niebuhr's editorial about the situation appeared in the May 7, 1957, issue of the Evangelical and Reformed Church's publication *The Messenger.* Eleanor Roosevelt's plea for Koinonia ran on July 31, 1958, in her syndicated column "My Day." (She later wrote a letter on behalf of the farm to the US Department of Agriculture.) Dorothy Day's account of her trip to Koinonia during the terror time appeared in the May 1957 *Catholic Worker.* One person who read the article and remarked on it was Flannery O'Connor. While she admired Day, the Georgia writer confided in a letter collected in *The Habit of Being: Letters of Flannery O'Connor* that she was dubious about the wisdom of someone riding a bus from New York to share in the sufferings of a group of southerners: "All my thoughts on this subject are ugly and uncharitable—such as: that's a mighty long way to come to get shot at, etc."

The letter I quoted from Martin Luther King Jr. to Clarence Jordan is dated February 10, 1957, and appears in volume IV of *The Papers of Martin Luther King, Jr.* Jordan spoke at King's church in Montgomery a little more than a year later; Jan Jordan remembered going to his house afterward for dinner.

A reporter for the *Times-Recorder* witnessed the motorcade of Klansmen who drove to Koinonia on February 24, 1957, to demand that it sell out and move. (Margaret Wittkamper also recounted the scene in her oral history.) The grand jury presentment attacking the commune ran in the newspaper on April 5, 1957. The bombing of the feed store that had been selling supplies to the farm was reported in large headlines on the front page of May 20, 1957. On the following Sunday, May 26, a group of Americus leaders met with Koinonia partners to propose that the farm relocate. We know exactly how it went because the session was tape-recorded. As the transcript in the Koinonia archives shows, the discussion got testy at times. When one of the Americus delegation suggested that 99 percent of the people in Sumter County wanted Koinonia to leave, Ora Browne asked whether he was including the slight majority of the population that was black, "or just the white people?"

Clarence Jordan's reflections on whether Koinonians were serving any purpose in letting people ride by and shoot at them appeared in *Faith at Work* magazine (April 1970), in a Q&A titled "The Legacy of Clarence Jordan: His Final Interview."

CHAPTER 4: THE CHILDREN'S HOUR

The lawsuit Koinonia parents filed to get their children into the Americus schools was covered in the Atlanta and Americus newspapers. Transcripts of the federal court hearing on the case—*William Wittkamper et al. v. James Harvey et al. and the School Board of Americus, Georgia*—are at the National Archives regional repository outside Atlanta, in Morrow.

My account of the hostility Lora Browne, Jan Jordan, and Billy Wittkamper faced at Americus High is based mostly on my interviews with them. Greg and Carol Browne detailed the harassment they encountered when they started at the school the following year. Greg's classmates Deanie Dudley, Celia Harvey, Joseph Logan, and David Morgan shed light on how he was viewed by the student body.

Margaret Wittkamper's oral history was a good source of information about her family's year away from Koinonia in North Dakota, as were my conversations with Greg and David Wittkamper. The changes at Koinonia when they returned are outlined in Lee's and K'Meyer's books. Almost fifty years later, Conrad Browne still found it hard to talk about his family having to leave the community.

A word about Clarence Jordan's "Cotton Patch Gospels," his translations of much of the New Testament into the common language of the South: they're wonderful—funny, folksy, pointed. To give a sample, here's his introduction of John the Baptist from Matthew 3:4: "This guy John was dressed in blue jeans and a leather jacket, and he was living on cornbread and collard greens. Folks were coming to him from Atlanta and all over north Georgia and the backwater of the Chattahoochee. And as they owned up to their crooked ways, he dipped them in the Chattahoochee." Jordan's writings inspired an off-Broadway play in 1981, *Cotton Patch Gospel,* by Tom Key and Russell Treyz, with music by Harry Chapin. I've seen it performed several times, none more memorably than when Key, a respected Atlanta actor and playwright, delivered an animated solo version at the Clarence Jordan Symposium in Americus in 2012.

CHAPTER 5: WELCOME TO THE REVOLUTION

Greg's pal Collins McGee is well remembered in Americus as a larger-than-life character. Greg, Sam Mahone, and Dobbs Wiggins were my principal sources of information about McGee, who also makes cameo appearances in several Koinonia histories and in the Jordan papers at the University of Georgia.

The Albany Movement is a familiar chapter in accounts of the civil rights era, tucked between the rise of the sit-ins and the riots over desegregation at Ole Miss. I relied on Taylor Branch's and Juan Williams's histories for an overview and on memoirs by Ralph David Abernathy and Andrew Young for particulars about Martin Luther King Jr.'s stay in the Sumter County jail. Young wrote that when he first met Jimmy Carter a few years later and heard him refer to Sheriff Chappell as a friend, it took him some time to form a better opinion of Carter. King made his remark about the sheriff being "the meanest man in the world" to a reporter for *Jet* magazine (January 4, 1962).

One of the best sources for understanding Koinonia's involvement in the civil rights movement is "Six Years Behind the Magnolia Curtain," an unpublished memoir by Dorothy Swisshelm, a social worker who lived at Koinonia and briefly shared quarters with Greg after his family had departed for North Dakota. Lora Browne kept a journal during those years that captures the youthful idealism of the Koinonia kids and the spirit of the mass meetings she attended. Vincent Harding, the Mennonite clergyman who set up the meeting between King and Clarence Jordan, recollected that encounter for me.

I spoke with three SNCC veterans about the spread of the movement to Americus: Sam Mahone, Don Harris, and John Perdew (whose memoir, *The Education of a Harvard Guy*, described the orientation session at Koinonia and his later jailing on insurrection charges). Zev Aelony, one of the other Americus Four arrested for fomenting revolution, wrote about his time at Koinonia in his alumni magazine at the University of Minnesota. He also discussed his experiences for the Freedom Riders 40th Anniversary Oral History Project at the University of Mississippi. (Aelony was a freedom rider, too—he got around.)

The story of the Leesburg Stockade—the extended jailing of almost three dozen girls arrested during protests in Americus—was the subject of a powerful article in *Essence* magazine by Donna M. Owens ("Stolen Girls," June 2006). I've interviewed several of the young women who were held in the stockade, including Robertiena Freeman, who later desegregated Americus High School. SNCC photographer Danny Lyon, who sneaked into the stockade and documented the awful conditions, has a chapter on Leesburg in his book *Memories of the Southern Civil Rights Movement*.

Claude Sitton's article summarizing the first months of protest and white resistance in Sumter County ran in the *New York Times* on September 29, 1963 ("Strict Law Enforcement Stifles Negroes' Drive in Americus, Ga"). The businessman who blamed all the unrest on Koinonia, it's worth noting, was also the foreman of the 1957 grand jury that investigated and condemned the farm.

CHAPTER 6: "NOT IN MY TOWN"

Greg and David Wittkamper told me about their experiences during the 1963–1964 school term, including the afternoon of the Kennedy assassination. The fire that destroyed most of Americus High on January 26, 1964, was covered exhaustively in the *Times-Recorder* and in the AHS newspaper, the *Paw Print*. David Morgan still had the February 3 issue, headlined: "A Lovely Day, Then—Tragedy." The old school was indeed a handsome building.

Jan Jordan described the punishment of one of her tormentors in speech class in an article she wrote for *Faith at Work* magazine (May–June 1965). Lora Browne had a similar experience in Mrs. Fennessy's class. Apparently, the lady didn't take any mess. (There were other teachers at Americus High who kept discipline; Robertiena Freeman recalled that Jimmy Hightower, the football coach, told his students that no one was going to harass anyone in his class, whatever they thought about the changes at their school. She appreciated his stand, although some of his players were among the worst harassers.) My account of Jan Jordan's graduation day came from her and from a letter her father wrote to the school superintendent later that summer (in the Jordan papers at the University of Georgia).

The panel that held hearings about school desegregation in Georgia was the Sibley Commission, named for its chairman, Atlanta lawyer John A. Sibley. His papers are at the Emory University Manuscript and Rare Book Library and include voluminous records of the commission's public forums in ten cities around the state. The first hearing was held in Americus on March 3, 1960. Warren Fortson told me the behind-the-scenes story of the desegregation of Americus High. John Perdew also contributed pertinent recollections. Robertiena Freeman, David Bell, Dobbs Wiggins, and Jewel Wise filled me in on how they came to enter the formerly white school.

CHAPTER 7: AMONG PANTHERS

My reconstruction of the first days of desegregation at the high school are based on news accounts and on my interviews with the participants. Each of the black students also wrote contemporary first-person pieces about their experiences for the civil rights newsletter *Voice of Americus*.

While there weren't as many protests in Americus during 1964, there were several outbreaks of racial violence after the passage of the civil rights act outlawing segregation in most public places. In his memoir, John Perdew told of his beating after he and several black people sat down at the Hasty House café. Homer Bigart of the *New York Times* reported on the tense mood of the city in an article on July 9, 1964: "White gangs, consisting mostly of teen-agers, foray nightly into the Negro residential district. Their object is to frighten Negroes from any further testing of the new liberties they may enjoy under the Civil Rights Act. Racing down the red clay roads, carloads of youths in battered automobiles pepper Negro homes with birdshot, firecrackers and rocks."

Years before I began this book, I had the pleasure of writing about Frances Pauley, a remarkable woman who worked for social change as executive director of the Georgia Council on Human Relations. She died in 2003, but through her papers at Emory University, I was able to read her reports about compliance with the civil rights law and about the progress of school desegregation across the state. She knew Americus well. Kathryn L. Nasstrom's biography, *Everybody's Grandmother and Nobody's Fool*, makes it clear that Pauley considered Sumter County one of her toughest nuts to crack.

CHAPTER 8: STILL STANDING

My account of the confrontation behind the baseball grandstand—and the events surrounding it—was based on interviews with Greg, Gladys Crabb, David Morgan, and Joseph Logan, whose written reconstruction of the scene in his 2006 letter to Greg was also helpful.

CHAPTER 9: A LESSON BEFORE LEAVING

Andy Worthy's suicide made the front page of the *Times-Recorder* on January 8, 1965. He was not the only member of the senior class to die that year; another boy perished in a plane crash later that spring.

Donnie Smith discussed his senior English paper about Greg during a taped interview at the class reunion in 2006. His classmates thought his choice of subject was the desperate act of a desperate student. The *Southern Patriot*, an education newsletter, ran an article about Greg in its November 1965 issue under the headline: "One Student Who 'Overcame.'"

The story of Robertiena Freeman's legal ordeal is based on interviews with her and her lawyer, Warren Fortson; on an oral history she did for the Sumter County Oral History Project at Georgia Southwestern State University; and on a case summary done by Frances Pauley for the Georgia Council on Human Relations.

The Americus High commencement was covered in the *Times-Recorder* (June 8, 1965) in a story that took note of the weather, the number of people in attendance, and the songs that were part of the ceremony—which is how I knew that they sang "You'll Never Walk Alone." I love small-town newspapers.

CHAPTER 10: THE NEXT SELMA

The election-day arrests that provoked the protests of 1965 in Americus were covered in the local, regional, and national media. My account was based on those reports; on retellings in Stephen G. N. Tuck's *Beyond Atlanta* and Laughlin McDonald's *A Voting Rights Odyssey*; and on an interview with the candidate who was arrested, Mary Kate Bell Tyner. I also heard her speak about that day during a panel discussion at Georgia Southwestern State University that included one of her poll watchers in 1965, Lena Turner-Fulton.

The near-fatal beating of Hosea Williams in Americus during the 1940s is mentioned in many articles about him, including his obituary in the *Atlanta Journal-Constitution* (November 17, 2000). The Atlanta papers wrote numerous stories about the turmoil in Americus during the summer of 1965. So did the *Times-Recorder*, which had virtually ignored the protests of 1963, no doubt reflecting the town leadership's wish that the movement would just go away. Willy Siegel Leventhal, a California college student who worked in Sumter County as a volunteer with the SCLC's SCOPE project, published a helpful book about that initiative and the strife he encountered in southwest Georgia, *The Scope of Freedom*. Warren Fortson told me about his ill-fated efforts to foster a dialogue between the races in Americus.

Greg's classmate Joseph Logan was remarkably candid about what he saw and felt and almost did during the disturbances of 1965. In some of the news photos, a line of young men can be seen standing atop the steps at First Methodist Church, ready to repel any unwelcome visitors—the same duty Joseph was drafted for. The efforts to desegregate the churches also figure in the memoirs of one of the men who was arrested, now Congressman John Lewis (*Walking with the Wind*). That was his ticket to jail in Americus.

The killing of Andy Whatley and the unrest that followed made national news and brought a new level of media scrutiny to Americus. Among the accounts I found particularly useful were ones in the *New York Times* (July 29, 1965), the *Los Angeles Times* (July 31), and the *Baltimore Afro-American* (July 31). I called Tom Brokaw because I had read that he regarded his brief conversation with a young protester in Americus in 1965 as perhaps the most memorable interview he had ever done. Some of the footage shot for his reports on WSB-TV in Atlanta and NBC can be viewed at the University of Georgia's Civil Rights Digital Library.

Warren Fortson's last, troubled days in Americus attracted the attention of two great journalists. Ralph McGill wrote a column about him leaving town in the *Atlanta Constitution* on September 16, 1965. Marshall Frady covered his tribulations for *Newsweek* and *Atlanta* magazine and included a profile of Fortson in his collection *Southerners* ("What Happened That Summer to Warren Fortson"). Frady found a lot of material in Americus. In the Newsweek Atlanta Bureau records at Emory University, there's a draft of a story he wrote after the Whatley killing that begins: "In the South's gazetteer of racial crucibles, the name Americus has a special viciousness all its own." And this description of Sheriff Chappell: "looks rather like a florid Boston terrier in glasses." Frady returned to Sumter County a few years later and wrote a kinder story about integration at Americus High for *Life* magazine ("A Meeting of Strangers in Americus," February 12, 1971).

CHAPTER 11: BREAKING AWAY

The story of Greg's singular college education comes from my conversations with him and from literature in his possession about the founding of Friends World College and the book donation campaign that paid for his tuition. The college is now known as LIU Global—part of Long Island University—whose website relates its roots in the Quaker tradition during the 1960s.

The account of Millard and Linda Fuller's arrival at Koinonia is based on interviews with them and on Lee's and K'Meyer's books about Koinonia, as well as on several histories of Habitat for Humanity. When I first interviewed Millard in 1987, he told me about the night he and the party from Koinonia were thrown out of First Baptist Church in Americus. When Greg told me the same story some twenty years later, from a slightly different perspective, I experienced a powerful feeling of déjà vu.

My telling of the James Meredith march was drawn from Taylor Branch's *At Canaan's Edge*, Aram Goudsouzian's *Down to the Crossroads*, and "The Meredith March," an article in *New South* magazine (summer 1966), in which writer Paul Good reported seeing a Mississippi state trooper threatening Morris Mitchell, the Friends World director.

The section about Greg's return to America and Americus was gleaned from my interviews with him and his brothers and from his mother's oral history.

The death of Clarence Jordan figures large in Lee's *The Cotton Patch Evidence*. Millard Fuller was codirector of the community then and told me about the hassles of dealing with the local authorities after the death. Jordan's passing was front-page news in the *Times-Recorder* and rated an obituary in the *New York Times* (October 31, 1969). The cabin study where he died has been preserved as a shrine—"Clarence's Shack," the sign calls it—where visitors to Koinonia can see his manual typewriter and his little desk.

CHAPTER 12: GROWING UP

The stories of Greg's classmates and how their attitudes changed after high school come from my interviews with them.

CHAPTER 13: ALMOST HEAVEN

My account of Greg's life after college is based on conversations with him, his brothers, Charles Browne, Carol Browne, and Greg's wife, Anne Gardner.

CHAPTER 14: GUILT AND GRACE

The story of the class members' decision to reconcile with Greg is based on interviews with David Morgan, Deanie Dudley Fricks, Joseph Logan, Celia Harvey Gonzalez, and Gladys Crabb. Deanie later told me about the Holocaust memoir by her friend Samuel Althaus that was fresh in her mind when she sat down to write Greg. I read the book and could understand why it moved her.

CHAPTER 15: BACK TO AMERICUS

I did not witness the class reunion in June 2006; I didn't even learn about it until a month or so after it had happened. Fortunately, I was able to view many of the weekend's events through the eyes of Faith Fuller, Millard and Linda's filmmaker daughter, who videotaped the lunch at Mrs. Crabb's house, the opening reception, and the reunion itself on the following evening. Faith generously shared a copy of her video with me; it was the next best thing to being there. (She included some of the footage in an epilogue for the tenth anniversary reissue of her 2003 documentary about Koinonia, *Briars in the Cotton Patch*.) My re-creation of the reunion was informed by interviews with the participants and by Greg's wife, Anne, who provided insightful narration from an outsider's perspective.

EPILOGUE

I accompanied Greg in August 2013 as he stepped back inside his high school for the first time in forty-eight years. I was with him during commemorations of the Sumter County Movement that year and in 2007, when we went to dinner with three of the students who had desegregated Americus High. We later visited the fourth one, Robertiena Freeman Fletcher, at her home in Perry, Georgia.

Greg and I also traveled to Americus for two Koinonia observances in 2012: the Clarence Jordan Symposium at Georgia Southwestern State University and a Koinonia family reunion later that autumn at the farm. We visited the Wittkamper House where his family used to live, climbed Picnic Hill where Clarence Jordan and Millard Fuller are buried, and walked the grounds where Greg and the other children were shot at while they were playing volleyball. As we were driving back to the farm one night after dark, a pair of headlights appeared in the rearview mirror and started drawing closer. "You might want to step on it," Greg said. "That could be the sheriff following us." I glanced toward the passenger seat and saw that he was smiling. There was a time when such things would not have been a joking matter.

SELECTED BIBLIOGRAPHY

Abernathy, Ralph David. *And the Walls Came Tumbling Down: An Autobiography.* New York: Harper & Row, 1989.

Althaus, Samuel. *Where Is God? Auschwitz-Birkenau to Dachau, 1942–1945.* Newport News, VA: self-published, 2000.

Anderson, Alan. *A Journey of Grace: A History of the First Baptist Church of Americus, Georgia.* Americus, GA: First Baptist Church, 2006.

———. *Remembering Americus, Georgia: Essays in Southern Life.* Charleston, SC: History Press, 2006.

Barnette, Henlee H. *Clarence Jordan: Turning Dreams into Deeds.* Macon, GA: Smyth & Helwys Publishing, 1992.

Berg, A. Scott. *Lindbergh.* New York: G. P. Putnam's Sons, 1998.

Branch, Taylor. *At Canaan's Edge: America in the King Years, 1965–68.* New York: Simon & Schuster, 2006.

———. *Parting the Waters: America in the King Years, 1954–63.* New York: Simon & Schuster, 1988.

———. *Pillar of Fire: America in the King Years, 1963–65.* New York: Simon & Schuster, 1998.

Brinkley, Douglas. *The Unfinished Presidency: Jimmy Carter's Journey Beyond the White House.* New York: Penguin, 1998.

Brokaw, Tom. *Boom!: Voices of the Sixties; Personal Reflections on the '60s and Today.* New York: Random House, 2007.

Bryan, G. McLeod. *These Few Also Paid a Price: Southern Whites Who Fought for Civil Rights.* Macon, GA: Mercer University Press, 2001.

Carson, Clayborne, ed. With the staff of the Martin Luther King, Jr. Papers Project. *The Student Voice, 1960–1965: Periodical of the Student Nonviolent Coordinating Committee.* Westport, CT: Meckler, 1990.

Carson, Clayborne, Susan Carson, Adrienne Clay, Virginia Shadron, and Kerry Taylor, eds. *The Papers of Martin Luther King, Jr.* Vol. 4, *A Symbol of the Movement, January 1957–December 1958.* Berkeley: University of California Press, 2000.

Carson, Clayborne, David J. Garrow, Bill Kovach, and Carol Polsgrove. *Reporting Civil Rights*. New York: Library of America, 2003.

Carter, Jimmy. *An Hour Before Daylight: Memories of a Rural Boyhood*. New York: Simon & Schuster, 2001.

———. *Turning Point: A Candidate, a State, and a Nation Come of Age*. New York: Times Books, 1992.

Coble, Ann Louise. *Cotton Patch for a Kingdom: Clarence Jordan's Demonstration Plot at Koinonia Farm*. Scottdale, PA: Herald Press, 2001.

Dittmer, John. *Black Georgia in the Progressive Era, 1900–1920*. Urbana: University of Illinois Press, 1977.

Egerton, John. *Speak Now Against the Day: The Generation Before the Civil Rights Movement in the South*. New York: Alfred A. Knopf, 1994.

Frady, Marshall. *Southerners: A Journalist's Odyssey*. New York: New American Library, 1980.

Fuller, Chet. *I Hear Them Calling My Name: A Journey Through the New South*. Boston: Houghton Mifflin, 1981.

Gaillard, Frye. *If I Were a Carpenter: Twenty Years of Habitat for Humanity*. Winston-Salem, NC: John F. Blair, 1996.

Garrow, David J. *Bearing the Cross: Martin Luther King Jr. and the Southern Christian Leadership Conference*. New York: William Morrow and Co., 1986.

Godbold, E. Stanley Jr. *Jimmy and Rosalynn Carter: The Georgia Years, 1924–1974*. Oxford, UK: Oxford University Press, 2010.

Goudsouzian, Aram. *Down to the Crossroads: Civil Rights, Black Power, and the Meredith March Against Fear*. New York: Farrar, Straus and Giroux, 2014.

Grant, Daniel T. *When the Melon Is Ripe: The Autobiography of a Georgia Negro High School Principal and Minister*. New York: Exposition Press, 1955.

Hedgepeth, William, and Dennis Stock. *The Alternative: Communal Life in New America*. New York: Macmillan, 1970.

Inscoe, John C., ed. *Georgia in Black and White: Explorations in the Race Relations of a Southern State, 1865–1950*. Athens: University of Georgia Press, 1994.

Jordan, Clarence L. *Clarence Jordan: Essential Writings*. Edited by Joyce Hollyday. Maryknoll, NY: Orbis Books, 2003.

———. *The Substance of Faith: And Other Cotton Patch Sermons*. Edited by Dallas Lee. Eugene, OR: Cascade Books, 2005.

Jordan, Hamilton. *No Such Thing as a Bad Day*. Atlanta, GA: Longstreet Press, 2000.

K'Meyer, Tracy Elaine. *The Story of Koinonia Farm: Interracialism and Christian Community in the Postwar South*. Charlottesville: University Press of Virginia, 1997.

Lee, Dallas. *The Cotton Patch Evidence: The Story of Clarence Jordan and the Koinonia Farm Experiment (1942–1970)*. New York: Harper & Row, 1971.

Leventhal, Willy Siegel. *The Scope of Freedom: The Leadership of Hosea Williams with Dr. King's Summer '65 Volunteers*. Montgomery, AL: Challenge Press, 2005.

Lewis, John, and Michael D'Orso. *Walking with the Wind: A Memoir of the Movement*. New York: Simon & Schuster, 1998.

Lyman-Barner, Kirk, and Cori Lyman-Barner, eds. *Fruits of the Cotton Patch: The Clarence Jordan Symposium 2012*. Vol. 2. Eugene, OR: Cascade Books, 2014.

———. *Roots in the Cotton Patch: The Clarence Jordan Symposium 2012*. Vol. 1. Eugene, OR: Cascade Books, 2014.

Lyon, Danny. *Memories of the Southern Civil Rights Movement*. Chapel Hill: University of North Carolina Press, 1992.

Margolis, Jon. *The Last Innocent Year: America in 1964, the Beginning of the "Sixties."* New York: William Morrow and Co., 1999.

May, Gary. *Bending Toward Justice: The Voting Rights Act and the Transformation of American Democracy*. New York: Basic Books, 2013.

McDonald, Laughlin. *A Voting Rights Odyssey: Black Enfranchisement in Georgia*. Cambridge, UK: Cambridge University Press, 2003.

McGill, Ralph. *The South and the Southerner*. Boston: Little, Brown, 1963.

McLaurin, Melton A. *Separate Pasts: Growing Up White in the Segregated South*. Athens: University of Georgia Press, 1987.

Miller, Timothy. *The Quest for Utopia in Twentieth-Century America*. Syracuse, NY: Syracuse University Press, 1998.

Miller, William D. *Dorothy Day: A Biography*. San Francisco: Harper and Row, 1982.

Morris, Kenneth E. *Jimmy Carter: American Moralist*. Athens: University of Georgia Press, 1996.

Nasstrom, Kathryn L. *Everybody's Grandmother and Nobody's Fool: Frances Freeborn Pauley and the Struggle for Social Justice*. Ithaca, NY: Cornell University Press, 2000.

Perdew, John. *The Education of a Harvard Guy*. Jonesboro, AR: GrantHouse, 2010.

Roberts, Gene, and Hank Klibanoff. *The Race Beat: The Press, the Civil Rights Struggle, and the Awakening of a Nation*. New York: Alfred A. Knopf, 2006.

Sams, Ferrol. *The Whisper of the River*. Atlanta, GA: Peachtree Publishers, 1984.

Sokol, Jason. *There Goes My Everything: White Southerners in the Age of Civil Rights, 1945–1975*. New York: Alfred A. Knopf, 2006.

Stoper, Emily. *The Student Nonviolent Coordinating Committee: The Growth of Radicalism in a Civil Rights Organization*. Brooklyn, NY: Carlson, 1989.

Talmadge, Herman E. *You and Segregation*. Birmingham, AL: Vulcan Press, 1955.

Teel, Leonard Ray. *Ralph Emerson McGill: Voice of the Southern Conscience*. Knoxville: University of Tennessee Press, 2001.

Trillin, Calvin. *An Education in Georgia: Charlayne Hunter, Hamilton Holmes, and the Integration of the University of Georgia*. Athens: Brown Thrasher Books/University of Georgia Press, 1991.

Tuck, Stephen G. N. *Beyond Atlanta: The Struggle for Racial Equality in Georgia, 1940–1980*. Athens: University of Georgia Press, 2001.

United States Commission on Civil Rights. *Survey of School Desegregation in the Southern and Border States, 1965–66*. Washington, DC: US Government Printing Office, 1966.

Warren, Robert Penn. *Segregation: The Inner Conflict in the South*. New York: Random House, 1956.

Williams, Juan. *Eyes on the Prize: America's Civil Rights Years, 1954–65.* New York: Viking Press, 1987.

Williford, William Bailey. *Americus Through the Years: The Story of a Georgia Town and Its People, 1832–1975.* Atlanta, GA: Cherokee, 1975.

Wills, Gary. *Lead Time: A Journalist's Education.* New York: Doubleday, 1983.

Young, Andrew. *An Easy Burden: The Civil Rights Movement and the Transformation of America.* New York: HarperCollins, 1996.

Youngs, Bettie B. *The House That Love Built: The Story of Millard and Linda Fuller, Founders of Habitat for Humanity and the Fuller Center for Housing.* Charlottesville, VA: Hampton Roads Publishing, 2007.

DISSERTATIONS AND UNPUBLISHED MANUSCRIPTS

Browne, Conrad. Unfinished memoir, loaned to author.

Browne, Lora. Diary and journal, loaned to author.

Chancey, Andrew S. "Race, Religion, and Reform: Koinonia's Challenge to Southern Society, 1942–1992." PhD diss., University of Florida, Gainesville, 1998.

O'Connor, Charles S. "A Rural Georgia Tragedy: Koinonia Farm in the 1950s." MA thesis, University of Georgia, Athens, 2003.

Snider, Joel Philip. "The Cotton Patch Gospel: The Proclamation of Clarence Jordan." PhD diss., Southern Baptist Theological Seminary, Louisville, KY, 1984.

Swisshelm, Dorothy. "Six Years Behind the Magnolia Curtain." Unpublished memoir, Dorothy Swisshelm Papers, Hodges Library, University of Tennessee, 1965.

MANUSCRIPT COLLECTIONS, ORAL HISTORIES, AND OTHER MEDIA

Civil Rights Digital Library. Walter J. Brown Media Archives, University of Georgia, Athens.

Civil Rights Movement Veterans. Website of oral histories, documents, and other materials assembled by Veterans of the Southern Freedom Movement, crmvet .org.

Frady, Marshall, Papers. Manuscript, Archives, and Rare Book Library, Emory University, Atlanta, GA.

Fuller, Faith. *Briars in the Cotton Patch: The Story of Koinonia Farm.* Script by Michael Booth and Faith Fuller. Cotton Patch Productions, 2003. Documentary film, 58 min.

Jamison, Gayla. *Enough to Share: A Portrait of Koinonia Farm.* Ideas and Images, Atlanta, GA, 1983. Documentary film, 16 mm, 28 min.

Jordan, Clarence L. "Clarence Jordan Tells the Koinonia Story." Cotton Patch Productions, uploaded to YouTube, 2011. Audiotape of a speech Jordan gave in Cincinnati, November 10, 1956, 46 min.

Jordan, Clarence L., Papers. Hargrett Rare Book and Manuscript Library, University of Georgia, Athens.

Koinonia Archives. Koinonia Partners, Americus, GA.

New Georgia Encyclopedia. Online reference by the Georgia Humanities Council in partnership with the University of Georgia Press, www.georgiaencyclopedia .org.

Newsweek Atlanta Bureau records. Manuscript, Archives, and Rare Book Library, Emory University, Atlanta, GA.

Pauley, Frances, Papers. Manuscript, Archives, and Rare Book Library, Emory University, Atlanta, GA.

Sibley, John A., Papers. Manuscript, Archives, and Rare Book Library, Emory University, Atlanta, GA.

Sitton, Claude, Papers. Manuscript, Archives, and Rare Book Library, Emory University, Atlanta, GA.

Sumter County Oral History Project. Thomas Cheokas Collection, James Earl Carter Library, Georgia Southwestern State University, Americus.

Swisshelm, Dorothy, Papers. Hodges Library, University of Tennessee, Knoxville.

William Wittkamper, et. al. v. James Harvey, et. al. and the School Board of Americus, Georgia. US District Court for the Americus Division of the Middle District of Georgia, National Archives at Atlanta, Morrow.

Wittkamper, Margaret. Oral history, in possession of Greg Wittkamper.

INDEX

Abernathy, Ralph David, 77
Aelony, Zev, 84–85, 88
African tour, 158–159
Albany Movement, 76–77, 95
Alcohol use, 75, 128, 163
All in the Family (television program), 171
Allen, Ralph, 84
Althaus, Samuel, 202–203
American Civil Liberties Union, 60–61
Americus Four, 85–87, 95
Americus High School
    ACLU lawsuit, 60–62
    commencement, 132–133
    desegregation, 4–5, 95–98, 101–104
    destruction by fire, 90–91
    Dobbs Wiggins's departure, 110
    football, 68–69
    Greg revisiting, 219–220
    refusal to enroll Koinonia children, 59–61
    students' antipathy to Koinonia community, 67–69
    See also Reunion
Americus-Sumter County Movement Remembered Committee, 220

Angry, Rufus and Sue, 48
Arson, 91
Auburn University, 150–151, 169–170, 172, 179

Barnum, Mabel, 142
Barnum's Funeral Home, 4, 84, 102, 142, 220, 227
Bass, Tommy, 64, 220
Beard, Ellen Marshall, 221–222
Bell, David
    Georgia Council on Human Relations award, 109–110
    integration of Americus High School, 4, 97–98
    leaving Americus High School, 130–131
    reconnecting with Greg, 223–225
Bell, Mary Kate, 139–140, 148
Birdsey, Herbert, 49
Black community
    Collins McGee, 74–76
    Koinonia membership, 29–30, 48
    response to violence against Koinonia, 47
    See also Civil rights movement
Black Power movement, 155–156

Black students
    desegregation of Americus High
        School, 4–5, 101–104
    desegregation of Sumter County
        High School, 163
    exclusion from commencement,
        93–94, 129–130, 132–133
    exclusion from reunions, 229
    Greg reconnecting with, 223–225
    Koinonia's support of, 17
    leaving Americus High School,
        130–131
    reconciliation, 225
    See also Bell, David; Freeman,
        Robertiena; Wiggins, Dobbs;
        Wise, Jewel
Blacklisting of Koinonia, 39–41
Bolden, Willie, 148
Bootle, William, 60–61
Bowen, Shelby Jean Bradley, 205
Boycotts, 39–41, 49, 59–61, 77–78
Brokaw, Tom, 147–148
Brown v. Board of Education of Topeka,
    35–44
Browne, Carol, 65
    expatriate community, 191
    life at Koinonia, 26
    posttraumatic stress, 194–195, 210
Browne, Charlie
    father's beating and arrest, 55
    expatriate community, 191
    marijuana and wine, 188–189
    posttraumatic stress, 191–192
    student violence against, 33–34
    West Virginia community, 187
Browne, Conrad "Con"
    assault on and arrest of, 54–56
    attitudes towards race, 30
    boycott of Koinonia, 40
    demilitarizing Koinonia, 31–33
    establishing Koinonia, 15, 25
    exclusion from Americus church, 25
    leaving Koinonia, 73
    violence against Koinonia, 43
Browne, John, 32–34, 43, 191

Browne, Lora, 63(fig.)
    attitudes towards race, 29–30
    boycott of Koinonia, 40
    civil rights movement, 78, 80–81
    physical attack on, 43–44
    reconciliation and amends, 222
    starting high school, 59
    student hostility towards, 62, 64
    violence against Koinonia, 43
Browne, Ora, 15, 25, 43, 47
Brownell, Herbert, 45
Buddhism, 161

Camp Koinonia, 38, 73
Carmichael, Stokely, 155–156
Carter, Jimmy, 39–40, 149, 226–227
Carter, Lillian, 106
Carter, Rosalynn, 39–40, 106
Chappell, Fred, 5, 42–43, 55, 77, 81,
    84–85, 103, 128, 164, 195
Children of Light, 28
Christian Brotherhood Insurance
    Plan, 47–48
Christian faith. See Religion and
    spirituality
Civil Rights Act (1964), 104
Civil rights movement
    ACLU suit foreshadowing, 61–62
    allegories in film, 125
    Americus Four, 85–87
    Birmingham demonstrations,
        79–80
    black voting rights, 139–141
    changing attitudes of Greg's
        classmates, 175–179
    classroom discussion, 124–125
    desegregation of Americus High
        School, 95–96
    Frances Pauley, 108–109
    Greg's return to Americus, 219–220
    growing rift between blacks and
        white supporters, 155–156
    Kennedy assassination, 89–90
    Koinonia's involvement, 78–79, 80
    nonviolent resistance, 84–86

prompting violence against
Koinonia students, 33–34
Robert L. Freeman's commitment to
change, 98
students' retrospect, 224
Sumter County protest movement,
76–79, 81–84
Civil War, 11, 31, 45, 167–168
Commencement exercises, 93–95,
129–130, 133–134
Communal living
future of Koinonia children, 191
Greg's exploration of European
communities, 184–186
West Virginia, 186–189
Community of the Ark, 184–185
Congress of Racial Equality (CORE),
85
Conscientious objectors, 15, 18–21,
152, 159, 183–184
Corporal punishment, 32–33
Crabb, Gladys, 116(fig.)
curiosity about Koinonia, 125–126
David Morgan and Greg, 197
David's reconnection with, 206
Greg's reunion with, 208–209
reunion weekend, 193, 207
Robertiena and, 228
student composition about Greg, 129
student outreach, 199, 201
violence against Greg, 115–117, 120
Crisp, Charles, 50–51, 96
Crutchfield, Richard, 221

Daniels, Mary Ellen Smith, 205,
208–209
Dating, interracial, 126–128
Day, Dorothy, 47
Dehumanization of people, 203
Democratic Party: backlash from the
Civil Rights Act, 105–106
Desegregation
Americus High School in 1969, 164
Americus High School in 2013,
219–220

Auburn University, 169–170
Civil Rights Act, 104
Collins McGee's exclusion from Jan
Jordan's commencement, 93–95,
129
Freeman's threat of violence, 220–221
Georgia State College of Business, 37
Joseph Logan's students, 170–171
of Protestant churches, 177–179
of Sumter County High School, 163
preparing the students, 4
Robertiena's exposure to violence,
228
Sumter County youth protests
against segregation, 81–84
violence at Americus High School,
101–104
Warren Fortson's transformation,
95–96
Draft resistance, 9–10, 159, 161, 183
Drug Enforcement Agency (DEA), 189
Drug use, 158–160
Dudley, Crawford, 177–178
Dudley, Deanie, 209(fig.), 212(fig.)
apologies and regrets, 6, 197–199,
202–205
personal journey, 176–179
psychology of bigotry, 209–210
regrets, 197–199
shunning Greg, 67, 106–107
the reunion, 208–209

Eisenhower, Dwight, 44–45
England, Mabel, 14–15
England, Martin, 14–15
Entertainment at Koinonia, 27–28,
30–32
Environmentalism, 53–54
European tour, Greg's, 146–149
Eustice, John, 27
Evers, Medgar, 80

Federal marshals, 62, 65
Findhorn community, 185–186
Fire at Americus High School, 90–91

First Baptist Church, 143, 148, 154,
    177
First Methodist Church, 67, 143–144,
    149–150, 168, 177
First Presbyterian Church, 177–178
Fletcher, Jeannie, 205, 214
Football, 68, 169–170, 224–225
Forest River farm, 70–72
Fortson, Warren
    ACLU suit against Americus
        schools, 60–62
    black voting rights, 142, 149
    civil rights protests, 95
    integration hearings, 96–97
    leaving Americus, 149–150
    Robertiena's arrest, 131–132
Frady, Marshall, 150
Freeman, Robert L., 142(fig.)
    background and philosophy, 98
    David Morgan's teaching career, 173
    integration hearings, 96
    Robertiena's arrest, 131–132
    threat of violence, 220–221
Freeman, Robertiena
    amends from classmates, 221–222
    arrest of, 131–132, 227
    desegregation of Americus High
        School, 4, 96–98
    personal and professional
        accomplishments, 227–229
    racism of Americus students, 130
    violence resulting from
        desegregation, 103
Fricks, Bill, 179–180, 197–199, 208
Friends World Institute, 152–156,
    158–162, 165, 183–185, 185(fig.)
Fuller, Faith, 212–213, 215–216
Fuller, Linda, 153, 162, 189–190, 212
Fuller, Millard, 153, 162, 166, 189–190,
    212, 225–226
Fuller Center for Housing, 226
Fund for Humanity, 162–163

Geeslin, Ann, 134
Georgia Council on Human Relations
    award, 108–110, 130

Gonzalez, Ron, 204, 210
Graduation, 129–130, 132–134,
    219–220
Grand jury review of Koinonia, 45–46
Gregory, Dick, 149
Griffin, Marvin, 37
Guns
    protest for black voting rights, 146
    retaliation for Andy Whatley killing,
        147–148
    Robert L. Freeman's temptation to
        resort to, 220–221
    toys at Koinonia, 30–32

Habitat for Humanity, 2, 162–163,
    189–190, 225–226
Harding, Vincent, 79
Harris, Don, 80, 84
Harvey, Celia, 174(fig.)
    apologies, 6, 198–199
    Greg's support for integration, 104
    personal journey, 174–176
    shunning Greg, 67
    the reunion, 210
Harvey, James, 174
Henry, Al, 135
Hispanic Americans, 204
Holocaust, 202–203
Homeschooling, 23, 60
Housing, Fuller Center for, 226
Hutterites, 70–72

Incitement, imprisonment for, 85
Ingram, Rosa Lee, 127
Insurance coverage of Koinonia, 39,
    47–48
Interracial dating and intermarriage,
    126–128, 210

James, Woodrow, 178
Jekyll Island resort, 109–110
John Birch Society, 143, 174
Johnson, Lyndon, 104–106, 140–141
Jordan, Clarence, 12(fig.), 166(fig.)
    ACLU lawsuit against Americus
        schools, 61–62

advocating self-defense, 112–113, 118, 150

blacks' exclusion from Protestant churches, 154

citizens' demand that Koinonia relocate, 52

civil rights meetings, 78–80

community acceptance of Koinonia, 226–227

death of, 165–166, 183

desegregation of Americus schools, 97

entertainment in Koinonia, 27

establishing Koinonia, 11–15, 25

Greg's appeal for books, 153

Habitat for Humanity, 162–163

Jan Jordan's commencement, 93–95

Jimmy Carter and, 39–40

KKK visit to, 16–17

Koinonia's appeal to Eisenhower, 44–45

Koinonia's quasi-capitalistic model, 72–73

police response to shootings, 43

racist violence in church, 17–18

The Whisper of the River, 174

university desegregation, 37

Jordan, Eleanor, 44, 59, 166(fig.)

Jordan, Florence Kroeger, 13–15, 17–18, 25, 166(fig.)

Jordan, Hamilton, 41

Jordan, Jan, 63(fig.)

attitudes towards race, 29

commencement exercises, 92–94, 129

expatriate community, 191

nonviolent protest, 88

protesting segregation in Americus, 83

reconciliation and amends, 222

shooting incident, 194

starting high school, 59

violence against Koinonia students, 62, 64

Jordan, Jim, 59

Jordan, Lenny, 163

Jordan, Thomas "T.J.," 114–116, 119–120, 123, 204, 206, 213

Kaigler, Emmarene, 228

Kennedy, John F., 80, 89–90, 96, 104

Kibbutz living, 186

King, C. B., 78

King, Martin Luther, Jr., 47, 77–79, 149, 155–156, 160–161

Koinonia community

agricultural methods, 15–16

appeal to Eisenhower, 44–45

backlash from *Brown* decision, 37–44, 42(fig.)

black members, 29–30

children's responsibilities, 25–26

citizens' demand for relocation of, 50–52

civil rights movement, 78, 80, 91

classmates' ignorance of, 66

David Morgan's acceptance of, 201

documentary film, 212

etymology and establishment of, 13–15

geography and functioning of, 11–12

Gladys Crabb's interest in, 125–126

Greg's parents' retirement, 189–190

Greg's quest for spirituality, 164–165

Greg's religious background, 9–10

Greg's unresolved pain, 192–193

growing acceptance of, 225–227

growth and development of, 25–29, 162

Habitat for Humanity, 162–163

KKK bombing in Americus, 49–50

pecan production, 54–55

posttraumatic stress in the children, 191–192

Quakers' visit, 152–153

quasi-capitalistic model, 72–73

radical ideas, 12–14

rejection from Americus High School, 59–61

struggle to survive, 70–72

students' antipathy to the community, 67–69

Koinonia community *(continued)*
  Sumter County youth protests
    against segregation, 82–84
  targeted assaults, 54–55
  the Wittkampers' move to, 21–22
  youth protesting segregation in
    Americus, 83–84
  *See also entries beginning with
    Jordan; entries beginning with
    Wittkamper*
Ku Klux Klan
  attack on Koinonia, 38
  bombing of Americus, 49–52
  driving black residents from
    Koinonia, 48
  Koinonia students' classmates, 30
  retaliation for Andy Whatley killing,
    147–148
  threatening Koinonia, 16–17
  violence against supporters of
    Koinonia, 49

Leesburg Stockade, 83, 97, 132
LeVias, Jerry, 170
Lewis, John, 85, 141, 143, 220
Logan, Alonzo Josephus, 167–168
Logan, Joseph, 68(fig.), 212(fig.)
  apologies, 6, 67, 198–199, 204–205,
    212–214
  backlash from the Civil Rights Act,
    105
  football, 68
  Greg's commitment to nonviolence,
    119–120
  ingrained attitudes, 143–144
  personal journey, 167–171
  segregation of Protestant churches,
    143–145
  shunning Greg, 73
  the reunion, 206, 216–217
  violence, 49, 150–151
Lynchings, 43, 145
Lyon, Danny, 83

Maddox, Lester, 149
Maendel, Joe, 70–71

Maendel, Mary, 70–71
Mahone, Sammy, 82–83
Marijuana, 155, 160, 163–164,
    188–189
Martin Theater, Americus, 27, 82–83,
    97, 105
Mathews, George, 51
McGee, Collins, 75(fig.), 127(fig.)
  black voting rights, 145–146
  exclusion from First Baptist Church,
    154
  exclusion from Jan Jordan's
    commencement, 93–95, 129
  Greg's depression, 88
  Greg's graduation, 133, 135
  Greg's self-defense lessons, 108
  Greg's social education, 127–128
  leaving Koinonia, 163
  life at Koinonia, 74–76
  nonviolent protest, 81–83
McGill, Ralph, 35, 150
McKinnon, K. W., 64–65, 108, 112,
    116–117, 120, 129–130
Media
  Americus Four, 85–86
  Birmingham civil rights
    demonstrations, 79–80
  classroom discussions on civil
    rights, 125
  desegregation of Americus High
    School, 101, 102(fig.)
  price of conscience in the South, 150
  violence against Koinonia, 45–47
  violence over black voting rights,
    146
Meredith, James, 155–156
Middle East, 159–160, 186
Mitchell, Morris, 153
Moll, Lloyd, 150
Money in Koinonia, 26–27
Morals offense, 131–132
Morgan, Dave (father), 172
Morgan, David, 133(fig.), 209(fig.)
  apologies, 2–3, 67, 198–201, 205,
    215–216
  backlash of desegregation, 101

conciliatory behavior toward Greg, 123–124
documentary film, 213
fire at Americus High School, 90
graduation, 133–134
Greg's commitment to nonviolence, 119
KKK attack on Koinonia, 41
personal journey, 171–174
reconnecting with Greg, 193–194
the reunion, 196–197, 208
Moyers, Bill, 105
Music
civil rights meetings, 78
freedom songs, 81
Greg's love of, 3–4, 27, 91–92
Greg's Swedish experience, 156–157
Hutterites' prohibition against, 71
interracial rock band, 163
the reunion, 213–214, 216

Nicholson, D. B., 17
Niebuhr, Reinhold, 47
Nightmares, Greg's, 210–211
Nonviolent protest
black voting rights, 145–146
Greg's commitment to, 112–113, 117–120
Greg's violent nightmares, 210–211
Joseph Logan embracing, 204–205
Koinonia and the SNCC, 81, 84–86
North Dakota, 70–72

Ole Miss, 155

Pacifism, 18–21, 30–33
Parable (film), 125
Parker, Susan, 229
Parks, Rosa, 149
Patton, George S., 141
Pauley, Frances, 108–109
Pecan production, 54–55
Perdew, John, 79–81, 95, 97, 105
Plains High School, 59
Pneumonia, 53

Police presence
Albany civil rights demonstrations, 77
black voting rights, 140
bombing in Americus, 51
brutality against civil rights protesters, 85
Greg's friendship with Collins McGee, 128
Greg's one-sided fight, 118–119
Jackson march, 156
violence against Koinonia, 42–43
violence against SNCC protesters, 105
youth protesting segregation in Americus, 82–83
See also Chappell, Fred
Polio, 53, 168
Pop culture, 27–28
Posttraumatic stress, 157, 191–192
Presley, Elvis, 27
Private education, desegregation and, 96, 164, 224–225

Quakers, 152–153. See also Friends World Institute

Racism
backlash from Brown decision, 35–36
boycotts against Koinonia, 39–40
Clarence Jordan's religious universalism, 12–13
Deanie Dudley overcoming prejudices, 198
friends of Koinonia youth, 30
ingrained attitudes, 169–172, 174–175, 179–180
Koinonia students' school fights, 33–34
media response to violence against Koinonia, 45–47
psychology of bigotry, 209–210
school fights, 33–34
Real estate, 188–189, 192
Reeves, Dan, 68

Religion and spirituality
  allegories in film, 125
  ambivalence over retaliation for
    violence, 55–56
  children of Koinonia's departure
    from, 191
  churches' failure to promote
    interracial relations, 143–144,
    149–150
  citizens' demand that Koinonia
    disband, 50–52
  Clarence Jordan's radicalism, 11–14
  Deanie Dudley overcoming
    prejudices, 198, 202–203
  exclusion of blacks from Protestant
    churches, 154, 177–179
  Greg's childhood, 9–10
  Greg's commitment to nonviolence,
    118–119, 185–186
  Greg's exploration of European
    communities, 184–185
  Greg's quest for spirituality, 161,
    164–165
  Hutterites, 70–72
  Joseph Logan embracing
    nonviolence, 204–205
  Joseph Logan's background, 168
  media response to violence against
    Koinonia, 46–47
  posttraumatic stress in Koinonia's
    children, 191–192
  racist view of, 172
  racist violence in church, 17–18
  school fights and, 33–34
  school violence threatening
    Christian faith, 64
  sojourners to Koinonia, 28–29
Republican Party: backlash from the
  Civil Rights Act, 105–106
Reunion
  apologies and amends, 214–217,
    221–223
  black students' exclusion from, 229
  Greg's anxiety over, 206–211
  Greg's open letter to his class,
    217–218

  student outreach, 193–194, 196
  the reception, 211–214
Rightmyer, C.W., 178
Rogers, Joan, 205
Roosevelt, Eleanor, 47
Rushin, Rosie, 127

Sams, Ferrol, 173–174
Sanders, Carl, 147
SCOPE (Summer Community
  Organization and Political
  Education project), 141
Segregation
  backlash from Brown decision,
    35–36
  black voting rights, 139–142, 147–149
  bus and train terminals, 77
  community's choice of high schools,
    59–60
  ingrained attitudes, 175
  Koinonia's logo, 16
  Margaret Wittkamper's convictions
    about integration, 19–21
  mixing races at Koinonia, 16–17
  of Protestant churches, 143–144
Self-defense, 112–113, 118, 150
Selma, Alabama, 140–141, 155
Sherrod, Charles, 78
Shiver, Willis, 39
Shunning behavior, 36, 66, 88,
  106–107, 121, 179, 209
Sitton, Claude, 85–86
Smith, Donnie, 128–129, 213
Sound of Music (film), 134, 157
Southern Christian Leadership
  Conference (SCLC), 77, 148
Southern Manifesto, 36
Southland Academy, Americus,
  224–225
Spain, 158
Staley Middle School, Americus, 173
State revenue department, 45
Student Nonviolent Coordinating
  Committee (SNCC)
  Albany Movement, 76–77
  black voting rights, 141

growing rift between blacks and
  white supporters, 155–156
Hasty House Diner violence, 104–105
Koinonia involvement, 81–82, 84
voter registration drive, 80
Suicide
  Andy Worthy, 123
  David's thoughts of, 89
  Greg's thoughts of, 70
Sumter County civil rights movement,
  76–79, 81–84
Sumter County High School, 130–131,
  163
Supreme Court, US: *Brown v. Board of
  Education of Topeka,* 35–36
Sweden, 156–157
Swisshelm, Dorothy, 78

Talmadge, Herman, 35–36
Thalean Elementary School, 23–24, 29,
  33–34, 43–44, 60–64
Thomas, Linda Mitchell, 205
Train station, desegregation of in
  Albany, 77
Tupperware, 175–176
Turner, Lena, 96, 127

University desegregation, 37
University of Georgia, 61

Vandiver, Ernest, 96
Veterans, 20, 31, 141
Vietnam War, 152, 160, 183
Violence
  ACLU suit against Americus
    schools, 60–62
  advocating self-defense, 112–113,
    118, 150
  against black veterans, 141
  against David Wittkamper, 88–89
  against Koinonia students, 33–34,
    62–64, 111–112
  against the Freeman family, 98
  ambushing Greg, 117–120
  backlash from the *Brown* decision,
    37–44, 42(fig.)

backlash from the Civil Rights Act,
  104–105
Birmingham civil rights
  demonstrations, 79–80
black voting rights, 141–142,
  145–149
Clarence Jordan's threat of, 17
Con Browne's beating and
  imprisonment, 54–55
David Morgan's response to, 119
desegregation of Americus High
  School, 101–105
Fortson's integration plan, 97
Greg's dreams of retaliation, 157,
  159, 210–211
Greg's senior year, 106–108, 135
KKK bombing in Americus, 49–50
Koinonia's appeal to Eisenhower,
  44–45
media response to violence against
  Koinonia, 45–47
retaliation for Andy Whatley killing,
  147–148
Robertiena Freeman's experience at
  Americus, 227–228
segregation of Protestant churches,
  144
student suicide, 123
Voice of Americus newsletter, 84
Voter registration, 80, 139–140, 149
Voting rights, 139–142, 145–146,
  148–149, 164
Voting Rights Act (1965), 140, 149

Wallace, George, 80, 105
Walters, Sherman, 168–171
Walton, Bessie, 228
West Virginia, 186–190
Whatley, Andy, 146–148, 150–151
*Where is God? Auschwitz-Birkenau to
  Dachau, 1942–1945* (Althaus),
  202–203
The Whisper of the River (Sams),
  173–174
White Citizens Council, 36, 39–40,
  143

White students
  as scapegoats, 2–3
  desegregation of Sumter County
    High School, 163
  supporting desegregation, 2
  violent backlash from the Civil
    Rights Act, 105
White supremacy, 82, 84, 147–148,
  169, 209
Wiggins, Dobbs, 109(fig.)
  backlash of desegregation, 101–102
  integration of Americus High
    School, 4, 97
  leaving Americus High School, 110,
    130
  reconnecting with Greg, 223–225
Williams, Hosea, 141
Wilson, Juanita, 229
Winter, Ernst Florian, 157
Wise, Jewel, 109(fig.)
  integration of Americus High
    School, 4, 97–98, 102–103
  leaving Americus High School, 131
  reconnecting with Greg, 223–225
Wittkamper, Anne Gardner (wife),
  192–194, 206–207, 211, 214, 217,
  222–223
Wittkamper, Billy (brother), 11(fig.)
  birth of, 20
  corporal punishment, 32–33
  high school, 59
  move to Koinonia, 21
  posttraumatic stress in Koinonia's
    children, 192, 194
  school fights, 34
  television, 27
  vandalism and violence against
    Koinonia students, 63–64
Wittkamper, Danny (brother)
  birth of, 25
  high school, 163
  polio outbreak, 53
  West Virginia community, 187
Wittkamper, David (brother), 11(fig.),
  187(fig.), 212(fig.)
  birth of, 20

  Clarence Jordan's death, 165–166
  Friends World Institute, 165,
    183–184
  Habitat for Humanity, 163
  high school, 163
  marijuana stash, 163–164
  move to Koinonia, 10
  North Dakota farm, 71
  student violence against, 88–89
  West Virginia community, 186–189
Wittkamper, Greg
  ACLU suit against Americus High
    School, 60
  apologies to, 6, 198–206, 210–211,
    221–223
  attack on Con Browne, 55
  backlash from school desegregation,
    103–104
  backlash of the Civil Rights Act, 105
  black voting rights, 143, 145–146
  Brown decision, 36
  civil rights movement, 78, 81
  Clarence Jordan's death, 165–166
  classroom discussion of civil rights,
    124–125
  Collins McGee and, 74–76
  commitment to nonviolence,
    112–113, 117–120
  corporal punishment, 32–33
  David Morgan's decency, 133–134
  desegregation of Americus High
    School, 102–103
  documenting police brutality, 84–85
  drive-by shooting, 43
  entering Americus High School,
    64–65
  European communities, 184–186
  European tour, 146–149, 158–159
  farm injury, 92
  fire at Americus High School, 90–91
  Friends World Institute, 152–156,
    161, 183–184
  Georgia Council on Human
    Relations award, 108–110
  Gladys Crabb's advocacy, 115–117
  graduation, 129–130, 132–134

his parents' deaths, 190–191
increasing depression, 87–88
intention to quit school, 121–122
interracial dating, 126–127
North Dakota farm, 71
open letter to his class, 217–218
photos of, 11(fig.), 26(fig.), 63(fig.),
    75(fig.), 127(fig.), 157(fig.),
    187(fig.), 209(fig.), 212(fig.)
posttraumatic stress in Koinonia's
    children, 192
protesting segregation in Americus,
    82–83
reconnecting with the black
    students, 223–225
religious background and childhood,
    9–10
segregation of elementary school,
    23–24
survival strategy, 65–66, 68–69
the move to Koinonia, 22
the reunion, 196–197, 206–208, 210,
    214–217
tour of Europe, Africa, and the
    Middle East, 159–162
toy weapons, 31–32
violence against, 34, 106–108,
    111–112, 117–120
West Virginia community, 186–189
Wittkamper, Margaret Gregory
    (mother), 11(fig.)
    boycott of Koinonia, 39–40

death of, 191
Gladys Crabb and, 193
Greg's intention to quit school, 122
Greg's travels after graduation, 162
KKK proposition to buy Koinonia,
    48–49
relocation to Koinonia, 20–22
relocation to North Dakota, 70–72
spiritual calling, 19–21
Wittkamper, Sallie (daughter), 192,
    207
Wittkamper, Sharon (wife), 188
Wittkamper, Stephanie (daughter),
    192
Wittkamper, Stephen (son), 192
Wittkamper, Will (father), 11(fig.)
    background and marriage, 9,
        18–20
    Clarence Jordan's death, 166
    death of, 190–191
    Greg's worldliness, 128
    move to Koinonia, 21
    pneumonia, 53
    relocation to North Dakota, 70–72
    transforming the poultry business,
        54–55
Women: black voting rights, 139–140,
    143, 145–146
Woodstock festival, 165
Worthy, Andy, 122–123

Yearbook, 197

Pam Auchmutey

JIM AUCHMUTEY spent twenty-nine years at the *Atlanta Journal-Constitution* as a reporter and editor, twice winning the Cox Newspaper chain's Writer of the Year award. He first visited Koinonia Farm in 1980 and has written extensively about the commune, the South, race relations, religion, and history. He lives in Georgia.